CENTRAL AFRICAN REP.

SUDAN

BANZYVILLE

EASTERN

EQUATOR

PROVINCE

STANLEYVILLE

★ COQUILHATVILLE

PROVINCE

REPUBLIC OF CONGO

KINDU

BUKAVU ★

RUANDA

GOMA

KIVU

URUNDI

LEOPOLDVILLE

★ KASONGO

TANGANYIKA

● TSHELA
ISANGILA ●
MATADI ●

○ LEOPOLDVILLE
KISANTU
THYSVILLE
KITONA

KIKWIT

KASAI

LULUABOURG
★
● TSHIKAPA

LUPUPA

BAKWANGA

ALBERTVILLE ●

LUPUTA

ANGOLA

KATANGA

● KAMINA

RHODESIA

KOLWEZI
JADOTVILLE
ELIZABETHVILLE ★

N. RHO

CONGO

Congo: Background of Conflict

NORTHWESTERN UNIVERSITY African Studies

Number Six

CONGO

Background of Conflict

Alan P. Merriam

Northwestern University Press

1961

This volume has been published with the aid of grants to the Program of African Studies by the Ford Foundation, which, however, bears no responsibility for any of the opinions expressed in this work.

TO

H.G.M., D.F.M., A.M.P.

and

B.W.M., V.C.M., P.A.M.

Preface

Until a few months ago most of the world was hardly aware that the Congo existed, but since June 30, 1960, when the Republic of the Congo officially gained its independence, its name has become almost a household word. In a most dramatic fashion, we have been made aware not only of the Congo but of all of Africa, for the Congo came into its independence in a state of turmoil which has effected the entire world. It has been the scene of tragic conflict and of a remarkable United Nations operation. It has, under the unsteady aegis of its first Premier, Patrice Lumumba, steered a course which has brought it at times perilously close to the permanent embrace of Soviet Russia. Because of the Congo, the very structure of the United Nations has been threatened, the cold war intensified, and American diplomacy challenged. Because of the Congo, neutralism has emerged as a real force in world politics, and our understanding of the role African nations will play in neutralism has come to be better understood. It is a truism that no event in today's world can long remain isolated; the Congo's troubles in the space of two short weeks became the troubles of all the world.

America has been slow to understand not only the Congo, but the new role which Africa is sure to play in world affairs. Traditionally, we have looked upon Africa as a remote Dark Continent inhabited by peoples with whom we felt we had no common cause, and who in any case held little interest for us. But all this is changed today, for Africa is coming with incredible swiftness to take its part in the world that now belongs to all of us, Africans, Americans, Asians, Europeans, and all the other peoples of the world. The so-called Afro-Asian bloc in the United Nations now numbers almost half the membership of that body, and in the United Nations every vote is equal.

Only history will tell us whether the chaotic emergence of the Congo is to be the pattern or the exception in Africa. Though it will probably be the latter, we have many lessons to learn from our look at the Congo. We see once again that man does not, indeed, live by bread alone, and that economic security cannot be successfully substituted for ideas. The Congo crisis is a tragedy both for the Belgians, whose dream of the perfect colonial enterprise leading smoothly to partnership with the Africans was rudely shattered, and for the Congolese, whose dream of freedom and independence was born in chaos. The reasons why these dreams turned to nightmares are not easy to find, but the purpose of this book is to try to determine them, to establish a background for this conflict.

No book, of course, is written as an isolate, as no world event can any longer be an isolate. In my own preparation I have found of special value the works of M.C.C. DeBacker whose publications for Inforcongo, the old Belgian Congo Information Service, have given me a wealth of documentation as well as sober analysis. The *Courrier Africain*, and the books of documents pertaining to the Congo published by CRISP, the Belgian Center for Socio-Political Research and Information (Centre de Recherche et d'Information Socio-Politiques), have been equally invaluable. I have had occasion to refer repeatedly, and with profit, to the series "Études Congolaises" and "Carrefours Africains," particularly the work of Paul Van Reyn, and also to the varied pamphlets and periodicals of the Belgian Information Service. Pierre Artigue's *Qui Sont les Leaders Congolais?* has been particularly valuable, and for those whose reading must be in English, Ruth Slade's little book, *The Belgian Congo: Some Recent Changes,* provides an excellent introduction. I have tried throughout this book to acknowledge my indebtedness to these authors whose thoughtfulness has contributed greatly to my own work, but it is a pleasure to do so here as well.

It is equally pleasant for me to acknowledge those Foundations which have supported my work in the Congo. In 1951–52, the Belgian American Educational Foundation and the Wenner-Gren Foundation for Anthropological Research made it possible for my wife and me to spend thirteen months in the Congo, during which time we traveled rather widely. In 1959–60, the National Science Foundation and again the Belgian American Educational Foundation sent me back to the Congo, and the Program of African Studies of Northwestern University made it possible for my wife to pursue her photographic and ethnographic studies as well. We are grateful for the support of these Foundations, as well as for the co-operation of l'Institut pour la Recherche Scientifique en Afrique Centrale (I.R.S.A.C.) which lent its assistance and friendship during both our trips.

The suggestion that I write this book at this time was made by

Robert P. Armstrong, a valued friend of long-standing; and although they probably do not know it, Professor Harold F. Williamson and Dean Moody E. Prior of Northwestern University said precisely the right things at the right time in the way of encouragement. Mr. Hans Panofsky, of the Africa section of Northwestern University's Deering Library, and his assistant, Mrs. Meno Spahn, were extremely generous with their time and thought.

In Chapter V of this book the impact of independence on two Congo communities is discussed; for the first, the village of Lupupa where I spent a year in 1959–60, I have, of course, drawn upon my own experience. For the second, Stanleyville, I have used the experiences of Mrs. Phyllis Fisher Neulist, a graduate student in the Department of Anthropology at Northwestern University, who spent a time period similar to my own in that city under a grant from the Ford Foundation. In addition, Mrs. Neulist has read the manuscript of the book and given generously of her advice; I am grateful to her on both counts, but particularly for the care with which she prepared some notes on Stanleyville for me and for allowing me to draw upon her experience.

As no book stands alone, neither does any man. My family is a part of me, and without its devotion, support and love, I should be far less than whatever person I am. They, too, are a part of this book; in fact, it is as much theirs as mine.

ALAN P. MERRIAM

Evanston, Illinois
4 October, 1960

ix

Table of Contents

Maps

Maps drawn by WILLIAM A. NORMAN

xiii

Congo: Background of Conflict

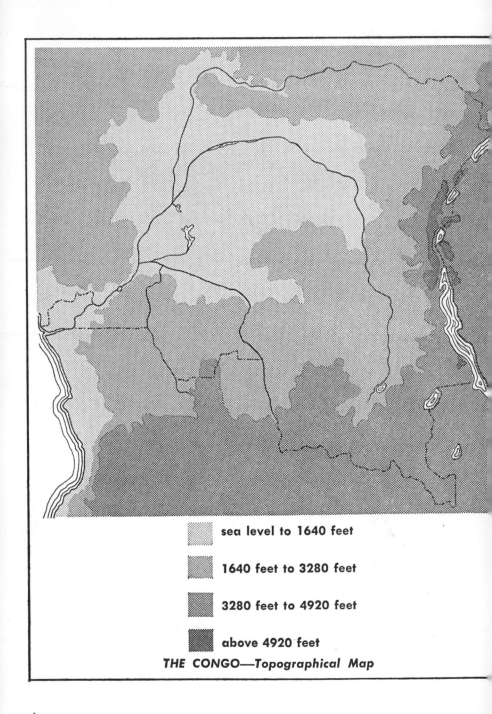

sea level to 1640 feet

1640 feet to 3280 feet

3280 feet to 4920 feet

above 4920 feet

THE CONGO—Topographical Map

CHAPTER I

Before Independence

There are few among us in the Western nations who know the Congo, and fewer still who, having visited it, have come away with an adequate picture of its immense variety. The Congo covers an area of more than 900,000 square miles, one-fourth the size of the United States, or equal to almost all of Western Europe. Its climate ranges from the hot and sultry Congo basin saturated with tropical rains to the high mountain ranges of the Kivu where vegetables of the temperate climate are grown and sweaters must be worn. Its people number somewhere around 13,000,000, from the pygmies of the Ituri Forest and other regions through the Bantu or true Negro populations who are primarily agriculturalists and whose ways of life present an ever-changing kaleidoscope of cultural patterns. Its history counts scandals and triumphs, the high adventure of exploration, determined campaigns against slavery, and now independence. Probably no one "knows" the Congo, and yet today we need desperately not only to know but to understand, for the problems of the Congo have become our problems; together with the Congolese, we must seek solutions which will give this new nation not only the answers to its own problems but the answers to some of ours as well.

Little is known of the prehistory of the Congo, although recent research carried out by individuals and by the Universities in the Congo will do much to unravel the mysteries of the past. Indeed, it was not until the nineteenth century that the Western world began to take a strong interest in the Congo. Before this time there had been only faint indications of its existence. We know, for example, that the geographer Eratosthenes of Syena (276–196 B.C.) was aware of the exist-

3

ence of lakes at the source of the Nile, but we do not know from where his information came. In A.D. 66, the Emperor Nero sent an expedition into the region—its objective, the source of the Nile, was never reached, for the group could not find a way through the swampy regions of the Sudan. Ptolemy's map of Africa, which dates to the second century A.D., shows two lakes as the source of the Nile, and these may well have been Lakes Albert and Victoria. His map also shows high, snow-capped mountains which were said to rise in the vicinity of these lakes: these were surely the Ruwenzori Mountains, which Ptolemy called the "Mountains of the Moon." We can only speculate on whether these early indications came from vivid imaginations or from early explorations in this region, and yet the accuracy of the placement of Lakes Albert and Victoria, as well as the Ruwenzori, would seem to indicate that some early exploration had taken place.

The first exploration in the Congo region of which we have a clear record is the discovery of the mouth of the Congo River in 1482 by a Portuguese explorer, Diego Cão, who named it Zaïre, a word supposedly derived from the African name Zadi, or "big water." On the right bank at a point since called Pointe Padrom, he erected a monolith bearing the coat of arms of Portugal and a cross. The marker was knocked over by early Dutch explorers in 1642, rediscovered by a Swedish traveler in 1886, and is now in the Museum of the Lisbon Geographic Society.

Cão returned in 1485 and made contact with the people along the river and also with the King of the Kingdom of the Kongo. In 1487 he returned again and sailed up the river as far as the first rapids above the present city of Matadi where he carved an undated inscription into a rock on the left bank.

At this time, the Kingdom of the Kongo covered a considerable territory on the south bank of the Congo River in the present countries of Congo and Angola; the capital, then

4

called Mbanza Kongo, was located at the present San Salvador in Angola. On contacting the King, Diego Cão established relations in behalf of the King of Spain, the King of Portugal, and the Pope in Rome. This, in turn, led to Christian proselytizing with the expedition of Ruy da Souza in 1491, and a bishopric was established at San Salvador; in 1582 a Portuguese, Eduardo Lopez, was sent to Portugal and Rome as ambassador from the Kingdom. This first occupation of the Congo was broken up by the end of the seventeenth century, because of struggles between the King and his enemies, and rivalries between San Salvador and Luanda and between the Dutch and the Portuguese. By the end of the century European occupation was restricted to the coastal regions with no missionaries remaining in the interior.

From this point forward, European exploration and penetration became increasingly active, and we can but résumé briefly some of the events in the Congo's history. In 1798 the Portuguese explorer Lacerda made the first penetration of the Katanga area. In 1816 Captain Tuckey sailed up the Congo for the British Admiralty, but the expedition failed due to the outbreak of disease. At about this same period the Arabs set out from the east coast and Zanzibar, and by 1840 they had reached Ujiji on Lake Tanganyika from where they crossed the lake and shortly thereafter reached the Lualaba. In 1860 Samuel Baker, an English explorer, reached Lake Albert with an expedition which was trying to find the source of the Nile, and in 1870 the German, Schweinfurth, explored the Upper Uele region in the northern Congo. From 1840 to 1872 the English missionary David Livingstone undertook a series of explorations in Africa, during which he sometimes traveled through parts of the Congo. On one trip he crossed the Kasaï and Kwango regions, moving from east to west, and in 1854 reached Luanda in Angola. On his last trip, in 1866–72, he discovered Lake Mweru and the Luapula River in the Katanga area. His death on May 4, 1873, was at Lake Bangweulu in Rhodesia. In 1874, Verney Lovett Cameron traveled across the southern part of the Congo.

Until this time, explorers had not penetrated into the interior of the Congo basin, except to touch some small portions of its eastern region. This feat remained for one of the most remarkable men in the history of the exploration of Africa, Henry Morton Stanley. Born John Rowlands in England, Stanley went to America in his youth, was adopted by an American merchant, and later became a newspaper reporter. Livingstone was then in Africa and had not been heard from for some time; the newspapers were full of the story, and the editor of the *New York Herald* decided to send Stanley in search of the missionary. Stanley later set down in his book *In Darkest Africa,* his reactions to his mission:

> When I was commissioned, while yet a very young man, for the relief of David Livingstone, the missionary, I had no very fixed idea as to what manner of man he was. The newspapers described him as worthy of the Christian world's best regard; privately men whispered strange things of him. One, that he married an African princess, and was comfortably domiciled in Africa; another, that he was something of a misanthrope, and would take care to maintain a discreet distance from any European who might be tempted to visit him. Not knowing whom to believe, I proceeded to him with indifference, ready to take umbrage, but I parted from him in tears. The newspapers were right in his case. (*104:*II, 228–29) *

Stanley's search after Livingstone resulted in the famous meeting at Ujiji on November 10, 1871, and probably one of the greatest sagas in the history of western exploration.

After this mission, which Stanley undertook from the east coast of Africa and thus did not cross the Congo, he was sent out again by the *Herald* and the English paper, the *Daily Telegraph,* to continue the geographic explorations begun by Livingstone. From this time until 1884, Stanley set up and fought through expedition after expedition.

* See page 357 for explanation of referencing system.

On September 12, 1876, King Léopold II of Belgium, who had become interested in the Congo through Stanley's work, convened the Brussels Geographic Conference, which had as its purpose the exploration of central Africa, the establishment of scientific and hospital stations to aid explorers, and the stimulation of efforts to abolish the slave trade which was being carried on in eastern Africa by the Arabs and in West Africa by European powers. The eventual result of this conference was increased exploration, including another trip by Stanley. In 1878, Stanley and King Léopold II met and established a "Survey Committee for the Upper Congo." Under the Committee's auspices Stanley returned to the Congo, established stations all along the Lower Congo region, including Vivi, the first capital; went on to Stanley Pool where Léopoldville which he founded, is now situated; and went inland to Lake Léopold II.

In 1879 this committee was replaced by the International Congo Association which adopted a flag of blue with a single gold star. Again Stanley returned to the Congo, this time in 1883, and with several chiefs entered into a series of treaties for recognition of the Association. During this trip he concluded 500 treaties, founded 40 posts, launched 5 steamers on Stanley Pool, and explored farther inland.

Various diplomatic difficulties were arising, however, and Prince Bismark called the Berlin Conference which took place from Nov. 15, 1884 to Feb. 26, 1885 and which had as its aim the settlement of African land disputes among the European countries. At this conference, Léopold II succeeded in persuading the United States and thirteen European powers to recognize the Association as a sovereign state. The Treaty regarding the Congo area laid down the following principles: freedom of commerce and navigation, neutrality in case of war, suppression of traffic in slaves and alcohol, obligation to improve the moral and material conditions of the Negroes, the necessity of effective possession of the country, and the

7

fixation of boundaries of the Congo. On April 30, 1885, the Belgian Parliament authorized the King to become the sovereign of the Congo Free State which became, then, not a Belgian possession but the personal property of Léopold II.

A great deal has been written about the 23-year rule of King Léopold II. Belgian sources hail it as an era of great progress which in some ways it undoubtedly was, but at the same time it was also an era during which the Congo was painted by outsiders as the worst possible example of brutality. Partly because of this, and partly because of the willed action of King Léopold II, the Free State was officially transferred to Belgium as a colony on August 20, 1908; it remained a colony until June 30, 1960.

Only passing mention can be made here of the anti-slave or Arab campaign in the 1880's and 1890's which resulted in the final suppression of slaving in the Congo, or of the East African campaign during World War I which resulted in the acquisition of Ruanda-Urundi under League of Nations mandate and later as a Trust Territory under the United Nations. Nor, except to note them, can we give special attention to the troubles which have occasionally plagued the Congo: the difficulties at the turn of the century during the ivory and rubber trade which were the targets of the Congo Reform Association, the difficulties at the Union Minière in 1942 when ninety Africans were killed, the religious repressions in the Eastern Congo in 1943 at Lubuta and Maisi, the revolt of the Force Publique in Luluabourg in the same year, or the religious difficulties at Matadi, in the Lower Congo, in 1944. These troubles are no more or less important than other events in Congo history—no colony has escaped them altogether.

The pivotal geographic feature of the Congo is its central basin: a depression in the center of the Congo drained by the Congo River and surrounded by a rim of higher ground. Geologically, it appears that the basin was once an inland sea which has left traces in Lake Léopold II, Lake Tumba, and in lake-like enlargements of the Congo River. The central plain of this basin has an average altitude of about 1,312 feet, its lowest level, at the lakes, is about 1,115 feet, and its highest level is near Banzyville and the Zongo Hills at about 2,296 feet. This central depression is covered by dense tropical forest, and is often marshy and always humid.

The central basin is surrounded by higher ground on all sides. To the north there is a slight elevation which separates it from the Great Tchad plain; this is a savannah region. To the west of the basin lie the Cristal Mountains, a chain with an average altitude of about 2,460 feet which runs through the Congo from Angola on the south into the former French Congo on the north. On the south the basin is rimmed by savannah, marked in the southeast by the Katanga highlands which form the Congo-Zambesi divide. The mountains here rise to about 5,500 feet; their higher parts are relatively bare while the lower parts are essentially bush. The eastern border offers the most striking physical aspect of the Congo, with its Great Rift Valley or Graben which is 869 miles long and 25 miles wide and extends from the Zambesi to the Nile. Lakes Nyasa, Tanganyika, Kivu, Edward, and Albert, of which the last four are in the Congo, lie in this great depression, and are separated from each other by low, warm plains situated between mountain ranges of 6,500 to 9,800 feet in altitude. The Graben is a great geological fault, probably at one time a single great water basin.

A further physical aspect of this eastern area is the Congo-Nile divide which runs through Ruanda and culminates in the Virunga chain of volcanoes. This chain lies across the Rift Valley with the Nile watershed to the north and the Congo watershed to the south. The Virunga chain is a group of active and extinct volcanoes rising to 10,000–15,000 feet. Finally, the Ruwenzori range is found somewhat farther north; it is about 80 miles long and 62 miles wide, running north and

9

south, with its highest peak reaching 16,794 feet, the snow line at 14,800 feet and the lowest saddles at 3,900 feet. It is perpetually snow-covered and boasts some rather extensive glaciers.

The principal river is, of course, the Congo which rises in the Katanga on the Congo-Zambesi divide at an altitude of 4,659 feet. From its point of origin it runs north and then turns to the west, comprising in this section several navigable stretches up to several hundred miles in length. At Stanleyville it runs over a series of seven cataracts known as Stanley Falls, and it is here that it enters the central Congo basin. At Stanleyville, too, the river, known to this point as the Lualaba, takes the name of Congo and begins a long navigable section of 1,077 miles. Its two biggest tributaries in this stretch are the Ubangi coming from the north, and the Kasaï which comes from the east and south and which, in turn, is fed by the Kwango. The navigable stretch of the Congo continues to Stanley Pool at Léopoldville, where it is broken by a stretch of 32 cataracts which drop a total of 870 feet out of the basin to the sea. These cataracts are broken by one navigable stretch of 80 miles at Isangile, but continues to Matadi, which is the terminus for seagoing craft. The last 92 miles of the Congo form a stretch called the Maritime Reach; at its mouth, between Pointe Padrom in Angola and Banana Point in the Congo, the river is about 6 miles wide with a depth of some 260 fathoms.

The climate of the Congo varies as markedly as the topography. In the central basin it is hot and humid with about 60–80 inches of rainfall during the year; this decreases toward the edges of the basin, where it is 40–60 inches. The annual number of days of rain in this region is about 130. As in all tropical areas, there are wet and dry seasons which vary depending upon the relationship to the equator. In the basin, the mean annual temperature is about 77°, and the range at the equator is from 60° to 100°. Humidity is always high in the basin, ranging from 65 per cent upward.

In the northern Congo, the rainy season lasts from approximately April 1 to October 30, and the dry season from November 1 to March 30, but there is much variation in this scheme, and in many areas there are two short dry seasons and two short wet seasons; on the southern side of the equator the seasons, are, of course, reversed. During the dry season it is relatively cool with an overcast sky and generally poor visibility due to dust particles in the air, while the rainy season is approximately the reverse.

The great climatic and floral zones include the Forest area comprised of the basin proper and marked by dense tropical forest; the wooded savannah is an open, park-like, grassland, which includes the Kasaï, Katanga, and far northern open forest areas; and the grassy savannah which is open country with relatively few trees, found in the far southern areas. The fauna, of course, is extensive and widely varied, including gorillas in the east, monkeys, chimpanzee, giraffe, elephant, zebra, buffalo, antelope and deer, a huge variety of birds and fish, snakes, beetles, bugs, and insects.

The principal reason for the Congo's prosperity is the mineral wealth which in pre-independence days accounted for one-third of the tonnage and two-thirds of the value of its exports. The metals include copper, found primarily in the Katanga where the Union Minière controls most of the production: at one time the Congo was the world's fourth largest producer. Gold is found in the Katanga, north of the Ituri region, and in other areas: its production is controlled by major holding companies and the Congo ranks among the world's first fifteen producers. Diamonds are found in the Kasaï; in gem stones the Congo is the world's second largest producer, and in industrial stones, its largest producer. Tin, found in the Katanga, manganese, zinc, wolfram (tungsten), tantalum, coal, and iron are of varying importance. The Katanga's pitchblende originally constituted almost a monopoly until the discovery of other sources in Canada, and the Congo at one time provided some 60 per cent of the free world's supply of uranium. Finally, the Congo has in recent years been producing an estimated 55–75 per cent of the world's supply of cobalt.

Mineral products are not, of course, the Congo's only wealth. A great variety of timber is cut in the Mayombe and other areas, copal, palm oil, coffee especially in the Kivu area, cocoa in restricted areas, rubber in the Eastern and Equator Provinces, quinine, pyrethrum, tea, sisal, sugar, perfumes, tobacco, cotton, stock raising, citrus fruits, and a variety of smaller crops such as peanuts, sorghum, soya, raffia, and kapok, all contribute to the Congo's prosperity.

Transportation is well developed, in comparison at least, with most other parts of Africa; in 1955 there were listed 88,-210 miles of road, about 2,800 miles of railways, 8–9,000 miles of navigable waterways, and a network of internal and external air connections controlled primarily by Sabena. Matadi provides a good port for ocean-going vessels, handling approximately 1,500,500 to 2,000,000 tons of goods annually.

Under Belgian administration, land was divided into three categories: the first, native land, was controlled by the Africans who had the right to do as they pleased with respect to the land's cultivation or with allowing it to lie fallow. In theory, at least, they also had the right to expand their holdings, and could cede their rights to the land through the administrative authorities. In fact, however, the land was not completely in the hands of the Congolese, for there were certain planting restrictions as well as quotas and general crop controls. The second category was Crown land which was held neither by African communities nor by private persons and which thus constituted the private estate of the Crown. The Crown could transfer such land or grant concessions "for purposes of development." On these lands, the Africans retained rights of harvesting, hunting, fishing, and tree cutting. The third category was registered land which consisted of concessions given through the Belgian government. Such land remained the property of the government but was conceded to a private company; the government usually retained mineral rights which were considered to be an asset entirely divorced from surface rights; thus prospecting in the Congo was strictly controlled.

During the reign of the Congo Free State, immense concessions were granted to private concerns who were thereby empowered to control the land in their concessions, to hold authority over the Africans living on the concessions, and to have a rather considerable say in the government, though not always officially. There were three such major concessions, the first of which was made to the Comité Spécial du Katanga (C.S.K.) which received its concession in 1891 when it was given a third of the territory of the Katanga, including mineral rights, for a period of 99 years; its concession covered the area of 111,111,111 acres. Special agreements of 1900 and 1901 established a common administration of the lands and mines by the State and the C.S.K. in joint ownership, and the government of the Congo appointed a third of the members of the board of the C.S.K. and split the profits evenly.

The second concessionaire was the Compagnie des Chemins de Fer du Congo Supérieur aux Grands Lacs Africains (C.F.L.) which was founded in 1902 with a 99-year lease for the purpose of building a railway linking the Congo River with Lakes Albert and Tanganyika. The original concession was 19,767,729 acres, since reduced to 370,645 acres at the time of independence. The C.F.L. also held mining rights although the lands were open to public prospecting. The third large concession was to the Comité National du Kivu (C.N.Ki.) which was established in 1928 with a concession of 741,290 acres of forest land on which it held exclusive mineral rights up to the time of independence. The importance of these private hold-

13

ing companies to the Congo is enormous, and their influence on the government was substantial in pre-independence days.

Administratively, the Congo was set up as a distinct identity from Belgium, with its own statutes, assets and liabilities: it was governed by the central metropolitan government with its seat in the colony. The Belgian legislature was supreme in matters of the Congo, but the legislative powers were delegated to the Crown which issued decrees and orders. There was a Minister of Colonies and a Colonial Council which was purely consultative and composed of fourteen councilors of which eight were nominated by the Crown and three by each of the two legislative Chambers in Belgium. Within the colony the Crown was represented by the Governor General, assisted by two Vice Governors General. There was also a Government Council which again was purely consultative: while it could submit resolutions and was consulted on major matters, it had no vote. Indeed, the Congo was set up as a voteless territory; neither Africans nor Belgians residing there had the vote, and the government was thus in no way controlled by the people of the Congo.

The country was divided into six provinces administered by Provincial Governors who ran their areas on much the same pattern as did the central government. The Provinces are the Katanga in the southeast, the Kivu in the central east, the Eastern in the northeast, the Kasaï in the south central, the Equator in the north and west central, and Léopoldville in the west and southwest. The Provinces were furnished with Provincial Councils which met once a year to shape policy but again only in a consultative capacity.

Each province was divided into Districts administered by District Commissioners. There was considerable shuffling of these smaller administrative units in the year before independence, but in 1956 there were 23 such districts. In addition to the districts there were towns which were separately administered. The Districts, in turn, were divided into territories. In 1956 there were 132 territories, each administered by a Territorial Administrator who was assisted by Assistant Administrators and Territorial Agents.

Each Territory was made up of a certain number of Native Areas which were called Chieftaincies or Sectors. On the same level were the Centres extracoutumiers, self-governing African townships in the vicinity of European towns. There were also the so-called Native cities. There were 445 Chieftaincies, 509 Sectors, 39 Centres and 13 Native Cities in 1956. The African communities were for the most part self-governing with their own courts, police, prisons, and exchequers. They conducted censuses, levied tax rates, and constructed their own administrative buildings and local roads. Wherever possible they shared in health, educational, agricultural, and other public services, but they were directed and supervised by Belgian Territorial Administrators.

Justice depended upon a system of Native Courts which included territorial courts presided over by the Territorial Administrator assisted by native judges, and the courts of Chieftaincies, Sectors, and lower courts. In each Territory, District, and Province, there was a European court. There were also two courts of appeal, one at Léopoldville and one at Elisabethville. The highest court was the Belgian Court of Appeal, and theoretically, at least, all cases could be carried to it.

The educational system was state controlled but administered to a considerable degree through both Catholic and Protestant missions. The mission schools of both denominations have been subsidized by the State in recent years, and the curriculum, in theory at least, was standardized by the State. In the past five years, two Universities have been established in the Congo, Lovanium at Léopoldville, and the State University at Elisabethville.

Health services were probably the best in Africa, and were organized under the direction of a Chief Medical Officer.

In 1956 there were 339 hospitals, including some subsidized by the State and some by private companies, 1,642 Rural Dispensaries, and 192 special units, all for Africans. There were about 65,000 beds.

The pre-independent Congo was heavily missionized. Official State policy was to remain neutral in all matters of religion, but in fact, Catholic missions tended to be heavily favored. Belgium and the Holy See entered into an agreement on mission endeavors in 1906, and the Congo was divided into thirty-four ecclesiastic territories with a high representative, an Apostolic Delegate, who resided in Léopoldville. There were some thirty different Missionary Orders of Catholics in the Congo. At the same time, there were also approximately forty-seven European and American Protestant denominations, of which all but four were non-Belgian. As of 1955, the extent of mission activity was given as follows:

	Catholic	*Protestant*
Number of posts	490	244
European missionaries		
Men	2,693	506
Women	2,285	851
African assistants		
Men	739	912
Women	511	—
Christians	3,455,084	704,254

As of January 1, 1955, the population of the Congo was listed as follows:

Province	*Area in sq. miles*	*Non-African population*	*African population*	*Density/ sq. mile*
Léopoldville	140,154	27,203	2,880,762	20.54
Equator	155,712	5,453	1,690,993	10.85
Eastern	194,786	13,500	2,331,613	11.86
Kivu	98,317	11,266	1,948,089	19.81
Katanga	191,878	28,457	1,456,383	7.59
Kasaï	128,006	6,881	2,029,486	16.34
Total	908,853	92,760	12,317,326	13.60

The most heavily populated parts of the country are, in order, from greatest to least density: Lower Congo, Middle Congo, North Kivu, South Kivu, Kabinda, Kwango, Kibali-Ituri, Kasaï. In these areas the highest population density is 41.44 per square mile, while the lowest density is 20.56 per square mile. The most sparsely inhabited areas, all with fewer than 7.77 inhabitants per square mile are the Lake Léopold II, Equator, Tshuapa, Tanganyika, Lualaba, and Upper Lomami areas.

The most recent figures indicate that approximately 23 per cent of the Congo's population is concentrated in urban areas, the remaining 77 per cent rural. In the newspaper *Kasaï* for August 8, 1959, the figures below were given for the joint African-European populations of the thirteen largest cities and towns in the Congo. The figures referring to the population as of December 31, 1958, are given on the left. On the right are listed the European populations of Congo cities which showed more than 1,000 Europeans as of the same date.

Total population		*European population*	
Léopoldville	390,000	Léopoldville	21,500
Elisabethville	183,000	Elisabethville	13,900
Stanleyville	80,000	Stanleyville	5,000
Jadotville	75,000	Jadotville	4,700
Luluabourg	60,000	Bukavu	4,300
Kolwezi	44,000	Kolwezi	4,200
Bakwanga	41,000	Luluabourg	3,100
Coquilhatville	38,000	Matadi	1,800
Bukavu	33,000	Albertville	1,500
Boma	32,000	Coquilhatville	1,400
Albertville	30,000	Boma	1,300
Tshikapa	28,000		
Kindu	21,000		

The same source gives a total population of 13,540,000 for the Congo for the same period: 125,000 of these were Europeans.

17

The problem of racial and linguistic affiliations of the Africans in the Congo is a difficult one, since terminologies have differed widely in the past and since summarizing materials are rarely available. However, it is generally conceded that the earliest inhabitants of the Congo were the pygmoid and perhaps small-sized Negroid peoples who arrived probably in the Paleolithic. It is surmized that these groups may have interbred and formed the earliest distinct racial group, the pygmies, whose name is derived from the Greek "pugmaios," which means "a cubit tall" (the cubit is an old measure of length referring to the length of the forearm, usually 21 inches). No one knows for certain from whence the pygmies came although they are mentioned by Homer, Herodotus, Aristotle, the ancient Egyptians, Pliny, and others. Many consider them to be one of the world's oldest populations. If we accept the fact that they were in the central area of the Congo in the Paleolithic, then we must assume that they were pushed back by the various Negro invaders and were gradually restricted to the less desirable parts of the area, the dense tropical forest. In any case, they have become a marginal population, and most are now racial mixtures called pygmoids. The pygmies are found in the Kibali-Ituri, the Kivu, Tanganyika, Lualaba, Tshuapa, Sankuru, and Ubangi regions, and it is estimated that they number some 80,000 in the Congo.

The remainder of the Congo population is made up primarily of Bantu, or true Negroes. It is generally thought that the earliest Bantu migrants to the area came from the northwest between Léopoldville and Coquilhatville, and from the west along the Atlantic coast. They established themselves in the regions of the Lower and Middle Congo, Kwango, Kasaï, Sankuru, and Lac Léopold II. Following this first invasion, other groups of Bantu came in waves between the tenth and fourteenth centuries. They came from the north, traveling down the Ubangi River, from the northeast to the southwest via the region between Lakes Albert and Tanganyika, and continued south through and out of the Congo as well. The Bantu established a number of great Kingdoms of which we have some record, including the Bakongo Kingdom which existed in the fourteenth century, the Baluba Empire founded by the Basongye in the fifteenth century, and the second Baluba Empire in the sixteenth century, the Lunda Empire in the seventeenth century, and several others.

In addition to the pygmies and Bantu populations, there are also some Nilotics in the Congo who are probably mixtures of Negroid and Caucasoid ancestry. These groups include the Hima in the Eastern Province, as well as some Tutsi in the Kivu; the large population of Nilotics, represented by the Tutsi, is found in Ruanda-Urundi.

As it is difficult to separate out racial groupings, so is it both difficult and, because of the problems inherent in over-simplification, dangerous to attempt a brief sketch of the cultures of the Congo. In general, however, the pygmy culture is usually characterized as one of great dependence on nature and as one of the few true food-gathering cultures. There is little or no agriculture, and no herding of animals; rather, the pygmies are primarily dependent upon what can be gathered in the forest and on hunting expeditions. There is little provision for storing food, and nourishment depends on what is gathered from day to day. The social structure is not particularly complex: the group of people which travels, hunts, and camps together has been called a "parentele" and is made up of a small group of families related by patrilineal descent. The oldest male is usually the informal head of the parentele, but his position is based upon personal rather than hereditary attributes. Marriage must take place outside the parentele, and residence is patrilocal—that is, the newly-married couple lives with the family of the husband. Monogamy seems to be the general rule, with polygyny rarely practiced. In religion there is a belief in a supreme being who is the object of some cult attention and who is the source of ethical life. Be-

19

lief in magic is strong and is tied in with the concept of a vital force in the universe. Aesthetic life is not particularly complex with little wood carving except for the production of daily objects such as drums, whistles, and stools. Music is rather involved, and there appear to be myths and stories about which not much is known.

Much has been written about the relationship between the pygmies and the Negroes; this is a symbiotic relationship between specific groups based upon the exchange of products. Out of the relationships come a social system in which most pygmy groups attach themselves to specific Negro groups. The Negro chief provides the pygmies with iron, household utensils, and agricultural products including bananas and plantains, and in exchange he receives various services, but primarily a meat supply. The relationships extend out from the economic sphere into the social, and thus pygmy children often take part in the Negro circumcision rituals and are sometimes admitted to their secret societies. There is also some marriage mixture, and this has created a situation in which the pygmies especially are becoming more and more genetically intermixed. It seems probable that over a period of time the pygmies will lose their identity as a racial group, moving to pygmoid status as is already the case in Ruanda, and finally disappearing altogether.

The pygmies obviously represent only a small proportion of the people of the Congo. The Bantu are much more numerous, and make up the great bulk of the population. Again it must be pointed out that the following description is highly generalized: there is in fact great cultural variation among the Congo's tribal groupings.)

Almost all the Bantu grow their own food, instead of depending on the free products of the country for their subsistence. Almost all groups also gather, hunt, and fish, but for the most part the foodstuffs produced in this manner are secondary. The basic agricultural practice is to cultivate a plot of ground over a period of several years until the soil is exhausted and then to move to another. The ground is usually prepared by cutting down the brush and, where necessary, the lower tree limbs which are left through the dry season. The dry material is then burned off and planting follows. The primary tool is the short-handled hoe. Principal crops are manioc, cereals such as rice, sorghum, and millet, peanuts, beans, yams, maize, sweet potatoes, sugar cane, and bananas.

Most agricultural peoples also keep small domesticated animals including pigs, goats, sheep, chickens, and ducks, but these are often kept as capital goods rather than being used as an immediate source of meat or milk.

The basic food supply then is vegetable, supplemented by animal products. The food resources are greater than those for the pygmies, but by Western standards most people are undernourished. Storage of food is rather widespread, but in most areas food is produced almost the year-around and thus storage is not a particularly critical problem.

The Congo is known throughout the world for its craft productions, including those in wood, such as masks, statuettes, and products of daily use. There is specialization in the various crafts, such as pottery making, iron working, basketry, and weaving.

Almost all Congo Bantu have a belief in a supreme being who is most often the creator of the world but who has usually chosen to retire from the world once the Creation has been accomplished. Probably more functionally direct in importance are the spirits of the ancestors who are thought to take an active interest in the activities of the living. A third belief is in spirits of nature, and a fourth in an impersonal force or power which can assert an influence in human affairs. Religious practitioners include priests who function as heads of cult groups with regular duties and calendars of events, magicians or sorcerers who control the magical side of religion, and divin-ers who, through a considerable number of techniques, are able to fortell the future and to answer questions regarding the various personal problems of their clients.

The basic social grouping, as in all societies, is the family, and above this grouping is the clan organization in which descent is most often traced unilaterally, that is, on but one side of the family. There are two major areas of clan group-ing in the Congo: in the north, the descent system is usually patrilineal, while in the south, it tends to be matrilineal. Mar-riage is usually a clan, rather than an individual affair, and the marriage form is polygynous with monogamy recognized and practiced widely. Political structures vary from organi-zations based on the individual village to the kingdoms and empires of former day.

In intellectual life there is usually a good deal of specula-tion upon problems of the environment and of life and life after death. Arithmetic systems are based upon systems of 5, 10, and sometimes 20. Weights and measures are standardized within the community, chronology is based upon the phases of the moon and the periodicity of the wet and dry seasons. Geo-graphic horizons are not usually wide, but local geography is very sharply known. The Congolese know the curative values of plants and herbs and use both internal and external reme-dies. There are specialists in curing who hold much local knowledge, and the healing arts are usually tied in with magi-cal practices.

The Congo, rich in all aesthetic life, is one of the great art areas of Africa, and indeed of the world. The plastic arts are represented by all sorts of objects: masks, statuettes, carved posts, batons, and other symbols of office. As an art area, the Congo has been divided into two major parts, the southern and the northern, based on certain stylistic characteristics. The graphic arts are less widespread but are found in certain areas in the form of house painting. Painting on canvas after the

European traditions of fine art has produced some splendid results. Music is characterized by an emphasis on rhythmic devices and techniques and a great diversity of instruments and styles. In some tribes, as for example the Ekonda around Lake Tumba, the music reaches heights of extraordinary complexity. Dance and drama are used to great effect, and the folklore is a highly complex system.

The problem of Congo languages is difficult since almost every tribal group has at least its own dialect. Belgian linguists see two major language groupings in the Congo, divided by a line running east and west roughly at the northern limit of the equatorial forest. To the south of this imaginary line are the Bantu languages, called Niger-Congo by the American linguist, Joseph Greenberg, and to the north are the languages called non-Bantu by the Belgian linguists and Macro-Sudanic by Greenberg. The possibility of a third language, that of the pygmies, is sometimes argued, but this remains in considerable doubt. At the same time, the vast diversity of languages in the Congo is solved to a certain extent by the use of four trade languages which are widely spoken as second languages by the Congolese. These include Kiswahili in the east, Kikongo in the west, Chiluba in the south, and Lingala in the north.

In attempting to classify the varied ways of life in groups of people around the world, anthropologists have developed the concept of culture clusters, a classifying tool which refers to peoples who usually live together, share common ways of life, and recognize the common bonds which unite them. (See 97:373–75.) There are a number of such clusters in the Congo: among the most important are the Kongo, Mongo, Kuba, Lunda, Luba, Warega, and Mangbetu-Azande. The cluster provides us with a simple means of grouping the major peoples of the Congo.

The Kongo Kingdom was formerly bounded by the Kwilu

in French Congo on the north, the Atlantic Ocean on the west, the Kwango River on the east, and the Kwanza River in Angola on the south. The origin of the people is said to be Lake Tchad, and the Kongo themselves claim that no one was in the present area when they reached it, although there is some archaeological evidence to the contrary. The Kongo apparently moved into the Kasaï region about A.D. 500, and during the next 300 years moved westward. By A.D. 1150 they were west along the Congo River to the Atlantic Ocean and were in this location when Diego Cão "discovered" the mouth of the Congo in 1482. In approximately A.D., 1550 the Yaka began pushing the Kongo westward from the southeast into their present location, and there is also evidence of internal migration which accounts for the formation of the various tribal divisions. The five major tribes which formed the Kingdom of Kongo were the Mbanda, Mpemba, Mbata, Nsundi and Mpangu; the Kingdom was at its height from approximately 1500 to 1650, while the period from 1650 to 1885 was marked by competition and disruption during which the Kingdom split into three major factions. In 1885 the Portuguese took over as political administrators, but at its height, the Kingdom of Kongo was a political, social, and cultural reality. It is upon the reality of this old Kingdom in the Lower Congo region that Joseph Kasavubu has based many of his claims as well as his political philosophy of ethnic separatism.

The Mongo, with a population of approximately 1,500,000 to 2,000,000 people, inhabit a large part of the central basin of the Congo. It is generally believed that they came originally from the northeast, and that they have occupied their present location for a few hundred years. Some of the people have the tradition of an ancestor, or a god, called Mongo, and some groups call themselves "the children of Mongo." The Mongo grouping has produced a number of political figures in the current political scene, of whom the most outstanding is Jean Bolikongo.

24

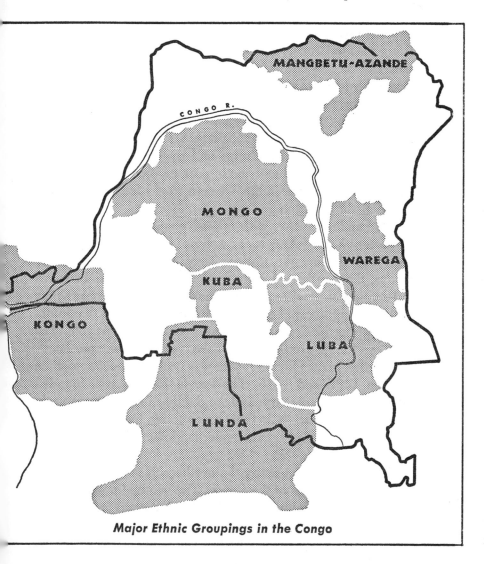

Major Ethnic Groupings in the Congo

The Kuba people, whose domain lies in the Kasaï area of the Congo, are constituted of a number of units including the Kuba proper, Shilele, Wongo, and others; population figures in 1947 showed 73,211 Kuba, 25,978 Shilele, and approximately 1,780 Wongo. Oral traditions pertaining to the group are numerous, and the genealogies of the Kuba kings go back 123 or 124 points in the succession with the rule of the ninety-third king dated somewhere between 1600 and 1610. Many theories exist as to the source of the group, the most likely placing their origin somewhere toward the west coast near the Kongo area. Their present location was possibly originally inhabited by Mongo and pygmoid peoples whom the Kuba subjugated and made part of their kingdom. The Kuba are best known in the Western world for their remarkable artistic traditions.

The Lunda, together with related peoples, occupy most of the eastern half of Angola, as well as smaller areas in Northern Rhodesia and the Congo. They are divided into three groups, the Northern Lunda in the Congo's Kasaï Province and contiguous territory about whom very little is known; the Eastern group located primarily in Rhodesia; and the Southern group in the Congo's Katanga Province and Angola. The Southern Lunda are thought to have come from the northeast, and the first known Lunda leader was probably born sometime between 1486 and 1515. The Lunda Empire was founded early in the 17th century, and the Southern Lunda were probably established firmly in their present area by 1750. The outstanding present-day Lunda leader is Moïse Tshombe, head of the Katanga.

The Luba people occupy the northern Katanga and southern Kasaï provinces of the Congo. The original population of this area was probably pygmoid, subjected at an unknown period to invasions of other populations from the north, probably the Kivu area, and possibly ultimately from Ethiopia. The Songye, Kunda, and Bui peoples settled in the northern portion of the present territory, and from a series of empires begun in the fifteenth century—the Songye and Bui founded by Kongolo, the Kunda, and the Kileondja—the Luba emerged. The present population of approximately 1,400,000 represents a rather varied mixture of peoples and cultures. The Baluba cluster, as we shall see, is the basis for Albert Kalonji's Mining State and as such it is playing an important part in the Congo situation at present.

The Warega group in the eastern Congo inhabits an area of heavy, hilly rain forest; its origin is considered to belong to the second of the three major Bantu migration waves from the northeast. It is sometimes postulated that Ethiopia is the ultimate point of origin in view of the known Lega group in that area, as well as a second Lega group near Lake Albert. The Warega cluster is composed of the Warega and the Bembe, and in addition some of the Songolo, Zemba, Bongo-Bongo, Babuye, and Tuku, the last of which is not a geographically contiguous group. Thus far the Warega have not produced any outstanding Congo leaders. They are best known to the Western world for their outstanding ivory sculpture.

The nucleus of the Mangbetu-Azande group, found in northeastern Congo and neighboring political states, was probably developed from Sudanic invaders who reached the present area before the sixteenth century. At this time the area was inhabited by proto-Momvu and late Momvu types who were invaded from the northwest by Sudanic peoples and from the south by the Bantu. The southern invasions resulted in the establishment of the Mangbetu about 1750–1800; the Azande invasion, possibly from Lake Tchad, came in approximately 1830. The result was the establishment of a considerable kingdom, but to date the Mangbetu-Azande cluster has not produced outstanding Congolese leaders.

This brief introduction to some of the major Congo groupings is not, of course, intended to be all-inclusive (see 97), but it does give some idea of the historic depth of the cultures of the Congo, as well as the traditional ethnic organizations of importance, not only in past times, but today as well.

Perhaps the greatest problem of the Congo today is its diversity. The shaping of a nation is difficult under any circumstances, but in the Congo the problem seems to be especially difficult both because of its natural diversity and because under Belgian administration very little was done to draw the various regions and peoples together under the flag of a single and unified state.

CHAPTER II

Preparation for Independence

As Western nations vary in their cultures and outlooks so have their colonial policies, so much so, in fact, that given an unknown colony an astute observer could probably identify the mother country from a study of the laws and statutes, the behavior of the colonists, and the pronouncements of ideals which he found in the colony.

The fundamental colonial policy which guided the Dutch was essentially one of nonassimilation. The Dutch tried to protect the native culture from foreign encroachment and to build on the basis of old traditions; they attempted to retain the native forms of government and to suppress any "radical" political agitation. In Indonesia, for example, one of the trade languages was used as the official *lingua franca*, and the Indonesians were not forced to learn Dutch or any other Western language. Indonesian customary law and religion were emphasized, and the educational system was organized on traditional lines wherever possible. The result of this policy was that the Indonesian people were isolated; when they finally did become aware of the outside world there was trouble, revolt, and abrupt loss of control by the Dutch.

The colonial policy of the United States was primarily one of Westernization of the peoples involved, and in general it was directed toward the goal of independence. United States policy has changed somewhat since World War II, however, as we continue to occupy certain areas, notably Okinawa and other Pacific islands, only for military reasons. The United States has lost considerable prestige in the world because of this type of action, although its stands on independence for other nations under colonial rule have become more vehe-

29

ment, often to the annoyance of some of its friends in Western Europe who still have colonial holdings.

British colonial policy has run through at least two major phases, the first existing from roughly the turn of the century until World War II, and the second since that time. Before World War II, it was taken for granted that most of Africa should, and would for a long time, remain under external control, but British colonial policy almost from the beginning has been guided by a firm and clearly stated principle that the objective of British occupation was eventual self-government for the peoples involved. Early in the history of African colonization by the British there had gradually developed the policy of "indirect rule" or the "native authority system." According to this philosophy, customary authorities in African society, such as chiefs and elders, were to be recognized and supported by the administration, their rule to be purged of "gross excesses," and the people to be assisted gradually in adapting themselves to a changing world and new needs resulting from British rule and general contact with the Western world. Great emphasis was placed on evils resulting from too rapid change; the ideal forms were those which least disturbed the traditional African life except in a controlled way.

Since World War II, there have been considerable changes in British policy, although they have not altered the basic idea of eventual self-government. The major changes have been the acceptance of the application of a Western parliamentary type of government, and of an immense speed up in the pace of developments. The consequences have been a greatly increased representation of the people in their own legislative councils, the formation of executive branches of government including or composed mostly of Africans, the replacement of the system of native administration by systems of African local government largely if not wholly elected, and a willingness to speed up economic development using both private and public capital. Thus, there has been an increasing speed in movements toward self-government in British territories since World War II.

French colonial policy has been based traditionally on the assimilation of the people, and thus France has never tried to halt social change in Africa; to the contrary, it has tried to accelerate it. The eventual idea was to make France and all the overseas territories a single political, economic, and cultural unity, with all its parts equally represented and equal in every way. Thus France attempted to create Westernized Africans who were given French citizenship. Interest lay not in perpetuating native cultures and languages, but rather in creating a French civilization in which all were to participate equally.

Since World War II, there has been a great extension of the rights of citizenship, especially legal rights. All tropical African territories sent deputies to the French National Assembly, although representation tended to favor the white French in the colonies over the Africans. The result of French policy has been a relatively stable set of colonies. When De Gaulle reversed the assimilation policy in 1958 and offered independence to any territory which wished it, the result was a basically orderly realignment of countries, most of which have retained close ties with France.

Of all colonial policies, those of the Portuguese and Spanish are probably the least clearly defined. The Portuguese have done as little for their African colonies as any colonial power, and their territories are poorly developed. Officially they have followed a weak assimilationist policy somewhat like that of the French; there exists a vague goal of making the colonies part of the mother country but little has actually been done.

Spanish colonies are small in Africa and Spain seems to have no policy toward them at all unless it is complete political subjugation and economic exploitation. It has been said that ". . . the colonial policy of Spain is one of utter rootlessness and lack of direction, and the Spanish dependencies are pathological specimens of abysmal backwardness" (*83*:335), and there seems to be no reason today to change this general assessment.

There has probably never been a Belgian policy formally equivalent to the British idea of eventual self-government or the French policy of eventual integration with French metropolitan life. Belgian policy has been sternly paternalistic, with control over the colony the paramount idea. The primary concern has been with economic development, and the colony has been controlled by a coalition of state, church, and business cartels in which the government owned large shares of stock. Control was exercised directly by Belgian administrators, with some evidence of indirect rule. Neither the African nor the Belgian residents of the colony had a voice in the government, and the colonial system was directly responsible to the Belgian Parliament in Brussels. At the same time, the Belgians early recognized the problem of labor provision in the new economy and launched a strong policy of technical training for Africans with the result that many Congolese held highly technical jobs. But there has not been an equal amount of liberal education and the Belgians justified this by a policy of "bringing all the people up together." Since the war, Belgian general policy has probably changed the least, until the political events noted in Chapters III and IV of this book forced the changes.

Colonial policies, then, have varied markedly from country to country with the Dutch stressing nonassimilation, the United States the Westernization of colonial peoples, the British indirect rule, the French assimilation, the Portuguese and Spanish no clear-cut policy, and the Belgians paternalism.

Paternalism is defined by the American College Dictionary as "The principle or practice, on the part of a government or of any body or person in authority, of managing or regulating the affairs of a country or community, or of individuals, in the manner of a father dealing with his children." No sharper definition of Belgian policy toward the Congolese exists. In looking back on the Congo before the movements toward independence began, one sees a "model" colony in which the Africans were regarded as children virtually incapable of guiding their own destinies, and in which the Belgians made provision after provision for the welfare of their charges. Indeed, the protective coating was applied so thickly and with such thoroughness that for a long time the Congo seemed impervious to any sort of outside influence. Ruth Slade remarks that:

> Even the maps produced in Belgium seem designed to convey this impression of an isolated island fortress; often they give only the sharp outline of that immense square of Central Africa, with its two tapering additions, the one pushing West to provide an outlet to the Atlantic, and the other south-eastward down into the Copperbelt. . . . From the maps they see in the schoolroom most Belgian children would be able to draw a passable outline sketch of their country's colony, but there would probably be few who could set it in its African surroundings.
> Until recently, of course, the need to place the Congo in relation to its African context was not particularly apparent; only now has this become inescapable. Theoretically the evolution of the Congo was to have taken place in a logical succession of slow and easy stages; mass education was to provide a literate population before education of an *elite* was considered, and a long apprenticeship in consultative councils was to prepare the way for democratic institutions at some remote date. At the same time a system of social welfare and the gradual creation of an African middle class provided satisfaction for the immediate future, and it was thought that a calm and peaceful discussion of economic and political emancipation could safely be relegated to some distant period. Theoretically the plan was perfect; and if the isolation of the Congo from the rest of the continent could have continued indefinitely it might have met with an outstanding success. (*103*:1–2)

This tendency toward the isolation of the Congo in political, economic, and social terms was implemented in a number of ways, whether consciously or unconsciously. One of these was the discouragement of white settlement in the Congo; while the express Belgian insistence here was, and quite rightly so, that the land should not be alienated by Belgian or other white settlers, the result was to minimize contacts Africans could make with other nationals, either European or African. Few white settlers actually owned land in the Congo, with the exception of the Kivu area, and in general technicians and officials were not encouraged to settle permanently in the colony, though some did of course. Those Belgians who wished to settle in the country could not do so without posting a sizeable financial bond which was forfeited if they were unsuccessful in establishing themselves. The results of this policy were at least twofold. In the first place, isolation was strengthened, and contacts between Africans and Europeans were kept relatively small. In the second place, the policy tended to make the Belgian inhabitants of the Congo feel temporary. Relatively few Belgians had adopted the country as their own, and the majority looked forward to a career in the colony, marked by the important event of a vacation, which most spent in Belgium every three years, and eventual retirement to Belgium. Considering this point of view, it is not surprising that few Belgians thought seriously of the future of the Congo, and that few were prepared to come forth with concrete proposals and suggestions for the country when the emerging fact of independence came to be realized. Indeed, this is one of the striking things about Congo independence: over a period of several weeks in June and July of 1960 I spoke earnestly and at considerable length with a great number of Belgians and I was struck with the fact that virtually no one had ideas as to what should be done. The almost universal reaction, on an intellectual level at least, was "There is nothing we can do about anything. It all depends now upon what America will do in the way of assistance. I will just have to sit back now and see what happens." To a certain extent this was true, for the Belgians in the Congo found themselves in a very difficult position, disfranchised apparently for all time by the agreements at the Round Table

Conference in Brussels in January and February of 1960, in serious economic difficulties because of monetary restrictions, and in danger of being uprooted and driven out of the country without having had a chance to make provision for such a move. But at the same time, in such a situation one has a right to expect ideas at least as to what could be done—the Belgians in the Congo in the late days of the colony and the early days of independence had virtually none. There were some exceptions in people who genuinely wished to remain in the Congo but if the Congolese, as we shall see, had little idea of what to do with their newly won independence, neither did the Belgians in the Congo.

This attitude was to some extent created and certainly reinforced by the fact that Belgians as well as Congolese had no voting rights in the Congo. The aim of this policy was partly democratic and partly protective. In the first instance, the administration felt that if the Congolese were not allowed to vote, neither should the Belgians, and this was simply a matter of honest democracy, although democracy in the reverse. As a protective measure, it was felt that legislative power should be reserved to the administration, not only because the Congo was not ready to vote, but because if Belgians were allowed the franchise they might exert a preponderant influence and thus put into jeopardy the welfare of the Africans in the colony. The non-voting policy in respect to Belgians certainly did much to stifle initiative, to intensify the feeling of the Belgians in the Congo that their stay was at best temporary, and thus to turn their thinking toward Belgium rather than toward the Congo.

The tremendous degree to which the Congo has been controlled essentially by outside forces, is emphasized in the three-pronged unofficial organization among State, Church, and business. We have already had occasion to note that the Congo was administered directly from Brussels. The Governor General was the representative of the Crown, all edicts and directives came from Brussels, and the Congolese were not consulted in the administration of their own affairs. Further, the Governor General was relatively little troubled by political affairs in Belgium, had no local legislative assemblies to guide or check his policies, and was responsible directly to the Belgian Parliament. The extent, then, of direction of the Congo on a governmental level from outside its own borders was immense, and local movements when they did exist were in a sense ignored because they represented local rather than Belgian views.

The Roman Catholic Church formed the second dominating power in the Congo, and this to some extent grew logically out of the fact that Belgium itself is more than 90 per cent Catholic. In general Catholics have been dominant in governmental positions, but their greatest influence came through the educational system which was administered in the Congo through missions. In 1925 the Belgian government gave the Catholic church an absolute monopoly on government subsidies to education, and this continued until 1945 when Protestant schools were included; the decree became effective about 1948. In general, then, Catholic influence has been strong in the government, not necessarily a bad thing in itself except as it has created something of an interlocking directorate between Church and State.

The third member of this directorate was business. In 1952 it was reported that five holding companies controlled approximately 70 per cent of all Congo business, a tremendous concentration of economic power. But further, in all five the State held a strong interest, ranging up to 50 per cent, and in other corporations a substantial, sometimes controlling interest. The result was that the State not only collected taxes from the companies, but dividends as well.

The five big companies were Brufina which controlled the Banque de Bruxelles as well as certain industrial organizations; Unilever, through its Belgian subsidiary Huilever, which controlled various vegetable products; Cominière, a mining and agricultural concern; the Banque Empain with strong interests in transportation; and the Société Générale which held mining rights and many other interests. John Gunther has commented on the Société Générale:

> This last immense and proliferating holding company was founded in 1822, has capital reserves of more than two billion Belgian francs ($40,000,000), and is the kind of colossus that might be envisaged if, let us say, the House of Morgan, Anaconda Copper, the Mutual Life Insurance Company of New York, the Pennsylvania Railroad, and various companies producing agricultural products were lumped together, with the United States *government* as a heavy partner. This is monopoly with a vengeance. The Société Générale is bigger than the other four companies put together. Its interests are extraordinarily multiform. It is much more than a mere bank or holding company. For instance it controls the CCCI (Compagnie Congolese [*sic*] du Commerce et Industrie) which in turn controls subsidiaries in cotton, sugar, pharmaceutical products, automobiles, and beer. It has interest in railroads, insurance, Sabena (the Belgian aviation company), diamonds, cattle, shipping, and cold storage.
>
> But none of this is what makes the Société Générale *really* count. What counts is the mines.
>
> . . . The financial structure is complicated. Under the Société Générale and the CCCI is an organization known as the Comité Spécial du Katanga. . . . Also an organization known as the Compagnie du Katanga is important. Underneath these is the celebrated Union Minière du Haut Katanga, one of the foremost and most successful mining companies in the world. The Belgian government owns a two-third interest in the CSK, which in turn owns 25 per cent of the Union Minière. . . . About 20 per cent of Union Minière stock is owned by the Société Générale. The Union Minière . . . pays, for instance, between 45 and 50 per cent of *all* Congo taxes. (75:661)

It should be pointed out that Gunther's last statement has been refuted by Jan Albert Goris who says that "the percentage is not higher than twenty per cent" (74:61), and a distinction should be clearly made that it was the Congo and not the Belgian government which was the owner of interests in Congo companies; according to Goris, ". . . this revenue is used only in the Congo."

In any case, the closed nature of the triumvirate is clear; the government of the Congo is directly responsible to Belgium; the Catholic Church is strongly supported by the govment which, quite naturally contains a high percentage of Catholic members; and the large companies are not only dependent upon the government for continued good favor but are also partially, at least, controlled by that government. Such an arrangement represents a strong power system; the Congo was definitely controlled, and almost the entire organization contributed, consciously or unconsciously, to the stifling of independence and independent thought on the part of both Congolese and Belgians.

The careful control and planning which the Belgians put into the Congo is further exemplified by the Ten-Year Plan approved by the Belgian Parliament in 1952 and intended to cover the period of 1950–1959. The objectives of the Plan were both economic and social:

> In drawing up the Plan, the Belgian government had as a main target the raising of the standards of living of the populations for which it is responsible. A quickened pace of social progress was essential if this was to be achieved. But if this progress is to be possible and permanent it must be based upon a stable and prosperous economy. The economic and social aspects of the Plan are therefore intimately related. (78:64)

The Ten-Year Plan, then, was designed to raise living standards through stimulation of the economic development of the country. This could best be achieved through development of power and transportation which would lay down a base for industry and thus stimulate the growth and stability of the economy.

> Economic development depends upon increases in the productivity of labor. Since the native population in the Congo is rather limited in numbers, increases in total production can

come only from increasing per capita output in the economy. It was thus necessary to provide for the gradual mechanization and rationalization of methods of production.

Two basic difficulties stood in the way of transforming methods of production—the lack of technical proficiency characteristic of the native industrial worker and the lack of organization in native agricultural production. To meet the first of these problems an extended program of vocational training was incorporated into the Ten-Year Plan. With regard to native agriculture, the Plan provided for a gradual conversion of the inadequate farming methods to a system of rational cultivation—from a purely extensive system of agriculture to an intensive one.

Finally, it was decided under the Plan to attack and quickly resolve a number of social problems, such as public health and hygiene, basic education of the native masses, and housing for the natives living in the large urban centers. Also, provision of public funds for investment in the fields of water supply and construction of silos, warehouses, and public buildings was incorporated in the general program. (*78*:64–5)

The Ten-Year Plan was a heavy investment for Belgium. It was originally estimated that government capital expenditures under the Plan would amount to about 25 billion francs, or about 500 million dollars, but the estimates proved too low and by the end of September, 1957, total work contracted for was approximately 37,393,000,000 francs or about 747,860,-000 dollars; the expectation was that the total cost would amount to some 48,114,000,000 francs, or 962,280,000 dollars. Under the Plan a great many projects were realized, and its importance to the Congo was tremendous. (See *35*:22–27.) It exhibited Belgium's willingness to invest in the Congo and its future in a precisely planned and controlled way.

Belgian precision, organization, and paternalism carried over into almost all aspects of Congo life. The Congolese were protected under a widespread social security system including sickness allowances and retirement pensions which covered all Africans employed in the Congo. The system was financed by employers' and workers' contributions, but the government also provided a subsidy for pensions to workers who were too old to participate in the contributory system. Perhaps the most clear-cut example of paternalism was the system of the ration or, as it is more widely known, *posho*. Under this system, all employers in the Congo were required to provide their workers with blankets, shorts, sweaters, and healthy and adequate food, and the system dates back as far as a decree of 1922, which was followed by a second decree of 1940. These decrees were made very specific by local laws, and in 1953, for example, in Stanleyville and Bukavu it was stipulated that the ration had to contain 90–100 grams of proteins (of which at least 25–30 per cent had to be proteins of animal origin), 500–600 grams of carbohydrate (a maximum of 15 grams of sugar), 70–75 grams of fats, 150 grams of vegetables or fresh fruit, 15 grams of salt, and other minerals and vitamins which would contribute to a well-balanced diet. These proportions were altered from time to time as research indicated the desirability of change. While the *posho* was originally intended to be given in kind rather than in cash, the latter form of payment came to be most common. No matter what the underlying philosophy, most employers were of the opinion that *posho* was paid in order to insure that the workers would have something to eat through each week, for it was felt that Congolese could not ration themselves and that if wages were paid at the end of the month in a single lump, the Congolese would waste it and would not have adequate food supplies. This extraordinary attention to detail was in part, at least, characteristic of Belgian rule in the Congo.

Paternalism also provided the Congolese with education, housing, medical care, and many other material benefits. Schooling, as has already been noted, was for the most part in the hands of missions, both Catholic and Protestant. Accurate figures on the number of schools in the Congo is difficult to obtain, for they change quite dramatically from report to report. Thus, for example, one source lists the number of schools in the Congo at the end of 1951 as 25,796, of which 9,463 were recognized and controlled by the government, 15,-769 were run by missions which did not receive any form of subsidy, and 564 were "free schools" organized by private societies. On the other hand, figures for 1955 indicate approximately 53 state-run schools, some 12,500 schools partly subsidized by the government, and perhaps 11,000 run exclusively by the missions. These figures refer, in both cases, to primary schools. Similarly, the figures on the number and percentages of children attending school vary from an estimate of 31 per cent in 1957 to 50 per cent in 1959. And finally, literacy estimates range from 42 per cent of the total population in 1959 to the UNESCO figure of a 30–35 per cent adult literacy in 1957.

Whatever the case may be, it is clear that Belgium made a tremendous effort to provide education for Congolese students. Requirements for teaching and for classroom facilities were changed constantly: the latest agreement was signed in July of 1959 between the Minister of the Belgian Congo and Ruanda-Urundi on the one hand, and representatives of the Catholic and Protestant missions on the other. This agreement provided for allocation of credits set aside for schooling, and stressed the decision that schools "must be both decently equipped and as cheap as possible. . . . As an example, it has already been determined that the six classrooms of a primary school, built on normal soil in a hot, damp climate, shall not cost more than 75,000 Belgian francs per classroom, equipment included" (*18*:10).

Basic colonial philosophy stressed the primacy of mass education, and thus emphasis was always placed upon the creation of more and more primary schools in which a larger and larger percentage of Congolese could be trained. The result was sometimes a dilution of standards, for the problem was immense and the policy of mass education difficult to realize. Most mission groups organized their classroom systems

around a central school at the mission station which was complemented by "out schools" scattered over the area served by
the mission. Unfortunately, the problem of teachers for the
out schools was often acute, and in more cases than were ever
made public, the first grade was being taught by a "teacher"
whose education went no further than the second grade.

Again there is nothing basically wrong with this, for education even through the first grade is, in the Western philosophy, better than no education at all. But this is one of the
reasons for the difficulty in establishing literacy figures, for
literacy can be defined in a number of ways, and it is doubtful
that a first grader taught by a second grader can truly be
called literate. It is further questionable how far the mass education program really developed, although the statistics are
impressive, and whether the problem was one which could be
solved even over a substantial number of years.

I should not care to press this point too far, for it is clear
that the Belgian effort toward education on the primary level
was considerable. The philosophy of mass education, however,
was based upon a deeper philosophy which held that the creation of an educated elite was an essentially bad policy which
would lead to difficulties as one part of the population came
to outstrip another, much larger part. The British program of
sending numbers of their colonial subjects to universities in
England, Europe, and America, was considered foolish by the
Belgians. Thus mass education meant exactly what it stated,
and the ideal was to bring the entire population through grade
and high school before any substantial elite could be created
by a university education. The result was that while millions
of Congolese did, indeed, attend primary school, very few had
gone through secondary schools before independence, and almost none through universities.

According to one source (*17*:24–5), in 1957 there were
some 1,250,000 pupils in about 26,000 primary schools, 20,-
000 pupils in some 300 secondary schools, and an additional

11,000 trainees in 340 technical schools and workshops. In these latter institutions, ". . . Africans can learn most trades and crafts or receive training for skilled jobs in such services as river navigation, meteorology, the postal services, etc. In a class apart are the remarkable schools for African medical and agricultural personnel. The higher technical training which they receive is on a pre-university level. The medical assistants, i.e., who have been graduated in Léopoldville since 1938, are not full doctors of medicine, but they give valuable help to the European medical staffs."

On the university level, education for Congolese was delayed for some time because of the Belgians' fear of creating an elite who would press for political independence before the mass of people was ready for it. Basil Davidson quotes the Belgian Colonial Minister as saying in April, 1954: "We have seen that those Natives who have been shown Europe, and given a very advanced education, do not always return to their homelands in a spirit favourable to civilization and to the Mother Country in particular" (*63:236*). Thus the first Congolese allowed to leave the country for university education was sent to Belgium in 1952, and Davidson could say, in 1955, that "no more than half a dozen Congo Africans have ever been allowed to go to European universities" (*63:236*). Although some Belgians urged that the number be increased and that special funds be set aside for the purpose, the government consistently opposed the move, and the eventual result was the provision of two universities in the Congo itself.

The first of these, Lovanium University, was officially recognized by a royal decree of February, 1956, but it had grown out of several preliminary steps. In 1925 a medical center was created at Kisantu in the Lower Congo by a number of professors from the Faculty of Medicine of the Catholic University of Louvain. In 1932 another group of Louvain professors created an intermediate agricultural college for the training of agricultural assistants. In 1936 a school was opened for medical assistants which offered a two-year preparatory course, four years of medical instruction and a two-year probationary period. In 1947, this program was further implemented by the creation of the Lovanium Congolese University Center, an organization which co-ordinated the different schools of Kisantu, and this project was formally recognized by a royal decree of 21 February, 1949. As the center developed, however, it became clear that Kisantu could not be used as a permanent site, and at the end of 1950 Louvain received from the government the concession of 675 acres on a hill, Mont Amba, situated eight miles from Léopoldville. On January 15, 1954, the first pre-university courses were begun and Lovanium University received recognized status in February, 1956, and opened its first full courses in October of the same year. Courses of study were set up in theology, medicine, philosophy, literature, pedagogy, general sciences, civil engineering, agriculture, and political, social, and economic science. Enrollment has grown steadily, as shown in the following table:

	1954–55 African	Non-African	1955–56 African	Non-African	1956–57 African	Non-African	1957–58 African	Non-African
Regular students	18	3	32	10	66	39	110	67
Students in general pre-university	12	0	43	0	50	0	58	0
Students in science pre-university	0	0	2	0	6	8	9	5
	30	3	77	10	122	47	177	72
Total	33		87		169		249	

The most recent figures for Lovanium, for the academic year 1958–59, show an enrollment of 236 students, comprising 89 Belgians, 104 Congolese, 38 students from Ruanda-Urundi, and 5 foreigners. The first degrees from Lovanium were granted in 1958.

44

Partly to counteract the fact that Lovanium is a Catholic university and partly because the need for a second university was clear, the Official University of the Belgian Congo and Ruanda-Urundi was created under state auspices in October, 1955, and opened its first classes in the fall of 1956. Its seat is at Elisabethville on a plot of 1,250 acres at the site of the former Elisabethville airfield some four miles from the city. Courses of study are offered in philosophy and letters, including philosophy, law, literature, social and commercial sciences; in a school of science including biology, geography, chemistry, natural and medical sciences, agriculture, and languages; and in a school of pedagogy. In the 1956–57 academic year the university enrolled 10 African students and 94 non-Africans for a total of 104; in 1957–58 there were 17 African students and 124 non-Africans for a total of 141; and in the 1958–59 academic year, there were 14 Congolese, 10 students from Ruanda-Urundi, 9 foreign students and 138 Belgians. Its first degrees were granted in June, 1960.

There have been a number of problems concerned with the two universities. For example, Lovanium, a private university, has nevertheless received State support which, coupled with its own resources, have allowed the creation of an extensive campus, faculty housing, and the installation of a good deal of technical scientific equipment including an atomic reactor, while the Official University is still struggling under rather limited funds to set up a building program. Both universities have had difficulty with the calibre of Congolese students accepted, and the percentages of drop outs and failures have been rather high. This has led to the establishment of pre-university courses which are designed to bring the Congolese students up to the university level. It may be noted here that the grant by the United States of 300 scholarships to Congolese made as an Independence Day present, while an exceedingly astute political and humanitarian move, may encounter difficulties, for it will not be easy to find enough qualified

Congolese to fill the openings. This, of course, reflects the emphasis which the Belgians placed upon primary schooling, and the relative slowness of a secondary program.

Another problem, though apparently not a serious one as yet, has been the natural division of students in the two universities. While Lovanium, for 1958–59 for example, showed an enrollment of approximately 44 per cent Congolese, the Official University in the same year counted but slightly more than 8 per cent of its student body as Congolese; both figures would be raised somewhat with the addition of the students from Ruanda-Urundi. There was danger in these figures, however, in that the two universities might have come to be popularly recognized as "one for Congolese and the other for whites," although given the present situation in the Congo, it is clear that with the departure of the greatest part of the Belgian population, the Official University will be the first to suffer heavy enrollment drops.

Still another problem has been the expense of university life for the Congolese, but this has been alleviated by the creation of annual scholarships. Students whose parents' income is under 150,000 Belgian francs received a grant of 20,000 francs and a loan of 10,000 additional francs per year. The amount of the grant and of the loans diminished in relation to the size of the parents' income, and was paid out periodically to the students.

A final problem which has plagued the educational system in the Congo is that of education for women. In the earlier days, education was directed exclusively toward males with a view toward creating assistants and clerks who would be useful to the administration, and education for girls and women was not encouraged. As a more or less educated group of men began to emerge, feeling toward the problem was mixed: some Congolese felt that wives should be the equals of husbands, and others, probably the majority, clung to a more African attitude that women should remain in a less prominent position than their husbands. The gap in education has not been appreciably narrowed, although strong efforts in this direction have been made. The system of *foyers sociaux* in which African women were given highly practical instruction in running the home, as well as the efforts of some of the educated Congolese to gain instruction in French for their wives have had only limited results. It was not until very recently that Africans in cities began to bring their wives with them to official mixed receptions and parties, and it was not until 1955 that the first Congolese woman was certified by the Central Examining Board as being prepared to enter university. The Congolese concept of the place of the woman in relation to the man is changing, it is true, but it will be some time before women are accepted and educated as social equals.

We have already had occasion to remark that the first Congolese allowed to leave the Congo for university training in another country was Thomas Kanza, who went to Belgium in 1952. In following years, the number studying abroad increased slowly. The Institute of International Education in 1957 listed two Congolese as currently attending American universities; both were males with private financial support, and one had begun his studies prior to 1955 and the other in the 1956–57 academic year. In contrast, the number of Nigerian students listed as studying in the United States at the same time was 222; Liberia showed 172, Sierra Leone 31, Kenya 17, and Ghana 154 (*51*:37). Nor was the number of visitors to other countries substantially increased at this time. Occasionally a Congolese visitor came to the United States, as for example Mr. Isaac Kalonji, who visited the cities of Richmond, Nashville, Atlanta, New York, Boston, and Washington, as well as Lincoln University in 1957, but such visits were few and far between.

Belgian educational policy, then, was an integral part of the paternalistic attitude toward the Congolese. The emphasis was placed upon mass education with the purpose of educat-

ing all the people at the same time; the creation of an educated elite was to be avoided and as a result, few students
ever attended overseas universities and university education
in the Congo itself was not provided until 1954. (See *49; 57.*)

It is, of course, impossible to discuss in detail all aspects
of Belgian colonial policy and its paternalistic nature. In
housing, the Congolese were able to secure loans and, as early
as 1952, the government made 3,047 individual loans totalling 1,860,000 dollars for this purpose. Much housing was
provided by private concerns, and housing built by Africans
in the cities had to conform to certain explicit standards. The
medical service, certainly outstanding in Africa, in 1957 had
a physician for every 20,000 inhabitants and a trained medical assistant for every 1,400. It had 560 hospital beds per
100,000 inhabitants, and the government regularly spent approximately 12 per cent of its budget on medical services. Almost literally, every Congolese was within walking distance
of a hospital or dispensary, and his fees for treatment were
either nonexistent or very low. Programs against tropical disease were spectacular; in 1930, for example, examination of
three million Congolese disclosed 36,000 cases of sleeping
sickness, while examination of six millions in 1956 showed
but 1,600 cases.

That the standard of living was high by African standards,
and growing higher, is indicated by savings accounts held by
Congolese. As of December 31, 1957, the Savings Bank of the
Belgian Congo and Ruanda-Urundi had 18 branches scattered
through the two countries, and African deposits rose from
1,123,000,000 francs as of December 31, 1956, to 1,603,000,-
000 francs at the end of 1957, while in the same year, the
average size of the individual account grew from 627 francs
to 762 francs. Accounts established by women were also present, and at the end of 1957 there were 139,857 accounts established in women's names.

Perhaps the clearest indication of the projects undertaken

48

and completed in the Congo for the Congolese can be given through a résumé of the work of the Fonds du Bien-Etre Indigène. The F.B.I. was founded in 1947 for the purpose of improving native living conditions in the Congo. Spending at the rate of 300 million francs or 6 million dollars per year on approximately twenty thousand projects, the F.B.I. in its first ten years constructed 28 hospitals, 369 dispensaries, 118 maternity hospitals, 124 consultation centers for children, 15 orphan asylums, 5 sanatoria, and 17 equipped medical centers. It provided 242 ambulances to serve the medical institutions, gave 60 million francs to the building and improvement of centers for treating leprosy, established three campaigns for insect extermination and hygiene, and distributed 100,000 kilograms (220,000 pounds) of powdered milk throughout the Congo. It set up at least one fish-breeding center in each province and its program totalled 8 such centers and 610 fisheries and ponds. Cattle raising centers were established, and stables and smaller centers were built in smaller communities. Community barns and warehouses were constructed, anti-erosion campaigns undertaken, experiments in light mechanization for agriculture conducted, and agricultural schools established. This is truly a remarkable record.

Such statistics could be continued almost indefinitely, and it is clear that the Belgian colonial system of paternalism, judged from the standpoint of material benefits, was unequaled in African colonial history. Why, then, should the Congolese ever have demanded independence? And why, when it did come, was almost unparalleled disaster the result?

It is trite to say once again that man does not live by bread alone, and yet it is as true now and as applicable to the Congo situation as it ever was. Paternalism fed the body and achieved remarkable changes in a relatively short period of time, but it did almost nothing for the intellect. The problems of the Congo do not derive from undernourishment of the body, they derive from undernourishment of the spirit, from the repression of ideas, from a lack of understanding on the part of the Belgians that the Congolese, too, were men and at the same time men whose ideas of liberty are much the same as ours but who differ in the ways it is achieved and implemented.

Paternalism itself relied on the assumption that political ideas will not flourish where there is economic contentment, and that opportunity withheld "until the time is ripe" means that opportunity will not be pursued. Paternalism, too, assumed that Belgian goals were equated with Congolese goals, and that Belgian ideas and ideals were clearly understood and accepted by the Congolese. Placing the blame is one of the Western world's most frequent games; in the tragic Congo situation the Belgians are to be blamed, and yet blame is a relative matter. That the Congolese were tragically unprepared for independence cannot be denied, but to say that Belgium deliberately fostered the conditions that led to it would be grossly unfair. Belgium apparently little understood the people with whom she was dealing, and yet who among us can cast the first stone in this regard? Colonialism is a dying giant in the world today and that Belgium did not see its demise quickly enough is evident, yet to forget what Belgium did contribute to the Congo would be unjust. Paternalism did not, in the end, work, and tragically, most of the real material accomplishments of Belgium in the Congo have been destroyed —destroyed by the thoughtlessness of the paternalistic system which created them. But what, in the long run, shall we vote for? Shall we condemn Belgium for being a colonial power in 1960 when almost all Western nations were colonial powers when Belgium acquired the Congo, and when we are faced today with a Russian colonialism of the most repressive sort? We do so, and we do so honestly, because we do not believe in colonialism any longer, no matter whether enlightened or repressive. Paternalism did not succeed, but has any other colonial system succeeded completely? Is it the type of system we wish to condemn or is it colonialism itself? It is, of course, the latter, for while we can accept leadership in the world we cannot accept control of one nation by another. And although colonialism is dying rapidly today, and rightly so, except for the newer Russian colonialism, this is not to say that we have nothing to learn from it. Belgian paternalism, on the face of it, was an extraordinarily successful system, and many Americans in high places were praising it extensively as little as five years ago, but it was a limited success and its weaknesses were exposed in tragic fashion. Let us examine those weaknesses for the light they can cast upon relations between people.

The basic weakness of paternalism was, of course, that it failed to prepare the Congolese for their independence; it failed to give them a sense of belonging to their own country; it failed to instruct them in the Western systems of government which, it was assumed, they would undertake once the fact of independence was established; it failed in race relations; it failed in education; it failed in understanding that decrees are not a substitute for real human relations; it failed because it established patterns of expectation which could not, in wildest dreams, be fulfilled.

Under the Belgian colonial administration the press was not free. The colonial Charter of 1908 recognized the following civil rights: individual freedom, freedom of religion, freedom of opinion, freedom of education, inviolability of the home, the right to petition, the secrecy of private correspondence, the right of legal action against public officials, the inviolability of private property, and freedom of employment. It did not recognize the right of meeting and association or freedom of the press. An official publication of Inforcongo comments, somewhat lamely: "Press censorship does not exist, but in the interior of the Congo the printing of some publications is subordinated to a system of authorizations, also subject to repeal. For reasons of public order, the authorities may also refuse the entry of certain foreign publications into the Congo" (*53*:69). The lack of a guarantee of freedom of the press was used by the Belgian government in its relations with the Congolese press; thus, for example, the weekly publication "Congo" was seized on August 24, and forbidden to publish on August 29, 1957, and individual numbers of some periodicals were banned from time to time, such as "Notre Kongo" the first number of an ABAKO periodical which was banned on October 29, 1959.

Such actions did not go unnoticed by the Congolese, who in the five years preceding independence had seen the emergence of an African press and were willing to fight for it. Thus in Joseph Kasavubu's speech of April 20, 1958, at his mayoral inauguration in Léopoldville he said:

> There is a surveillance which is . . . systematically exercised over our budding press . . . We protest energetically against this inhuman attitude and demand the immediate liberation of the native press . . . Our counsellors must understand that confidence is never gained gratuitously. It must be earned and merited. (*68*:167)

And commenting on the suppression of "Congo," Thomas Kanza wrote:

> The ordinance by which the authorization to publish was taken away from the founders-directors of "Congo" gave no justification. It was arbitrary and conformed to the colonial law. Sole master after God, he who held the power to give authorization to publish a journal was, in the Congo, the same who had the liberty to take it away when he wished and when it pleased him . . . The authorities forgot, however, that for the Africans, the conclusion was evident; the motive of this serious governmental measure could not be discussed. The paper was banned because the truths of colonial reality are not to be published and divulged—they are simply to be borne with joys and smiles. . . . This suppression was a grave political error for the Belgians and a mistake which fell to the profit of the Congolese in their struggle for emancipation. (*81*:32–3)

Belgium apparently never recognized this mistake for in September, 1959 a new decree relating to "freedom of the press" was signed by the King. It superseded all previous legislation and consisted of five articles. The first of these stated that "any person who publishes a periodical must give prior notice in writing to the Provincial Governor," stating the name of the periodical, its objectives, aims, directors or managers, and a precise list of the editorial staff. Article 2 authorized the Governor General or his delegate to prohibit the introduction and circulation within the Congo of periodicals or other written material which was published in any language outside the Congo, and which might be such as to disturb the public order. Article 3 provided that the Governor General or his delegate might suspend for a maximum period of six months the publication of any newspaper or periodical which might in his judgment compromise the public order. Article 4 enumerated the sentences which applied to infringement of the decree, and Article 5 abrogated all previous legislation regarding freedom of the press.

A similar decree signed at the same time dealt with freedom of association which was not guaranteed in the Colonial Charter. It might have been expected that by 1959 restrictions would be lessened, but to the contrary Article 1 provided that "every association must, within thirty days of its constitution, be declared to the District Commissioner or the head burgomaster of the town in which it has its headquarters." Such declaration, as in the case of publishing, had to contain the name and office address of the association, its objectives and aims, and a precise list of the persons involved in its management or on its board of directors. Article 2 allowed the Provincial Governor, after due warning, to dissolve any association whose activities, in his judgment, might compromise public order, and in emergencies lesser functionaries were given the same right subject to notification of the Provincial Governor who was required to review the action within sixty days. Legal sentences were also stipulated (*19:5–6*).

Far from liberalizing the situation—and it must be remembered that this was late in 1959 when provisional government, although not independence, had already been promised to the Congolese—the Belgian administration tended to tighten it by these decrees. Their motive directed toward controlling the situation, may have been admirable, but their public relations were not. In a country already seething and, by that time clearly on the road to independence, it would seem wise to allow the freest possible circulation of ideas if for no other reason than to provide a safety valve. That Belgium did not see it this way is a further index of the extent to which the Congo's situation was visualized as one which must be controlled at all costs and in all possible ways. As late as September of 1959, control rather than guidance seems to have remained paramount.

The Congo press situation, though always tightly controlled, was rather remarkable in respect, at least, to the number of publications appearing in the country. In February, 1958, a directory of the press listed over 400 publications currently distributed in the Congo, about half of them newspapers. A press association, open to Belgian and Congolese journalists was established in 1955, and both the Belgian press agency, *Belga,* and the French *France-Presse* were permanently stationed in Léopoldville. Of the approximately 144 news organs, it is perhaps significant that roughly 40 per cent were published in Léopoldville Province, and another 20 per cent in Katanga Province. Among these were listed nine daily papers, all published in French or in French and Flemish; three French bi-weeklies; one French paper published thrice weekly; twenty weekly papers of which nine were published in French and nine in both French and a vernacular language, one in Flemish and one in a vernacular language; twelve fortnightly papers, ten in French and vernacular, and two in the vernacular; ninety-one monthly papers, five in French, eighty-three in French and the vernacular, two in the vernacular, and one in French and Walloon; one journal published every two months in French and Flemish; two French language quarterlies; five irregular periodicals, two in French, two in Flemish, and one in French and a vernacular; and about ninety smaller journals specially published for Congolese either in one of the four Congolese vehicular languages or in tribal vernaculars.

The sheer number of publications in the Congo is indeed extraordinary, and it must be said that suppressions were relatively few and that articles critical to the administration were often tolerated. But a democracy—and the Belgians were striving for a democracy—is not nourished by a controlled press, and the press decrees of 1959 did not contribute to the establishment of confidence on the part of the Congolese. (See *50:9–13; 106.*)

If the press remained contained, and if outside publications were restricted, so was the radio, although in this case, outside sources could not really be controlled. The Congo radio system was organized by the state in the form of Radio Congo Belge which was centralized in Léopoldville with transmission stations in the provinces. Programs were directed toward Congolese listeners and often broadcast in the trade languages, and a number of Congolese were employed in the system as broadcasters, disc jockeys, and technicians. In late 1958 it was estimated that the number of radio sets in working order owned by Congolese was 70,000, and that there were 400,000 listeners. The African broadcasters on Radio Congo Belge were said to receive over 30,000 letters a month from their Congolese audience.

Radio Congo Belge was perhaps a greater success with its African than with its Belgian listeners. Most, though not all of the Belgians I knew were somewhat suspicious of the Congo radio and preferred to listen to Radio Brazzaville which, they felt, gave better, more detailed, more accurate, and more frequent news programs. Africans did not seem to be so involved with this particular problem, but they, too, listened to Radio Brazzaville as well as Radio Congo Belge.

Other stations were heard in the Congo, too, including Radio Cairo and Radio Pekin, and the latter had one of the clearest direct beams into the Congo. The Voice of America was heard, but it did not usually come in strong, and those with whom I spoke complained that the VOA had too few programs in French and none in African languages; the VOA beam was not direct to the Congo but picked up from European broadcasts. Radio Congo Belge was, of course, as tightly controlled as was the press in the Congo, and the result was that listeners turned to other channels; this is not to say, of course, that it was not heard in the Congo—it was widely heard, but it was not widely trusted.

The Belgian colonial regime had its difficulties, too, with race relations. As an African middle class began to emerge after the war, its members began to ask themselves and others some questions about human relations between Africans and Belgians in the Congo. As Ruth Slade has noted, "They became aware that while the whites had taken seriously their task as 'tutors,' had striven in various ways to introduce new and western forms of culture, and to a certain extent to europeanize the Africans, there was a point at which they seemed determined that the process should stop. When it came to inviting Africans to a meal, to buying meat at the same butcher's shop, to travelling next to an African in the train, to letting their children sit on the same school benches as young Africans, to the great bitterness of the *évolués* the Europeans objected. All had been well as long as the Africans had remained as children who were to be taught and encouraged . . . but the limit was reached at the adolescent stage, when Africans began to want to be treated on terms of equality, as adults, to be regarded as brothers rather than sons . . ." (*103*:11–12).

These problems were augmented by the fact that discrimination did exist and in the legislation of the colony itself. There were distinctions between black and white in the penal code, by which Africans, for example, could be flogged while Europeans could not. There were distinctions in government service which prevented Africans from rising above a certain level. The very physical arrangement of the cities was an affront to Congolese; in Léopoldville, for example, the European city hugs the edge of the Congo River while the African cities are spread out on the plains behind. If there had been justification for this, as claimed, on hygienic grounds, these justifications were fast becoming obsolete, but the fact of the separation was there.

Once the problem of racial distinctions became clear, the Belgians did a considerable amount to legislate them out of existence. The first African family moved into the white section of Léopoldville in the summer of 1958, statements by the dozen in the mid-fifties made by various government dignitaries indicated changes on the official level in many spheres of race and human relations, and in a decree of December, 1957, the suppression of racial hatred was made official: "whosoever shall manifest racial prejudice, racial or ethnic hatred, or commit an act liable to provoke such prejudice or hatred, will be sentenced to one month to one year of imprisonment, and a fine not exceeding 3,000 francs, or one of these penalties only." And there were, further, a number of moves in private sectors toward implementing amicable relations between Congolese and Belgians.

But race relations are not, unfortunately, a matter of legislation alone; real amity lies in the hearts and minds of people, and such amity on the side of the Belgians, and the Congolese as well, was lacking. My own experience in the Congo led me to believe that those Belgians who truly felt friendship for the Congolese on an equal basis were few and far between. Belgians in my experience seldom had true African friends, seldom invited Africans to their homes, seldom felt that Africans were their intellectual equals. On the contrary, the sentiments most often expressed were that the Congolese were, in truth, savages, and I could not count the number of times that their differing cultural behavior was explained to me in terms of the "fact" that "they were up in trees just fifty years ago."

Partly this is direct and individual racial discrimination, but partly, too, it is the heritage of colonialism. People cannot often quite believe that their teaching has achieved results, or that they have actually succeeded in changing the ways of another group of people. And more than this, cultural differences are remarkable, and despite the teaching of generations of anthropologists the man in the street still sees such differences in terms of higher and lower, of superiority and inferiority. It is difficult for a Westerner to believe deep in his heart that polygyny does work or that an African system of religion does in truth have merit and efficacy. What the scientist can accept as fact and as a matter of course, the man on the street may listen to, he may even nod his head in agreement, but in his heart he remains unchanged—too often savagery is African, and Africans are still savages to him.

Thus the underlying and prevailing opinion of the Africans on the part of the mass of Belgians in the Congo was one of superiority-inferiority, and such a feeling cannot be masked, no matter how hard the bearer tries, nor can it be legislated out of existence. And more than this, Belgians could not believe in their own successes: an African who, as a child was sent off to school with a paternalistic pat on the back, was received, as he returned home, with the same paternalistic pat, although his whole gamut of attitude and behavior may have changed in the meantime. Paternalism looked at the African as a child to be led; when the child became an adult, he expected to be treated differently, and in the vast majority of cases, he was not.

Paternalism failed, too, in that it moved too slowly. The Belgians often moved quickly to repair damage once it had been done, but their policies did not seem to be directed toward anticipating and preventing problems which might arise in the future. As a result, when the winds of independence began to blow across the world, not sparing the Congo in their course, Belgium was unprepared and so were the Congolese. The history of the last five years before independence is not a history of Belgium's anticipation of what was to come, but rather a history of Belgium caught in a press of events, fighting hard to stabilize the situation, but fighting always a rearguard action, bowing to the demands of the Congolese, patching things up after they had happened, and being pushed, shoved, jostled, forced by events which they had not anticipated and which swept them up in an ever-increasing pace of action which they clearly disliked but could not control.

Perhaps the most serious lack in Belgian preparation of her colony was the failure to build up a group of educated Congolese who could participate in government and, as it turned out, give the country mature and considered leadership in independence. We have already seen that Belgium's policy was to educate all the people together; as a policy, this is not necessarily a poor idea in theory, but in fact it did not work, for when the time came for leadership from the Congolese, there was none equipped to lead. The average level of education of the Congolese at the Round Table discussions in January and February of 1960 was something less than high school; the cabinet of the first government of the independent Congo, while including a very few university graduates, was not much higher. The Congo was filled with first class carpenters and mechanics, but there were no engineers; there were bishops, journalists, accountants, medical assistants, teachers, civil servants, pharmacists, but no attorneys or architects. There were no doctors, no people trained at a university level in what we would call a liberal education, no social scientists, no humanists; there was simply no group of truly educated people who were prepared to give enlightened leadership. The two universities existed, it is true, but they were established far too late, and the number of university graduates is pathetic in proportion to the entire population.

Thus it was to a group of uneducated people that the Congo was turned over to independence. But the problem went deeper than this, and it is a problem which plagues the Western world, the Belgians not excepted. This is the fact that deep in our hearts we do not truly believe that Africans are capable of governing themselves. We fail to realize that when colonial powers turn over governments to the people of the former colony, we expect those people to govern themselves in ways laid down by and acceptable to us. Our hesitation about the capabilities of African peoples stems partly, at least, from the fact that Africans in the past have not usually chosen to run their traditional governments along our Western political lines. For us, it is normal and natural to accept those political structures which derive from the Greek and Roman states, and we simply have little experience in thinking of other possible systems of organization. Further, we make a large assumption, indeed, that other peoples will follow us, that is to say, will follow the developed Greek and Roman patterns which we consider "normal" and "natural." It does not often occur to us to think otherwise. And finally, we do not realize that in the formation of new independent African states it is world pressures and, most specifically, the pressures of the colonial power that in actuality force the new states into Westernized molds.

It is precisely at this point that Belgium failed, for not only was the assumption made that the Congo would, obviously and naturally, become a political state in the Western sense, but the assumption was made in the face of considerable evidence to the contrary. There was, after all, an almost complete lack of training and explanation of what a Western political organization is.

This, in turn, led to another assumption, namely that the

Congo was a political entity in the minds of the Congolese, and quite possibly, nothing could be farther from the truth. What is "natural" and "normal" to the Western world—in this case, the political boundaries of a state called the Congo which was created in 1885—is not necessarily "natural" and "normal" to the Congolese. The reality for them is not the centralized state, but rather a mixing of the political with the social structure in a formulation which rests upon villages, tribes and, at the most, regions. And given this, why indeed should the Congolese see the Congo as a unified political state? In any case it is a political artificiality which cuts across ethnic and regional lines, and the Congolese are perfectly aware of the fact. For them, the unity of the Congo is not in fact logical; much more important is the ethnic reality of the old Kingdom of the Kongo which grouped together the Bakongo people and their satellites but which, in Western terms, crosses political boundaries into Angola on the south and Cabinda and the French Congo on the north. Or equally important is the reality of the old Baluba Empire created in the fifteenth century, or the Lunda Empire, or the Mangbetu-Azande grouping, all of which cut across the arbitrary boundaries created for the political accommodation of the Western colonial powers. And this is why few Congolese political parties really had a united Congo at the heart of their campaigns.

Belgium failed to see that this political organization which it finally declared for the independent Congo was a foreign organization, and, beyond this, it failed to make the Congolese understand the workings of Western democracy. Perhaps we can overlook the failure to understand the changes in organization that Belgium was proposing, though any one of their anthropologists could have told them so, but we cannot overlook the fact that the Congolese were utterly unprepared to assume the Western type of responsibilities which were quite abruptly thrust upon them. The country was simply not prepared to be a country, and part of the Belgian legacy was not only political but ideological vacuum so far as Western and world political organization was concerned.

Perhaps this is the time to state flatly that the Congolese are not stupid people. All the anthropological evidence we have at our disposal tells us that no racial group as a group differs significantly in intellectual capacity from any other group. What we often fail to realize is that it is our actions which make other people seem stupid. We do not see that the demands we make on Africans, for example, are substantial in that what we ask them to do is to unlearn their own ways of life and learn ours instead. We seldom consider the difficulties we would have were the positions reversed and were we being asked to make our way confidently through an African society. We assume that our way of life is better; we assume that because of our conquest of arms over Africa we have the right to insist on a conquest of human behavior as well. We cannot search for a resolution of our difficulties by resorting to damning Africans for a lack of intelligence; we must look as well to ourselves and to the demands we make upon Africans to absorb our values and act according to our standards of behavior. We in the West need to see that Africans have their own values and standards, and we need to understand that Africans will inevitably form their own governments in their own ways and with their own unmistakable stamps. We may regret it, for if they were only carbon copies of us our relations with them would be much simpler, but we must understand that Africans do not wish it this way and will not have it this way, and it is time we faced that fact.

Another legacy of colonialism which applies as much in the Congo as it does in any other African sphere is the wide split between political activity in urban and rural areas. When we speak of unpreparedness, it is one thing to talk about the cities and quite another to speak of the countryside. In Lupupa, for example, a small village in the eastern Kasaï

Province, no one reads a newspaper; in Elisabethville during the Independence Day celebrations, copies of the daily newspapers were bought by Congolese almost as fast as they could be dispensed. In the villages, understanding of what independence was and what it would mean to the people was at best only dimly recognized; in the cities, there was a far greater degree of political awareness. This country-city split is a problem which all nations face, but it is especially acute in the Congo and other emerging African nations where the urban groups tend to control the situation and, to a considerable extent, lead and manipulate the rural population. In the Congo the cry for independence came from the cities, and in the rural areas which I knew the cry was far more muted and many of the people were uneasy over the political developments insofar as they understood them. In assessing the Congo situation, this fact must never be forgotten.

A final result of paternalism is the deep-seated feeling on the part of the Congolese that Europeans are to give and Africans are to receive. This is much more than a superficial attitude: it is a real philosophy of life in African-European relationships. That it has grown up out of paternalism is evident, for under the paternalistic system almost everything was given without really asking much in return. The philosophy operates not only on the individual level but on the governmental level as well. In individual relations with Congolese, the Westerner is besieged with requests of all kinds, some reasonable and some not so reasonable; the attitude is often that the Westerner should do things for the Congolese that the latter is able but unwilling to do for himself. On the governmental level we have clearly seen this attitude at work since independence. Mr. Lumumba made it abundantly clear not only that he expected aid from other nations but that it was his right and prerogative to receive it. Moreover, it was clear that he regarded it as the duty of other nations to keep his government supplied and in power. His attitude toward the United

Nations was not one of thanks for sustaining him in a situation which he could not control himself, but rather one that almost stressed his being the center on which the world turned. What emerged was his feeling that the United Nations was obliged to sustain him and that there was no reciprocal responsibility on his part.

In fact, though we must lay the basic blame to the Belgians for the ugly situation in the Congo, the behavior of the Congolese has hardly been exemplary. We look in vain for responsibility of action; in his weeks in office Lumumba failed completely to govern his nation. Throughout the history of the past five years the Congolese in an overwhelming majority of cases contented themselves with demanding further concessions from Belgium and failed almost completely to offer constructive suggestions aside from nationalistic ones. It seemed that a strong psychological situation had emerged in which the Congolese were simply and flatly against anything which Belgium proposed. And this in no small part arises, I am sure, from paternalism in which the African was to take, and the European was to give without demanding any responsibility of the taker. This is one of the most serious problems which faces the Congo. How long will it be before it is realized that communication is a two-way street and that life in the wider world demands responsibility as well as reasonable return for favors given.

It is not difficult to see opportunities gained and lost after their time has passed, but what is puzzling in the Congo situation is that Belgium did not see it before it happened. Others saw it; as early as 1953 George Carpenter, speaking of the Congo, wrote:

> It is clear that as long as the people remain quiescent under a paternalistic regime which makes no provision for their progressive training in the direction of autonomy, while at the same time the economy of the colony becomes increasingly complex, demanding ever higher levels of managerial ability and skill, the gap between proved African competence and the de-

mands of high level leadership continues to widen rather than become less. There was until recently hardly any real thought of transferring effective responsibility from European to African shoulders. It was believed that the present pattern of relationships might continue more or less unchanged for a century or more. (*60*:309–10)

Chester Bowles saw it at least as early as 1953:

The weakness of the [Belgian] program appears to be their reluctance to allow the African to secure an advanced education . . . for fear that he will then demand a growing share of responsibility in the shaping of his future . . . The danger lies not so much in the possibility that the Belgians will not compromise eventually with the force of nationalism, but that when they do they will find the Africans almost totally inexperienced in handling the responsibilities which they are certain to demand and eventually to get. (*75*:662)

Even some Belgians saw it, and Gunther says, "I asked a man who is quite possibly the single most powerful living Belgian how long Belgium could hold the Congo, how long the rule of the white man was going to last. He replied, 'Sooner or later we will have to have elections. After that, five years' " (*75*:668). The only fault to find with the prediction is that, though astute, it also was too controlled.

CHAPTER III

Toward Independence

On July 1, 1885, Belgium recognized the Congo Independent Free State under the personal domination of King Léopold II and twenty-three years later, on October 18, 1908, took over the Free State as its own colony. On June 30, 1960, the Belgian Congo became the Congo Republic, free and independent, to take its place as a sovereign nation among the other sovereign nations of the world. Thus, in the space of seventy-five years, the Congo changed from an almost unknown spot on the map to a country standing in the center of the spotlights that illuminate the current struggle between East and West. Yet the movements which brought independence to the Congo can be traced throughout those seventy-five years only with difficulty; the history of independence as such dates back only to 1955 and to the foment caused by a plain-speaking Belgian professor.

Before 1955 there had been very few indications either of what was to come or of what the Belgian government planned for its colony. But as early as 1947 there had been some tentative beginnings of African participation in the government of the Congo with the appointment of two Congolese to the Governmental Council which theretofore had been composed entirely of Europeans. By 1951, African interests were cared for by the government appointment of eight African members, and, as we shall see, these tentative beginnings grew in 1957 into some local governments elected by the people.

Hand in hand with the gradual movement toward some political independence came a slow awareness to a few Congolese of the outside world and what it might mean to them.

Thus Thomas Kanza, who later became the Congo Republic's first Minister to the United Nations, was in 1952, in his own words, "the first Congolese ever sent abroad to a European University," in his case to Belgium (*69*:1:1). In 1953, a group of fifteen Congolese representing almost all geographic areas of the Congo, was taken on an extensive one-month trip through Belgium where they were shown many aspects of Belgian life of which they had previously had little if any idea. Two of these men were later named to Lumumba's first government, and several of them took active part in the drive toward independence (*36*).

The slow awakening was furthered by King Baudouin's visit to the Congo in 1955. Arriving in Léopoldville on May 16, the King was warmly greeted by a crowd estimated at 200,000 Congolese and 15,000 Europeans. During his voyage in the Congo, the King traveled to Coquilhatville, Luluabourg, Kamina, Kolwezi, Jadotville, Elisabethville, Usumbura, Bukavu, and Stanleyville, as well as to three cities in Ruanda-Urundi. Everywhere he went, he was received by the Africans with loud acclaim and rising hopes (*71*:75–86). Ruth Slade has written that "for the Congolese, the King was in their country not as the representative of Belgium, but as their own great chief, someone who was interested in their social welfare and in the difficulties of their daily lives. . . . The King appeared to the Congolese in the form of a liberator who would put the Europeans in their place, sweep away the social barriers dividing white and black, and usher in a happier state of affairs. It was thus a bitter disappointment to many to find that all did not immediately change after his visit" (*103*:19).

On returning to Belgium the King made some tentative gestures toward political evolution, but these were couched in the form not of independence but of the strengthening of relations between Belgians and Congolese and the emergence of a joint Belgo-Congolese state.

> The time will then come—the date cannot yet be determined—
> to give our African territories a status which will guarantee, for
> the happiness of all, the continuing existence of a true Belgo-
> Congolese community, and which will assure to each, white or
> black, his proper share in the country's government, according
> to his own qualities and capacity. Before we realize this high
> ideal, Gentlemen, much remains to be done. (*103*:19–20)

It is not unfair, I think, to point out the extremely tentative
nature of this 1955 declaration by King Baudouin, the emphasis not on independence for the Congolese but on a joint
Belgo-Congolese community in which, practically speaking,
the responsibilities and rewards would for many years inevitably rest with the Belgians, as well as the careful hedging
that white or black would "share in the country's government,
according to his own qualities and capacity," and finally, the
statement, made but five years ago, that "much remains to be
done" before even these modest goals could be reached. We
may note also that no promises were made, no timetables created; rather, there was but a grain of hope that given the
proper circumstances and enough time, something would be
done about the Congo and its political evolution. The remarks indicate clearly in their cautious and tentative nature
how little thought had been given by mid-1955 to the Congo
as an independent state.

To the end of 1955, then, the situation in the Congo was
one of unsuspecting calm, unbroken by almost any suggestion
of independence for the Congo or even of any concrete thinking about future aims. In December of 1955, however, much
was changed with the publication of A. A. J. Van Bilsen's *Un
Plan de Trente Ans pour l'Emancipation Politique de
l'Afrique Belge* (A Thirty-Year Plan for the Political
Emancipation of Belgian Africa) (*105*:164–202). Van Bilsen was at the time a forty-six-year-old professor at the University Institute for Overseas Territories in Antwerp; he had
a doctorate in law and had traveled in the Congo and other
parts of Africa. His Thirty-Year Plan was not couched in

completely specific terms, that is, there were no dates given at which any particular stage should be reached. Rather, he argued persuasively that the Belgian government was following no determined plan at all: ". . . lacking firm directives and the vigorous support of the metropole, the colony is not being developed following any predetermined line or any doctrine for which [the Belgian] parliament takes responsibility" (p. 164). He further criticized what he felt to be an unbalanced growth of industrialization, and pointed out the lack of higher-echelon Congolese prepared to take a place in running the government: "It is our fault, not theirs [the Congolese] that there are no doctors, veterinarians, engineers, functionaries or officers among them" (p. 165), and he contrasted this situation with the success of the missions who had, to that time, trained hundreds of priests and a bishop. In similar vein he went on to implicate Belgian policy in saying that "a traditional fault of colonial authorities is to make concessions [only] when they can no longer do otherwise" (p. 171), and to add that "a second classic fault consists in giving too little attention not only to the formation of competent indigenous elites, but above all to the awakening among them of the sense of their responsibilities toward the general good" (pp. 172–173). With these points in mind, Van Bilsen then argued that since almost nothing had been done, it would take thirty years to prepare the Congolese for the responsibilities of independence.

> In the Congo and Ruanda-Urundi the formation of an elite and of responsible directing cadres is a generation behind the British and French territories.
> In thirty years, the children born between now and 1960 will form the active base of the population. Among the elites, the youngest will have completed their university studies or their preliminary education. What the Congo will be in thirty years will be the function of what we do between now and 1960 or 1965. If we wish it, in a generation our African territories will be in a position to take their proper destiny in their own hands. It is our duty and in our interest to see that this is done. If we

do not create and execute a plan, we will not be able to do what is necessary in time.

    If we do not have a plan . . . in fifteen or twenty years, if not before, we will find ourselves faced by tensions and irresistible movements in several parts of our territories. (p. 176)

Finally, Van Bilsen proposed that the structure of the future Congo state should be "a grand Congolese federation" including Ruanda and Urundi. His arguments for this form of government were three: (1) that the physical size of the Congo made a centralized government virtually impossible; (2) that Ruanda and Urundi were too weak economically to stand alone as independent states; (3) that a federal system held many points in common with the already-created Belgian administration (pp. 183–89). This argument for federalism was later to appear as one of the chief problems in the Congo, both before and after independence.

    In summary, then, Van Bilsen's plan represented a "call to arms" not so much for the Congolese as for the Belgians. For the first time the problem of the future of the Congo and what Belgium was to do with it was faced and some practical suggestions made. Predictably, the response from Belgium was not for the most part enthusiastic. Thus Mr. Raymond Scheyven objected on the basis of what a fixed timetable would mean to the future:

> I see a danger in fixing a time limit. How can one say to a capitalist, a technician, "Come and settle down, invest your money, your energy, and your intelligence, but look out, in ten, twenty, or thirty years, your time will be ended." How can you encourage a young man to come work in the Congo if you tell him at the same time that he hasn't even before him the time to make a full career? (*62*:16)

And Mr. Buisseret, the Minister of the Congo at the time, spoke with some scorn as late as 1957 of the "irresponsible strategists who fix dates: such an attitude shows that they either know nothing or that they understand nothing of Africa" (*62*:18). Not all response from Belgium, of course, was neg-

70

ative. Van Bilsen had undoubtedly made a contribution to the future of the Congo, and both the Socialist Party and the Roman Catholic Social Action Group reacted favorably to his ideas.

But if the reaction in Belgium was mixed, the reaction of those few Congolese who were aware of the Thirty-Year Plan was almost unanimously enthusiastic, and Van Bilsen's ideas led for the first time to an eloquent vocal statement on the part of the Congolese themselves. This was the Manifesto published in the July–August, 1956, issue of a small African paper in Léopoldville, the *Conscience Africaine.* The *Conscience* had grown out of a cultural group formed by the Abbé Joseph Malula in 1951 at which were discussed various philosophic, psychological, and sociological questions. In time these discussions were mimeographed and reproduced under the editorship of Joseph Ileo who later became one of the outstanding leaders in Congo politics. Gradually the publication grew, and from 1953 on it was published somewhat irregularly under the title of *Conscience Africaine.* The Manifesto was published in a special issue and according to *Africa Special Reports,* "the response . . . was electric. Word swept Léopoldville's African 'city' and filtered deep into the Congo bush . . . Africans who couldn't read pasted treasured copies on their walls. The Manifesto was sold at a football game, and amazed Europeans watched African fans buy it up like pieces of Chickwanga bread" (*3:2*).

Viewed from the perspective of five years, the Manifesto seems an almost innocuous document. Always polite, though firm and never threatening, its points are made in somewhat flowery language, though its intent is perfectly clear. It was unsigned, but most observers tend to credit it primarily to Joseph Ileo.

> We have done this in a spirit of sincerity and with a desire to produce a constructive piece of work. What is more, we do not

71

lay claim to any monopoly either of the love of our country or of clairvoyance for her future.

The present manifesto is only a point of departure. We will sharpen and complete it together with those who come later to join us.

In the history of the Congo, the last eighty years have been more important than the millenniums which have preceded them. The next thirty years will be decisive for our future. It would be vain to base our national sentiment on attachment to the past. It is toward the future that we turn our attention.

Running strongly through the Manifesto is the desire of its writers to create something new and distinctively African which would synthesize two civilizations; the idea of being a carbon copy of Belgium is flatly rejected.

We will only find this new equilibrium in the synthesis of our African character and temperament with the fundamental riches of Western civilization. . . . we wish to be civilized Congolese, not dark-skinned Europeans.

But at the same time:

We understand well that the Europeans wish to maintain their own way of life . . . We reject with vehemence the principle of "equal but separate" . . . Out of the civilizing actions of Belgium in the Congo will develop a new civilization which will be ours.

This strong attitude toward the desire to see all racial and color attitudes disappear, and to create a new, different, and, we assume, essentially African state is widespread in African independence movements.

The Manifesto continued in a more purely political vein:

An increasing number of Congolese want to take more responsibility and more initiative in the future of their country. They wish to assimilate in their national life other basic values of Western civilization which are still absent or insufficiently developed; respect for the individual and for his fundamental liberties without racial distinction, a more intense pursuit of social justice, a true democracy based on the equality of all men and the participation of the people in the government of their country.

72

The Manifesto rejected the idea of the Belgo-Congolese community remarked upon by the King, in the fear that it could and would be used to slow down the complete political emancipation of the Congolese and "to perpetuate indefinitely the European's domination or at least preponderant influence, and thus form a privileged caste."

The moderate tone continued:

> Belgium must not consider that there is a feeling of hostility in our desire for emancipation. Quite to the contrary, Belgium should be proud that, unlike nearly all colonized people, our desire is expressed without hatred or resentment. This alone is undeniable proof that the work of the Belgians in this country is not a failure . . .
>
> But to achieve that the Belgians must realize now that their domination of the Congo will not go on forever. We protest energetically against opinion sometimes expressed in the press that does not make an essential distinction between the presence of the Belgians in the Congo and their domination of the Congo.

Political change was tied directly to Van Bilsen's Thirty-Year Plan which was noted in the Manifesto and which "has become a necessity. . . . Only an unequivocal declaration on this point will preserve the confidence of the Congolese toward Belgium."

> On the one hand, existing institutions must become more and more representative by replacing progressively the present system of nominations with a system in which the population itself will designate its representatives. On the other hand, the councils which are now purely consultative must receive a true power of decision and control in increasingly extended matters in order to arrive finally at a responsible government . . .
>
> We are not asking only for a plan of political emancipation but for a full plan of total emancipation.
>
> At each stage of political emancipation there must be a corresponding stage of economic and social emancipation, as well as progress in education and culture. The parallel realization of these steps is an absolute necessity if political emancipation is to be sincere and effective.

From this point, the Manifesto went on to augment social and economic aims. Higher salaries were made a strong

73

point, as was assistance to agriculturalists and other workers; and equal pay for equal work with Europeans was demanded. Belgium was assured that independence would be worked out in co-operation with Belgium but definitely not by Belgium alone. Europeans in general were assured that their co-operative effort was desired, and the general aims of an orderly and peaceful effort were stressed. But in summary, the point was once again stressed: "We ask specially to be directly concerned, in the most formal way, in the elaboration of the contemplated thirty year plan. Without this participation, such a plan could not have our assent."

Considerable stress was placed on the necessity for unity of purpose and of politics, the newspaper was offered as a rallying point for further discussion of the ideas expressed in the Manifesto and the final paragraphs emphasized a dignified call to action:

> Through our dignified, intelligent and courageous attitude, through our respect for authority and for the men who represent it, we wish to merit esteem and confidence in order that all will rally to the cause we wish to promote.
>
> We have full confidence in the future of our country. We have confidence also in the men who must live in it in concord and in happiness.
>
> With all the sincerity and all the enthusiasm of our hearts we cry out: Long live the Congo! Long live Belgium! Long live the King!*

To summarize, the Manifesto of the *Conscience Africaine* stressed the desire for an end to discrimination of any sort, for the creation of a state which would reflect Congolese aspirations and desires rather than for a state structure imposed by Belgium, for a true democracy based upon the equality of men and the participation of the people in the country's government, for the recognition of a clearcut distinction be-

---

* Complete English text will be found in Appendix I; a complete French text in *84*:251–64.

tween the presence of Belgians in the Congo on the one hand
and Belgian domination of the Congo on the other, for sincere
co-operation and understanding between Belgians and Congolese, and always, for eventual emancipation structured not
only by Belgians but by Belgians and Congolese together with
the Congolese consulted at every step of the way.

In retrospect the Manifesto seems a rather mild document
with reasonable aims and yet it, and the later Counter Manifesto of the ABAKO party, caused considerable stir. The excitement was engendered not so much by what the Manifesto
said as by the fact that a group of Congolese dared to say it
at all. It was only a few weeks later that there appeared the
second, so-called Counter Manifesto which was considerably
more demanding in tone. Where the first Manifesto was
largely the work of a Bangala association which thus gained
certain advantages in being in the forefront of demands for
political evolution, the second or Counter Manifesto was the
product of Joseph Kasavubu and his ABAKO group, made
up primarily of Bakongo people. Speaking at a public meeting on August 23, 1956, for an ABAKO commission which
had been set up for the study of the *Conscience Afraicaine*
Manifesto, Kasavubu laid down the counterattack. The published document was at first conciliatory:

> Our friends of *Conscience Africaine* have produced a docu-
> ment worthy of this period when peoples' spirits are restless for
> a change in the colonial system. We can only congratulate them.
> However, everyone is aware that no human work is perfect. The
> principal aim of our study is to set off the weak points and to
> furnish points of support for this document.

At this point, however, the ABAKO severely criticized the
first Manifesto as idealistic in the matter of politics. It
urged politics as a necessary part of the democratic process
and asked how these "soldiers who love victory but renounce
arms" intended to win the victory. Where the first Manifesto
had envisaged a single political party about which all would

75

unite, the ABAKO saw the struggle among political parties as vital to the emergence of the Congo.

Belgium, too, was sharply criticized for her colonial actions, especially for the control of the Congo from Brussels, and the Counter Manifesto says: "Our position is clear and we demand: 1. Political rights; 2. All the liberties of the individual—of thought, of opinion, and of the press; liberty of assembly, of association, of conscience, and of worship."

As for Van Bilsen's Thirty-Year Plan, the ABAKO found itself diametrically opposed to the *Conscience Africaine* group:

> For us, we do not wish to collaborate in the elaboration of this plan, but purely and simply to annul it because its application would serve only further to retard the Congo. In reality, it is only the same old lullaby. Our patience is already exhausted. Since the hour has come, emancipation should be granted us this very day rather than delayed another thirty years.

At the same time, the ABAKO was in agreement with another of Van Bilsen's suggestions which had also been supported by the *Conscience Africaine* group. This concerned the political formation of a federated Congolese state, and in supporting it the ABAKO took cognizance of certain historic, ethnic, and linguistic facts about the Congo which have often been ignored in Congo and Belgian politics. Further, ABAKO supported the *Conscience* group in emphasizing that the Congolese must have full say in the creation of future political institutions. The ABAKO ridiculed the idea of the Belgo-Congolese community, and suggested that the Congo might possibly become part of a commonwealth in the British pattern. Attention was paid to the question of salaries and standard of living, education, and the Africanization of existing political institutions in the government, and the Counter Manifesto closed by quoting Van Bilsen.*

In neither of the Manifestos did the word "independence"

---

* See Appendix II; the complete French text may be found in *84*:263–75.

appear; even in the strongest language used by the ABAKO group, the word employed was *émancipation:* ". . . il faut nous accorder aujourd'hui même l'émancipation plutôt que de la retarder encore de 30 ans" (*84:*270). The Congolese were not asking for independence so much as for freedoms, political rights, participation in government, realization of their legitimate aspirations. But even more important is the fact that for the first time the Congolese had spoken for themselves; if independence was not yet being used as a slogan, the Manifestos were a definite step toward the future.

In some quarters this new political expression was bitterly attacked, and thus Labrique wrote scathingly that the Manifestos would create racial bitterness and the Balkanization of the country. He spoke of the authors of the Manifestos as "playing at the game of the sorcerer's apprentice," and said:

> . . . The "leaders" of these movements, the supposed authors of these Manifestos do not come from the heart of the population. They are people who have nothing to lose, but everything to gain from the agitation and disorder that they create. They make a name for themselves; they give themselves a notoriety which they would never have otherwise gained in their profession. They do not take account of the catastrophe toward which they are taking their people and, in consequence, themselves. . . .
>
> Let us distrust the bad shepherds, the irresponsibles, those who search not the public good but their personal profit.
>
> Let us distrust those who demand or promise the moon in order to assure themselves of taking it. Let us distrust those who divide in order the better to rule. (*84:*109, 110)

Whatever the case may be, Ruth Slade has noted that "the excitement aroused by these two Manifestos seemed to die a natural death; it did not in fact result in the creation of political parties at that period. Under the surface, however, the evolution of ideas proceeded rapidly. Whereas in 1956 the evolues were asking for planned emancipation by gradual stages, in 1959 they were demanding independence for 1961" (*103:*17).

But if the Manifestos themselves "died a natural death," their effect lingered on, and the emerging political awareness made itself felt in the communal elections of December, 1957, and in their aftermath in Léopoldville through a speech by Kasavubu in April of 1958. By governmental decree of March 26, 1957, a change was made in the political organization of some cities in the Congo. Thus, the Governor General was empowered to give the rank of "city" to any agglomeration which he felt justified the title: in 1957 Léopoldville, Elisabethville, and Jadotville were so named, followed in 1958 by Coquilhatville, Stanleyville, Bukavu, and Luluabourg. The cities were then divided into communes (African or European), and each was to elect its own communal council on a three-year mandate. Voting was restricted to males of twenty-five years or older who had resided at least six months in the city and who had incurred no prison record; of 50,958 registered voters, 43,180 voted. The bourgomaster was to be nominated by the Governor of the Province who thus kept a certain degree of control over the city organization.

The most important elections from the political standpoint took place in Léopoldville in December of 1957. Here the population was split into two major factions, on the one hand the Bangala ethnic grouping, and on the other the ABAKO which represented primarily the Bakongo people of the Lower Congo region. Ruth Slade has made some extremely cogent remarks on the voting pattern:

> On the whole, voting in the African communes followed tribal divisions; a man tended to vote for a candidate who belonged to his own tribe rather than for one of whose programme he approved. Often enough a candidate did not put forward a programme at all, although sometimes he might—in Elisabethville for example—label himself as a Liberal or a Socialist. Again, there were the few who put forward a programme of local improvements. One candidate at Stanleyville proposed a three-point programme to the electorate at the end of 1958. There was to be discipline on the roads, with a strict enforce-

ment of the speed limit and the provision of street-lighting (there had been five after-dark murders in the commune during the preceding six months); there was to be discipline in the sphere of recreation, with an attempt to empty the bars of the large numbers of men who congregated there even when they were not actually drinking, together with the provision of a football field; and there was to be more discipline in general— one of the points under this head being that the gardens around the houses were to be cared for instead of being left to run wild. But the majority of candidates did not present themselves as having any particular attachment to the Belgian political parties, nor having any special plans for local improvements, but simply as having sufficient education and ability to represent the electorate before the Europeans. (*103:* 25–6)

In Léopoldville, the ABAKO and the Bangala represented about equal proportions of the electorate, but the ABAKO won a smashing victory. Depending upon which source one consults, they took 62 per cent (*107:*29) or 70 per cent (*62:*22) of the popular vote, 8 out of the 10 available bourgomaster positions, and 120 (*39:*2) or 129 (*107:*29) of the 170 available seats on the communal councils. Van Reyn (*107:*29) offers the following "official" explanation for the victory:

> The ABAKO, which formed a coherent party and which was directed by the hand of a master, had carefully prepared for the elections. Its members had quite clearly cast a vote on a tribal basis. On the other hand, the Bangala were divided, and moreover they had not taken the elections seriously believing that the administration would use the results only as indicative and would divide the seats proportionally between the groups.
>
> But the administration was bound to democratic rules. It was thus obliged to consider the results as the expression of the sovereign will of the electorate and to proceed accordingly.

Kasavubu, who became the mayor of the commune of Dendale in Léopoldville, took the occasion of his inauguration on April 20, 1958, to deliver a blistering speech against the Belgian administration. In it he demanded the creation of scholarships for Congolese, the admission of Congolese to European universities, recognition of the Congo as a nation, and freedom of the press. But his most eloquent demands were directed toward the installation of a democratic regime:

> But democracy will only be established when we obtain autonomy. Democracy is not present when functionaries continue to be named in place of those elected by the people . . . Democracy is not established when we see no Congolese police commissioners in the police force. And similarly in the militia, we do not know of any Congolese officers, nor are there any Congolese directors in the medical service. And what about the administration of education and its inspection? There is no democracy when the vote is not general. The first step is thus not yet accomplished. We demand general elections and internal autonomy.*

In response to this challenge, the Belgian government named a Study Group which was to examine the political situation and to draw conclusions which would later serve as the basis for governmental action. Despite the clear call from the Congolese in both Manifestos that any action should and must be bilateral, the commission was constituted in Belgium of completely Belgian membership. In any case, the commission did not arrive in the Congo until October 20, 1958, and its report did not appear publicly until February, 1959.

In the meantime, during the summer and fall of 1958 there occurred a number of events which served to strengthen the movement toward independence. One of these was the International Exposition in Brussels which counted among Belgium's contribution seven Congo pavilions. These pavilions were staffed by several hundred Congolese from all parts of the Congo and Ruanda-Urundi, and other Congolese were invited to attend the Fair as guests. Here, for the first time, people from widespread parts of the Congo could mix together, exchange views political and otherwise, observe the Belgians and compare them with the Belgians in the Congo, and search among themselves for common political ground. Housed to-

---

* The complete French text may be found in *68*:163–69.

gether at the grounds of the Musée Royale du Congo Belge, the opportunity to learn more of the Congo as a whole and to develop new ideas was almost ideal. Thomas Kanza has remarked clearly on the Exposition and the Congolese impressions gained from it. Speaking of "La Belgique Joyeuse," a section of the Exposition devoted to drinking, dancing, and other entertainments, he says:

> It was in la Belgique Joyeuse that many colonial tourists learned what they had pretended to ignore—to know that man is everywhere the same, that human qualities as well as virtues and faults are not the monopoly of any people or any race.
> In the splendor of the park at Tervuren . . . life went on until late at night. The people there were already divided into two groups: those who would return immediately to their native country and those who had decided to know Europe better before returning. . . . Among the first group were a number of actual political leaders of the Congo. They had lived in Belgium but they could honestly boast of having met the peoples of almost all the countries of the earth. (*81*:34, 35)

The effects of the meetings of Congolese at the "Expo '58" have been somewhat underestimated in the past. Surely this first opportunity for contact among emerging politicians who had never previously met each other or, indeed, even been exposed to each other's ideas, was of capital importance to the future of the Congo.

A second event in the summer of 1958 which had considerable impact upon the formation of Congolese political ideas was the visit of General de Gaulle to Brazzaville, just across the Congo River from Léopoldville, and his speech there on August 24, in which he said: "Whoever wishes independence can have it as soon as he wishes." It has been remarked that "the visit of the chief of government at Brazzaville was noted at Léopoldville . . . with as much intensity as in the capital of French Equatorial Africa. The words of the general touched the Congolese of Léopoldville with equal vigor. And when General de Gaulle spoke of independence frankly, with an open heart, explaining the pros and cons of it, there was an inevitable reaction on the Congolese side. 'Why don't the Belgians speak this way to us?' " (*101*:36).

This general response was made specific two days after De Gaulle's visit to Brazzaville in the form of a Motion to the Minister of the Belgian Congo, Mr. Petillon, dated August 26. The Motion was notable not only for its conclusions, but also for its expediency and for the fact that it was signed by a number of Congolese who were either at that time or were later to become leaders of several of the political parties: Diomi and Pinzi of the ABAKO, Adoula of the Action Socialiste, Lumumba, Mbungu, Ngalula, Nguvulu, Ngwenza, and Ileo of the future MNC, and Bariko and Motingia of the Bangala. The Motion took cognizance of the two Manifestos, but its objective was the independence of the Congo. Its specific demands were the association of Congolese in the Study Group appointed in Brussels, an accelerated program of economic, social, and political reforms, a statement from Belgium of the stages, with dates, of "decolonization and total emancipation," and the rejection of regional federalism in favor of a united Congo (*107*:37). Van Reyn has called this document "the Declaration of Independence of the Belgian Congo" (*107*:38).

The third event of importance at this time was the Pan-African Conference held in Accra, Ghana, in December of 1958. Belgian authorities did not place difficulties in the way of the ABAKO and MNC leaders who had been invited to attend the Conference, but Mr. Kasavubu failed to make the trip because of certain difficulties with his inoculation certificates. Congolese participation, then, was restricted to three members of the MNC, Patrice Lumumba, President of the MNC, Joseph Ngalula, editor of *Présence Congolaise,* and Gaston Diomi, bourgomaster of the Ngiri-Ngiri commune of Léopoldville.

The three men were received and treated in the grand manner by the Ghanaians and the other members of the Congress.

No longer was the Congo an African isolate, for in Accra the delegates learned at first hand of the independence movements in other parts of the continent. Lumumba was made a member of the permanent organization set up at the conference, and his contacts with other African leaders—Nkruma. Sékou Touré, Houphouet-Boigny, and others—could hardly have failed to impress him. During the conference Lumumba made a short speech (December 11, 1958) in which he gave a résumé of developments in the Congo to that date, pronounced irrevocably that the aim of the MNC was "the liberation of the Congolese people from the colonial regime and their accession to independence," cited the Universal Declaration of Human Rights of the United Nations charter as the basis of his demands, scored Belgium heavily for "injustices and abuses," came out strongly against Balkanization of the Congo, and closed: "Down with colonization and imperialism! Down with racism and tribalism! Long live the Congolese nation; long live independent Africa!"*

Upon the return of the three delegates from Accra, Kasavubu and Lumumba were publicly reconciled, and on December 28, 1958, Lumumba made a fiery speech in the commune of Kalamu in Léopoldville before a crowd of 7,000 people. Beginning with a résumé of the work of the Accra Conference, he cited the Conference conclusion:

> . . . The Conference demands immediate independence for all Africa and that no country in Africa remain under foreign domination after 1960 . . . We state with satisfaction that the resolutions of the Conference coincide with the views of our movement.
> The independence that we claim in the name of peace cannot be considered any longer by Belgium as a gift, but to the contrary . . . it is a right that the Congolese people have lost.
> The objective . . . is to unite and organize the Congolese masses in the struggle for the amelioration of their lot, the liqui-

* The complete French text can be found in *68*:169–72.

dation of the colonial regime and the exploitation of man by man.

It is high time that the Congolese people prove to the world that they are cognizant of the realities of the "autonomy-gift" which the government is preparing and promising. We don't want this autonomy. . . . The Congolese people must stop sleeping and waiting for our independence and liberty.

The Congo is our country. It is our duty to make it greater and better. (*94*:158–61)

Much has been made of the fact that the serious riots in Léopoldville of January 4–7, 1959, broke out seven days after Lumumba's speech, but the connection between the two events will probably never be clearly established. On the one hand Lumumba's abilities to stir a crowd and his unenviable record of sowing riot and dissent in many parts of the Congo would seem to indicate the possibility at least, of a connection. But on the other hand, it is equally clear that other considerations must be examined.

Foremost among these is the problem of unemployment. Léopoldville, which in 1900 was little more than a collection of huts, had grown by 1939 to a population of 50,000, and by the time of the riots to at least 350,000 with perhaps as many as 100,000 additional illegal dwellers. This tremendous urbanization movement was general throughout the Congo; in 1938 only about 8 per cent of Congolese Africans lived in cities, but by the time of the riots the figure had increased to approximately 23 per cent. According to Ritner, 40 per cent of adult male Congolese lived in towns in 1959 (*101*:133). Belgian sources placed the number of unemployed in Léopoldville at 15,973 as of June 30, 1958, a figure which the same source says had increased to 19,000 by the end of August, and 25,000 by February of 1959 (*22*:3). The Belgian government undertook stringent reforms, including programs of public works, the voluntary return of 4,352 persons to their rural communities and, after controls, the return of 7,788 persons to their original homes. By October of 1959, the Government was able to announce that unemployment in Léopoldville had dropped to 11,375, as against an estimate of 27,000 who would have been unemployed had not the government actions been taken (*56*:9–10).

According to Ritner (*101*:142) the beginnings of trouble were to be foreseen in December:

> Then, in December, the insults began; groups of idlers, hanging around in front of the miserable little shops, began to howl at passing Europeans in their cars. Little spontaneous meetings congealed at this or that intersection, lining up in improvised processions that marched down the avenues and threw stones. Nocturnal lootings commenced.

The first real incidents of the riots themselves took place on Sunday, January 4, following the banning of an ABAKO meeting on YMCA premises in the Kalumu commune. According to Belgian sources, "this meeting had been convened . . . without the permission of the building superintendent and the latter requested the police to have the building evacuated" (*28*:1). The purpose of the meeting had been the presentation of a report by Mr. Pinzi on his recent visit to Belgium. From this point, the accounts grow confused. Ruth Slade says:

> The Abako supporters . . . grew excited and talked wildly of independence; M. Kasavubu, who was also present, failed to calm them. The police arrived and resorted to the use of firearms; anger spread throughout the native city, and the cry of independence was taken up; the pent-up fury of many months was unloosed; Europeans were attacked and churches, schools, hospitals, and social centres destroyed. The Europeans gave way to panic, the Army was called in, and the repression was violent. Casualties among the Europeans might have been much heavier had not some of them been hidden and protected from the crowds by individual Africans. They might have been lighter, however, had not Radio Leopoldville played down the gravity of the situation, and reported that all was calm in regions where rioting was in fact in full progress. As a result, unsuspecting Europeans became involved in the riots when they could have avoided the affected neighborhoods. (*103*:49–50)

A somewhat different view is provided by the Belgian Congo Information Service which picks up the story after the report that the building superintendent had called in the police.

> There were a few moments of indecision before the situation rapidly worsened and a police vehicle was set on fire. A band of men marched to the Portuguese commercial district with the aim of sacking, looting and burning shops.
>
> After some consultation and in view of the increasing danger, it was decided to place the city under martial law and bring in troops.
>
> During the night of January 4 to 5, public buildings, private residences, shops, social clubs, schools, missions and stores were attacked in Leopoldville and surrounding suburbs. Cars were set on fire and passers-by molested. . . .
>
> It was necessary to resort to armed force, and the native troops and the police were obliged to shoot on several occasions in the evening of January 4 and during the days of January 5 and 6, either to defend their own positions or to prevent acts of robbery and looting, or to advance in the course of their mopping-up operations, or again to rescue molested Europeans.
>
> Although the outbreak began as a political demonstration, subsequent events showed that the baser elements of the population took advantage of the situation to commit acts of banditry and vandalism. Xenophobia was more in the nature of a pretext than a motive. (*28:*1–2)

According to a background story in the overseas edition of the *New York Times,* "A mob assembled and M. Kasavubu tried to soothe it. He thought he had calmed them. But the mob assembled again in the afternoon. M. Kasavubu was not there to caution it and violence erupted in Léopoldville" (*31*). A final account gives somewhat more information.

> But when, on January 5, the mobs spilled over to the main market place of the town the government stepped in massively. Armories were opened up and guns, along with from thirty to fifty rounds, were issued to any European who presented himself at the door. In addition to arming themselves, the colonists formed into voluntary platoons and regiments which took over the guarding of vital spots like oil dumps and railroad yards, while the regular army and the police—with armored cars and mortar units—took on the African townships themselves. A curfew and an illegal-assembly law were decreed, and for two nights every African on the streets—individual or part of a mob

—was fired upon. A paratroop unit already on the high seas, returning to Belgium, was hastily flown back to the colony. (*101*:142)

The number of casualties resulting from the riots is somewhat difficult to establish with complete accuracy: Van Reyn (*107*:42) lists 42 dead and 250 wounded, while Slade (*103*:50) cites 49 African deaths, 49 Europeans and 330 Africans wounded. A résumé of the official report says that "on the European side there were 49 wounded, 15 of whom were hospitalized and 34 who returned home after first-aid treatment. . . . As for the Congolese, 49 were killed (including 12 wounded who later died in hospital), 101 wounded and hospitalized, and 140 slightly wounded who were not taken to hospital" (*38*:4).

The immediate result of the riots was a Parliamentary Commission of Enquiry, made up of nine members who arrived in the Congo four days after the rioting began. Their report was honest and frank: as Legum has noted: "The Commission discarded the propaganda, the pretence and deception and the bogus claims about the advantages of paternalism over democratic political rights" (*86*:90). It was divided into four chapters, the first dealing with the immediate and underlying causes of the incidents.

> Amongst the social causes [are] cited: human relationships between Europeans and Natives; the irregular migration of the rural population towards the cities and the resultant overcrowding and unhygienic living conditions; the unemployment arising out of the recession; insufficient schools for children and young people; labour conditions; and the influence exerted by the trade unions.
> As for political causes [there are mentioned] Government incompetency, inefficient administration, the various nationalist movements; religious friction, inadequate news services and foreign influence (such as the Accra conference, etc.). (*38*:1)

The second chapter is a history of the events which took place on January 4 and 5 before military intervention was ordered; reorganization of the police force is stressed. The third chapter deals with the military intervention and its conduct with some recommendations for possible future operations, and the fourth discusses what should be done to prevent future outbreaks of the same kind: improvement of human relationships, improvement of communications media, adoption of a clear-cut long range political policy for the Congo, modification of the town electoral system, a program to combat unemployment, the establishment of a national labor council, increase of educational facilities, and the promotion of youth movements, are cited among other suggestions.

A second result of the riots was the dissolution of the ABAKO movement and the arrest of its principal leaders. Those arrested, however, were never brought to trial, and instead were gradually released. On March 14, 1959, the last six were liberated, three of whom were allowed to return home, while the other three, Joseph Kasavubu, Daniel Kanza, and Simon Nzeza, were suddenly sent to Belgium where they arrived on March 17. Though always under the surveillance of the Sécurité, they were allowed full liberty in Belgium and, indeed, took the occasion to travel throughout the country; but it was not until almost two months later, May 13, that they were allowed to return to the Congo. (See *81*:40–45.)

On January 13, 1959, the Congo received a governmental declaration as well as a message from the King concerning its future. Much controversy has been engendered over the timing of these announcements, with some holding that it was the Léopoldville riots which forced their issuance. This seems to have no basis in fact, however, for it is clear that the pronouncements had long been planned for that particular date. There has also been some speculation that the riots themselves were planned for January 13 but got out of hand and took place nine days early: there has not been any proof of such a possibility.

The King's message was rather general in its form but the broad aims of Belgian policy toward the Congo were restated:

"The aim of our presence on the dark continent has been defined by Léopold II: to open these backward countries to European civilization, to call their populations to emancipation, liberty and progress after having freed them from slavery, illness and misery." But it continued: ". . . our firm resolve without undesirable delays but also without inconsidered precipitation, [is] to lead the Congolese people to independence in prosperity and peace." The significance of this statement lies in the use of the word "independence"; it is the first time that the word was used in an official statement, and it marked a change in government policy. It is also significant to note that for the first time a clear-cut statement was made which accepted the idea that the future of the Congo would involve African adaptations rather than Belgian-imposed ideas: ". . . far from imposing on these populations solutions which are entirely European, we shall favor original adaptations which respond to the proper character and traditions which are dear to them."*

The Government Declaration of January 13, 1959, was in some ways as vague as the King's message, and the specific date of independence for which the Congolese had hoped was not forthcoming. On the other hand, the change in government policy was made clear and "independence" was spoken of in more concrete terms:

> Belgium intends to organize in the Congo a democracy capable of exercising its prerogatives of sovereignty and of deciding on its independence.
> As a co-signator of the Charter of the United Nations our country has moreover confirmed its wish to lead the people of the Congo to the point where they will be capable of governing themselves. All our action in the Congo is directed toward this line of conduct.

Heavy emphasis was placed upon universal suffrage, elections, and the democratic process, and a section was devoted

---

* The complete text of the King's message can be found in *108*:3.

to stress upon racial equality, equal pay, and equal opportunity for all. Politically, the declaration promised that the municipal councils as well as the majority of members of the rural councils would be elected by universal suffrage, and that the basic regional units, the territories, would be governed by councils which again would be elected. The two sets of councilors would form an electoral college which, in turn, would appoint the majority of provincial councilors. It was promised that the elections for these various councils would take place toward the end of 1959, and that the provincial councils would take effect in March of 1960.

A new governmental structure leading to independence was formulated. The Provincial Councils would, of course, form the basic governmental bodies on the provincial level. At the same time, a nascent Chamber of Deputies, or General Council, would be named by an electoral body composed of town councilors and members of the Territorial Councils. Finally, at the meetings of the Provincial Councils in March of 1959, two members would be designated from each province to serve on a Legislative Council which was planned to be the forerunner of a future Senate. Until such a program could be put in motion, consultative groups to the Governor General and to the Governors of each province were to be appointed immediately.

Thus the future Congo government was to consist of local, territorial, and provincial councils on the local level, and of a Chamber of Deputies and a Senate on the national level. Elections at the end of the year 1959 were to name the local councils, the date of formation of the Chamber of Deputies was not fixed, while the nascent Senate was to be elected in March, 1959.*

These promises representing concrete moves toward inde-

* The complete French text can be found in *108*:4–6, and an English translation in *4*:55–59.

pendence through the transfer of government to the Congolese were a substantial step forward, and both African and European comments were for the most part favorable. Certainly this represented a clear-cut promise of independence, though no date was mentioned, and the question thus became one of time: the basic struggle had been won.

The Governmental Declaration had been based to a considerable extent upon the report of the Study Group which had been appointed in July of 1958, did its work from October 21 to November 14, and submitted its report to the government which made it public in February of 1959. The group held its sessions in each provincial capital and consulted a total of 462 people of whom 212 were African and 250 European. Its report urged a clearer definition of Belgium's intentions toward the Congo, stated what its final objectives should be, and discussed the rate of progress toward independence, the question of a fixed date, and various social and economic problems. But the last part of its report was devoted to the establishment of fundamental reforms and the creation of the new governmental institutions discussed above. (See *27:5–7*.)

By this time the proliferation of political parties in the Congo had reached full phase, and general lines of battle were being drawn between competing politicians and parties with an eye toward future power in the independent Congo. On April 7–12, 1959, under the general aegis of Patrice Lumumba, a meeting of eight political parties took place in Luluabourg. The sessions were not public and out of them came a series of six motions calling for the formation of various commissions, commenting on suffrage, and instituting ideas which came to be rather basic "planks" in the platform of the Mouvement National Congolais headed by Lumumba. Of special importance, however, was the first motion which stated flatly that "the Congress demands the installation in January, 1961 of a government to determine at what date the Congo will accede to its total independence." For the first time, a definite timetable had been demanded, and for the first time, too, Africans from all parts of the Congo had come together in a political meeting to discuss their political future. (See *65:15–26.*)

This congress was followed swiftly by another meeting in Léopoldville in June of 1959 which resulted in the granting of a collective audience to the parties involved by Minister Van Hemelrijck on June 24. Noting that "no Congolese organization was consulted in the formulation of the governmental declaration of January 13," and that "that declaration was timid and did not fix all the stages required to lead the Congo to its independence," the group set forth four points. The first called for immediate implementation of public and individual liberties as guaranteed under the United Nations Charter. The second demanded the creation of supervisory commissions to oversee the coming elections, while the third called for universal suffrage in those elections and the eradication of the plan to include appointed members. It is the fourth resolution, however, which is most important and most striking, for it proposed a detailed timetable for independence:

4. Timing for independence
    1959: October: Installation of supervisory commissions
           December: Communal and territorial elections
    1960: March: Provincial elections
          June: General elections on a national scale
                          Formation of a parliament
                          Formation of a provisional government
                            responsible to the parliament
      1 December: Referendum for the adoption of the
                            constitution
                          Dissolution of the parliament
                          End of the provisional government
    1961: January: General elections on a national scale
                          Constitution of parliament
                          Formation of a responsible government
                          (See *65:73–77; 25:14,* for English
                          translation.)

Events were now becoming primarily political and on the same date (June 24) as this declaration which was engineered by the MNC and Lumumba, the ABAKO, over the signatures of Kasavubu, Kanza, and Nzeza, sent to Minister Van Hemelrijck a "project of government" for the Lower Congo region in which the group coolly announced: ". . . as of the month of January, 1960, the Province of Léopoldville will become an autonomous state which will be called the 'Republic of Central Kongo.' It will be a democratic and social republic, and its capital will be Léopoldville." The document went on to set forth in some detail the organization of the proposed government.

On June 26, two days later, Van Hemelrijck answered that ". . . the Belgian government cannot look favorably . . . on facilitating action on your plan. . . . I would add that sanctions toward you would have to be taken if you continue to implement this program . . ." In turn, ABAKO replied on July 2 and hedged to the extent of saying that its plan would now be put into action ". . . as part of a federated Congo." (See *65:*70–72.) It may be added here that the ABAKO threats of secession continued sporadically during this period, and were used consistently to threaten the Belgians when the ABAKO considered that things were not moving swiftly enough. (See, for example, *8.*)

Official response to these programs, which called for greater haste as well as the division of the Congo into units held together through a federal system, was given at a lunch held by the Belgian Congo and Ruanda-Urundi Press Association on June 24, 1959, for Minister Van Hemelrijck. Among other remarks, he spoke strongly against both greater haste and the possible Balkanization of the country:

> Law and order must be maintained. Troublemakers, whoever they are, must be brought to their senses. The time has come for firmness. We shall permit no departure from the Government Declaration, which will be fully implemented. It is vain, there-

> fore, to cast doubts upon the unity of the Congo and publish programs which acknowledge differences of opinion. "Balkanization" of the Congo would put an end forever to any possibility of the Congo's occupying a preponderant place among the Central African nations. It is also vain to launch into dangerous improvisations by hastily setting up a provisory government which, for lack of any representative value, would be unable to render the services expected of it. (*65*:65)

On the other hand, Vice-Governor Schöller, on September 2, 1959, acting at the time in the absence of Governor General Cornelis, sent a telegram to the Minister in which he urged that for various practical reasons the concept of federalism for the Congo should not be abandoned completely, and that the drawing up of the constitution of a Congolese government should be accelerated. (*40*:2–5; *108*:22)

Finally, the new Minister of the Belgian Congo and Ruanda-Urundi, Mr. Auguste de Schrijver, who succeeded Mr. Van Hemelrijck on September 3, 1959, attempted to clarify further the government's January, 1959, Declaration. In his statement of October 16, Minister de Schrijver began by outlining three steps toward independence. The first was the reconfirmation of the government's intentions to hold elections in December of 1959 at which city and territorial councilors would be elected by the Congolese. The second step would be the creation of provincial councils which would come into being as soon as possible after the December elections. Sixty per cent of the members of the provincial councils would be elected by the members of the territorial and municipal councils, while 30 per cent would be co-opted by those first elected; the final 10 per cent would be appointed, presumably by the Belgian government. "The Provincial Councils, established by a 90 per cent majority of members elected by the people, will be given extensive authority in the Provinces; . . . At the head of the Provincial Councils there will be a Provincial Government and a permanent deputation selected within and by the Provincial Councils" (*34*:3–5). The third step would come in the creation in 1960 of two legal assemblies and an executive body, thus a central government for the Congo.

The organization of the national government remained much as it had been outlined in the first announcement, save that some further details were given. The Chamber of Deputies was envisaged tentatively by Mr. De Schrijver as consisting of approximately 100 members elected under a system of proportional representation, although it was not settled whether this would be by direct vote or by the vote of elected territorial and municipal councilors. The Senate would have a more restricted membership and be formed through election by the provincial councils: each province would have the same number of seats. For the first time, an executive branch was mentioned in concrete terms. Under Mr. De Schrijver's tentative plans, the executive powers would be exercised by a Council of Ministers, possibly assisted by Under Secretaries, and presided over by the Governor General; members would be appointed by the King. Both the assemblies and the central executive council, it was promised, could be formed by August or September of 1960, and thus the formation of a government was set forward considerably.* Indeed, it was generally understood that the provisional government would be in power by the fall of 1960, and that complete sovereignty would be in effect by 1964.

In the midst of these various pronouncements in the summer and fall of 1959, other kinds of trouble began to manifest themselves as rioting appeared on a general scale. The first troubles grew out of an extremely complicated situation in Luluabourg, capital of the Kasaï Province, as tensions arose between the Baluba and the Bena Lulua tribes. As early as May 6, 1959, Chief Kalamba Mangole Sylvestre had demanded that the administration recognize the existence of a Lulua kingdom—a move generally felt to be directed against

---

* For complete French text see *108*:24–27; in English, *34*:3–5; *32*:1–7.

the Baluba. Without going into detail, it can be said that the Baluba were latecomers to the area, had in some instances been slaves to the Bena Lulua, and to a certain degree had been dependent upon them for land concessions. But the Baluba had kept up with the changes made by the Belgians and had come to dominate administrative and business positions, and the Bena Lulua rather belatedly found themselves in a position of being overwhelmed by a people whom they regarded as relative newcomers and strangers.

On June 29, 1959, the Governor of the Province appointed a commission to study the tense situation in Luluabourg, and a report was filed on July 8. On the same day, the report was stolen from the administrative offices, apparently copied, and returned; the move was political and probably made by the Mouvement Solidaire Baluba. The result was a sharp letter to the administration signed by Evariste Kalonji and Justin Kasanda, President and Secretary, respectively, of the MSB. The letter accused the Belgian administration of playing favorites, specifically of favoring the Bena Lulua, and of deliberately fomenting discord between the two groups. The situation grew more and more tense, and on August 3, Albert Kalonji, President of the MNC-Kasaï, Evariste Kalonji, and Albert Nyembwe were placed under arrest. Shortly thereafter rioting broke out in Luluabourg and it has continued with increasing violence to the present time.

The problem of who is at fault in the Baluba-Bena Lulua conflict cannot be solved here. The Baluba faction tends to blame the Belgian administration which it accuses of favoring the Bena Lulua. The Bena Lulua faction tends to blame the Baluba. One thing, however, is certain: whatever the background of the dispute, it has gone far beyond the original difficulties and become a war of hatred which will not be easily resolved. The Baluba-Bena Lulua fighting has continued off and on in Luluabourg for well over a year with literally hundreds if not thousands of casualties. It has spread to almost every part of the Congo where there are Baluba and Bena Lulua together: Tshikapa, Bakwanga, Albertville, Jadotville, Elisabethville, Léopoldville, and smaller local areas have all seen rioting and casualties. In truth, the rioting was not primarily political in the sense of rioting in the cause of Congo independence against the Belgian administration, but inevitably political overtones entered into the situation and it is doubtful that the conflict would have broken out in calmer times. In any case, the fact that it has continued stronger than ever since independence marks it clearly as an internal conflict, but it formed an ugly backdrop to the political events which were convulsing the Congo in the latter half of 1959 and the first half of 1960. (See *61; 80; 2:6–8.*)

The rioting in Luluabourg which spread to other areas found an echo of itself in Matadi on October 14 where twenty-eight people were hospitalized after the police moved in to break up a meeting of a prophetic religious movement. While the difficulties seem to have had no direct relationship to political movements of the times, it is again somewhat doubtful that they would have occurred had not the times been troubled. (See *30:1–21.*)

A third set of problems broke out in Stanleyville as an aftermath of Lumumba's MNC Congress there on October 23–29. The Congress itself made a number of startling demands, including the postponement of elections, the opening of new negotiations between the Congolese and Belgium, and the formation of a single assembly in place of the Belgian two-house plan. On October 30, a final meeting of the Congress was addressed by Lumumba, and the result was heavy rioting which caused the deaths of twenty-six Africans (the exact figure varies from report to report), and the wounding of more than one hundred Africans and Belgians. A warrant for Lumumba's arrest was issued, but he was hidden for two days by two Europeans and the arrest was not made until November 1. These troubles in Stanleyville were the beginning of a long series of ugly incidents in that area which continued sporadically throughout the remainder of the pre-independence period. Further riots broke out, cars were stoned, Europeans assaulted, and threats made, but in this case the motivation was clearly political.

Beginning in Luluabourg, Matadi, and Stanleyville, and spreading from each of these centers into the towns and countrysides around them, these incidents formed a melancholy background to the serious political negotiations going on between Belgians and Congolese. They also provided a certain sense of urgency to the negotiations as relations seemed to degenerate further and further. The pressures they engendered certainly contributed to the continually faster pace of the negotiations and to the eventual decision to grant independence long before the date originally contemplated by Belgium. The African upheavals also resulted in the decision of King Baudouin to make another visit to the Congo; the decision was made so abruptly that even the Belgian parliament was not informed of it until after the King had left Belgium. Arriving in Stanleyville on December 17, Baudouin was greeted by demonstrations which necessitated the dispersal of an airport mob by tear gas. His visit included all six of the provincial capitals and, judging from newspaper reports, he was treated to frank talk from the political leaders who demanded immediate independence in Stanleyville and Léopoldville, and warned that the Bas-Congo was close to explosion in Léopoldville. Nowhere, however, was the King personally troubled, except for the more or less usual difficulties in crowd control. In many places, for example Coquilhatville, he received extremely enthusiastic greetings which demonstrated again his personal popularity with the Congolese.

During the King's visit, the December elections for city and territorial councils took place all over the Congo. The King discreetly withdrew to Ruanda-Urundi on election days in order not to influence the vote: the elections were completed without violence or bloodshed, perhaps because difficulties had been expected and preparations made. Voting took place during almost the entire month of December. The results were very interesting, especially as they revealed patterns of voting which clearly depended on local situations. Thus, for example, in the Province of Katanga, of a total of 1,685,571 inhabitants, 362,520 were registered on the voting rolls; of these, 297,321, or 82 per cent actually voted. On the other hand, in Léopoldville, where the elections had been boycotted by the ABAKO, the nine African communes had a total of 76,924 voters of whom only 24,131, or 31.37 per cent voted: a large part of these were non-ABAKO members of course. In Stanleyville, as expected, Lumumba's MNC scored heavy successes; in Luluabourg, where 91.39 per cent of the electorate voted, the MNC-Kalonji came out ahead, although in the province as a whole the vote was split. The Katanga Federalist Union, Conakat, was successful, as predicted, in the Katanga, while in Kivu Province the vote was almost entirely local. The Equator Province also voted on local bases.

It is worthwhile to note some specific election figures which indicate the extreme localism of the voting and at the same time the kind of "majorities" gained by individual parties. In Katanga Province 484 seats were at stake and, of course, the Conakat gained the highest number, 84 seats. In addition, however, 191 seats went to local candidates who were considered favorable to Conakat. Conakat's major opponent, Balubakat (Baluba du Katanga) gained only 27 seats. Thirty-eight seats went to more or less nationally known parties, while 144 seats were scattered on purely local bases among independents who could probably not be counted upon to support any specific national or provincial party. Thus of 484 seats, Conakat gained a clear victory in only 84 contests, with a probable supporting total of 275 seats in all, or a bare majority given the optimistic view that the 191 renegade seats would indeed support the Conakat. The December elections, then, showed clearly the almost completely local nature of the vote, the extreme fission in any given area, and the dependence of the turnout of voters on circumstances which were definitely not national, but local. It has been estimated that about 1,870,000 people voted, and that of these about 1,300,000 cast their ballots for local candidates who were not affiliated with national political parties. (See *20*:5–7; *1*:2–9.)

The next important event, indeed the most important in the history of the independence of the Congo, was the Round Table Conference held in Brussels from January 20 to February 20, 1960. The idea of the conference had grown out of a number of suggestions made both by Congolese and Belgians, and the question of an exact date for its opening had been the subject of considerable dispute, with the Belgian side insisting that mid-January was the earliest possible date, and some Congolese, notably ABAKO leaders, insisting that it must take place early in January. A number of other difficulties were encountered and overcome such as seating of delegates, procedural rules, and so forth, and when the conference opened, 55 Belgians and 96 Congolese were in official attendance; in addition, 18 Europeans served as advisors to 15 specific parties (*9*:62–3). It is interesting to note that of 72 Congolese members specifically interviewed by CRISP, only 12 had had any formal education beyond the high school level and most of these in theological studies, although philosophy and law were also represented. Of these same Congolese delegates, there were 12 chiefs or notables, 25 clerks, 1 teacher, 5 accountants, 2 planters, 2 public defenders, 6 merchants, 5 state functionaries, 2 journalists, 1 judiciary agent, 1 administrator of a co-operative, and 2 without profession. Their average age was thirty-five years (*12*:9–10). Despite these difficulties (and the additional difficulties of personality and political problems which went on throughout the conference,

100

especially on the part of Mr. Kasavubu), agreements were reached, and sixteen resolutions were passed.

The first twelve of these resolutions concerned political problems. Resolution 2 stated, "As of June 30 next the Congo, within its present frontiers, shall become an independent State whose inhabitants shall, under conditions to be enacted by law, have the same nationality and shall be free to move about and establish themselves within the confines of the said State, and in which goods and merchandise may also circulate freely." The new state was set up on the basis of the six provinces long-established by Belgium, and it was arranged that the first Congolese government would be formed from the results of the provincial elections scheduled for May. The two-house organization, long since proposed, was continued with a Chamber of Deputies to be elected directly by universal suffrage on the basis of one representative for each 100,000 inhabitants, and a Senate formed essentially of members designated by the provincial assemblies on the basis of fourteen members per province, at least three of whom were to be tribal chiefs or leaders. French was named the official language of the parliament, and the first term of office was set at not less than three years nor more than four unless the parliament was dissolved for special elections under the Constitution. The Constitution was to be drawn up by both Houses no later than June 30, 1960, and the same body was to decide upon a Chief of State who was to hold office until the new Constitution became operative. A number of principles were set up to guide the Constituant Assembly,

1) the equality of all in the eyes of the law;
2) the right of every individual to life and to corporal integrity;
3) the guarantee of individual liberty, with the exception of sentences pronounced by the judiciary . . .
4) freedom of thought, conscience and religion;
5) freedom of speech;

PROPOSED LEGISLATIVE ASSEMBLIES
(As provided by the resolutions at the Round Table Conference)

PROVINCIAL ASSEMBLIES*

Léopoldville	90 seats
Equator	60 seats
Eastern	70 seats
Kivu	70 seats
Katanga	60 seats
Kasaï	70 seats

Members of the provincial assemblies are elected by universal suffrage or by the elected representatives of the people. In addition, each assembly will co-opt traditional chiefs whose number will constitute no less than 10 per cent or more than 15 per cent of the total assembly.

PARLIAMENT

Chamber of Deputies (137 members)

Elected in each province by universal suffrage on the basis of one representative for each 100,000 of population, plus an additional representative if the population figure over the nearest 100,000 is greater than 50,000.

Province of Léopoldville 33 elected	Province of Equator 18 elected	Eastern Province 25 elected
Province of Kivu 23 elected	Province of Katanga 16 elected	Province of Kasaï 22 elected

Senate (84–96 members)

Each provincial assembly elects fourteen senators, among whom must be included from each province at least three traditional chiefs or notables. Eventually, a maximum of twelve senators may be co-opted by the elected senators, but these must be distributed equally among the provinces.

CENTRAL LEGISLATIVE POWER

Chief of State

Chamber of Deputies   Senate

* Basis for calculating the division of seats in the provincial assemblies is as follows:

less than 2,000,000 inhabitants:	60 seats
2,000,000 to 2,499,999 inhabitants:	70 seats

6) freedom of education and all of its corollaries;
7) right of public meeting and freedom of association;
8) the inviolability of correspondence and of postal, telephone and telegraph communications;
9) freedom of work;
10) the right to own property . . .
11) the inviolability of the home.

The resolutions provided that until June 30, the basic law would be in the hands of the provincial authority, and distinctions of powers and duties between the provincial governments and the central government were clearly drawn. Resolution 11 defined the electoral system which stipulated that all voters must be males, twenty-one years or older, six-month residents of the area in which they voted, and Congolese. Belgians were not given the vote, nor were prisoners or persons interned or hospitalized by reason of mental derangement. Candidates for office were required to be Congolese, twenty-five years old for election to the Chamber of Deputies, and thirty years old for the Senate; Belgians were again excluded. Resolution 12 provided for the exercise of executive authority until June 30 by appointing six Congolese members to the staff of the Governor General, and three members to the staff of each Provincial Governor. The appointments to the Governor General's staff included one representative from each province: Katanga, Rémy Mwamba; Léopoldville, Joseph Kasavubu; Eastern, Patrice Lumumba; Equator, Paul Bolya; Kasaï, Pierre Nyanguyle; Kivu, Anicet Kashamura. A further commission of six members was established to remain in Brussels to draw up draft laws, edicts, decrees, treaties, conventions, and a draft constitution.

Resolution 13 promised a general treaty of friendship between Belgium and the Congo to be signed as soon as possible, as well as a Belgian technical mission to the Congo. The following resolution spoke in rather general terms of economic problems and provided for an Economic Round Table conference, while Resolution 15 put the Belgian civil servants in the Congo under the authority of the Congolese government, although their right to resign rather than work under a foreign power had already been made clear. The final resolution provided for the exercise of judiciary power.

Although some questions were left unanswered, the sixteen resolutions of the Round Table Conference provided a statesmanlike approach to the difficult problem of independence. In general, they were greeted with enthusiasm by the Congolese and with incredulity by the Belgian population of the Congo itself.*

Laws based upon the sixteen resolutions were quickly passed in the Belgian parliament. A law of March 8 specified that the Congolese would participate in the administration of the Congo during the transitional period between that time and June 30. On March 23 a bill defining the organization of the legislative and provincial elections was passed, and on May 18 two bills were passed, the first dealing with public rights and the second with the structure of the Congolese State. The latter act replaced the Colonial Charter of 1908 under which the Congo had been governed since its acquisition by Belgium.†

Resolution 14 of the Round Table Conference had provided for a second conference to discuss economic, financial, and social questions as well as arrangements for agreements between Belgium and the Congo regarding technical aid and economic co-operation. This Economic Round Table Conference took place in Brussels from April 26 to May 16, 1960, and was attended by five governmental and twenty parliamentary delegates from Belgium and about sixty delegates of the various Congolese political parties as well as the members of

* See *45*:4–20; *9*; *11*. The resolutions will be found in Appendix III.
† The organization of the new state based upon the Round Table resolutions is discussed in detail in *99*.

the Executive Council attached to the Governor General. Also represented were observers from the area of private business, delegates of trade associations, and from Ruanda-Urundi. The final result was eighteen resolutions proposed by two working committees. The resolutions of the first committee were very general in nature and consisted for the most part of the reference of various economic problems to further study committees. The second committee also set up future studies and made broad recommendations, but some of its provisions were more specific. Thus the committee dealt, in Resolution 2, with possibilities of expropriation, a move which it left open to possibility. Resolutions 3 and 4 dealt with the creation of various committees, while Resolution 5 suggested ways in which Belgo-Congolese disputes might be settled. Other resolutions concerned technical co-operation between Belgium and the Congo, the Congo's relations to the European Economic Community, trade relations between the Congo and other states, and powers of concession. Resolution 11 dealt strongly with social problems, recommending the end of all racial discrimination, the establishment of universal social security, and the guarantees of all freedoms by the new Congolese government. The last resolution concerned land tenure but left open the question of the concessions previously granted individual companies. The Economic Round Table probably raised more questions than it answered, but at the same time it did clarify many of the problems facing the Congo, and undoubtedly contributed to the awareness of the economic picture on the part of the Congolese who attended the conference. (See *52; 53.*)

Between the end of the Economic Conference in mid-May, and the accession to independence on June 30, a number of significant events took place in the Congo. One of these was the beginning of the movement of Belgians out of the country. No figures are available concerning how many left the colony before June 30, but Sabena, the Belgian airline, was booked almost solidly throughout May and June, and as independence came closer, was forced to borrow equipment from other world airlines in order to put on many extra flights. The anxieties and doubts as to the future stability of the country probably explain the exodus more than any other factor. Fully as important, however, were two economic measures which made life difficult and unsure for the Belgians. The first of these was a decree that no resident of the Congo could send out of the country a sum totalling more than 10,000 francs (200 dollars) per month. Although this was later modified to allow for exceptional cases, it worked a certain hardship especially on those Belgians who had families to support in Belgium. Much bitter complaining was heard in the Congo about this currency restriction, primarily on the basis that it penalized the small businessman unnecessarily, since "all the big money has already been allowed to escape," and also because the mechanics of making the transfer were difficult. At first forms had to be filled out each month, although this was later modified to allow a single form for a regular monthly transfer. The process moved slowly, and applications were sometimes seemingly arbitrarily denied. The fact, however, that a person leaving the Congo definitively could liquidate his resources and transfer them to Belgium intact undoubtedly contributed to the exodus. The second financial problem which faced Belgian colonists early in 1960 was the stifling of credit in the Congo. In mid-April the central Chamber of Commerce announced that it had advised all its members to stop credit acceptance as of May 1; the result was that almost all businesses, whether members or not, cut credit. In Kabinda in the Kasaï, where most of my own major supplies were bought, the credit cut had the effect of an almost immediate shortage of goods: within a matter of two weeks, no gasoline, salt, powdered milk or matches were available, although most of these items did eventually return. But more evident was the fact that, since businesses are successful and can expand only in an atmosphere of credit, the future began to look even more difficult. Stores could not obtain the goods necessary to their daily functioning, and in some cases there was simply not enough cash to carry on a business. It was the economic situation, then, the insecure future, the almost untenable financial situation in regard to obligations in Belgium, and the lack of credit, which combined to force many Belgians to make their plans to leave the country, and the last two months before independence saw a growing wave of departures.

A second event of major importance was the appointment in May, 1960, of Mr. Ganshof van der Meersch as Resident Minister of Belgium in the Congo. This appointment grew out of the relative vacuum in Belgian government in the Congo, especially since the Round Table discussions, and was probably designed to restore the confidence of all concerned. At about the same time, the Belgian government had decided to strengthen Belgian bases in the Congo by sending in further aviation, commando, and parachute divisions. This move had contributed to the lowering of general confidence; the stated purpose was that "we must see to it that Belgium cannot be reproached with having granted independence in chaos." In any case, Minister van der Meersch's job was defined to "co-ordinate measures relative to the maintenance of order, watch over the normal functioning of the judicial apparatus, and stimulate the activity of the administration"; in short, to keep order.

In the meantime, incidents of violent nature were taking place all over the Congo, particularly in the Luluabourg area where the Baluba-Bena Lulua conflict continued to break out sporadically spreading almost throughout the Kasaï Province. In this atmosphere of tension, political movements continued. In a letter addressed to King Baudouin, the ABAKO demanded the immediate formation of a provisional government and threatened "to solicit a foreign body to keep order and to boycott all the resolutions of the Round Table Conference." In the name of the MNC, Lumumba followed suit in a telegram to the Minister of the Congo, demanding that the executive colleges both on the national and provincial levels be transformed into a provisional government, and that the Round Table directives be modified to allow the Chief of State to be elected directly by the people rather than through the two Houses. The government rejected both appeals and their rejection coincided in time with the decision to reinforce the military bases, thus suggesting to Congolese leaders the conclusion that the Belgians were planning to set up a puppet government backed by military force. In a press interview May 18, Lumumba protested and called for "the immediate departure of the metropolitan troops as well as those stationed at the bases of Kitona and Kamina. They constitute an affront to the Force Publique of the Congo . . . and to General Janssens (commander of the Force Publique). The Force Publique, with its thousands of Congolese soldiers and its Belgian officers is an ample force." He also leveled a number of accusations against the Belgian government: "The principle objective of the Belgian government is to see constituted a puppet government which Belgium will control . . . The immediate liberation of the country and the immediate transfer of powers is the sole possible means for avoiding serious incidents, incidents for which Belgium will be responsible before the world." So saying, Mr. Lumumba on May 19 handed in his resignation to the Executive College, but faced with a solid front by his colleagues and undoubtedly aware that in so resigning he compromised his own political future, he returned to this position later in the month.

Toward the end of May the results of the general elections were made known, and it appeared that the MNC-Lumumba had won a weak victory for, with its allies, it could now hope, at least, to control the provincial governments of the Eastern, Kivu, and Kasaï provinces. In the Chamber of Deputies the

MNC won 38 seats; in addition 26 other seats were won by parties or individuals considered to be favorable to the MNC (13 PSA, 10 CEREA, and 3 UC of the Kasaï, all part of a new coalition). It must be noted specifically, however, that this did not represent a majority (69 seats of a total of 137 required), and also that the MNC had no representation in the Katanga province which was to cause so much trouble for Lumumba after independence.

The first two weeks in June were given over to the formation of the provincial governments and the national assemblies. During this period two lines of power formed. The first, based on Mr. Lumumba's policies, included his own party, the opposition party of the Katanga, the principle party of the Kivu, and a fourth rather general party. The second was an anti-Lumumba cartel formed of three major political parties. The maneuvers of these two groups were to have considerable influence in the struggle to form a central government.

On learning of the results of the May elections Lumumba had demanded that the King call on the MNC to form the new government, and on June 13, Minister van der Meersch gave Lumumba a directive authorizing him to seek out the possibilities. On June 14, Tuesday, Lumumba ran into the first difficulties when the anti-Lumumba cartel, as well as Mr. Kasavubu refused flatly to meet with him. The following day a meeting was arranged but agreement could not be reached on the selection of ministers, and the ABAKO refused to move from its position regarding the Chief of State. On June 16, Mr. Lumumba reported back to the Minister on the problems which faced him, and the Minister himself agreed to assist in the negotiations. However, on making contact with the leaders of the opposition cartel, the Minister was so impressed with the extent of their determination that he dismissed Mr. Lumumba and turned on Friday, June 17, to Mr. Kasavubu.

Mr. Lumumba immediately reacted by calling a press conference at which he charged a plot, attacked the Minister and the King, and announced a boycott of all parliamentary institutions. The following day, June 18, as Kasavubu encountered difficulties similar to those suffered by Lumumba, Lumumba announced that he would form an independent popular government. Sunday morning, June 19, Kasavubu announced that he had formed a coalition government which represented all political parties save Lumumba's MNC, and the Minister, feeling that success was at hand, prepared to leave for Brussels to seek Belgian sanction. But during the day no less than three major parties protested that they were not part of Kasavubu's government, and the Minister postponed his trip. That evening he called Lumumba and Kasavubu together but no accord could be reached between them. Kasavubu offered Lumumba the post of Premier in a government to be formed by Kasavubu, but the offer was refused. Monday, June 21, passed in fruitless maneuvering, but on Tuesday the Chamber was called upon to express its opinion through the vote, and the result was a clear-cut victory for Lumumba. In consequence, the duty of forming the government was that evening withdrawn from Kasavubu, and returned to Lumumba.

Wednesday and Thursday, June 22 and 23, were passed in political jostling but by Thursday afternoon, Lumumba had put together a government which in theory represented 120 out of 137 seats in the Chamber. On a final vote that evening, however, he obtained only 74 votes: 1 vote was cast against him; 5 abstained from the vote; and there were 57 absences of which most, if not all, were considered to be deliberate. The Senate also confirmed the government by a vote of 60 for, 12 against, and 8 abstentions, and the government was formed. Finally, on June 24 Mr. Kasavubu was overwhelmingly elected as the President of the State, and a Congolese government was completed just five days before Independence Day (*24*). It remained only for Belgium and the Congo to sign a treaty of mutual assistance, friendship, technical co-operation, diplomacy, military dispositions, and commerce; this was done on June 29 and the following day the Congo was no longer a colony.

We have seen that in the short space of five years the Congo's status changed from that of a colony whose owners had hardly contemplated the question of independence, to an autonomous republic. Belgium has received her share of brickbats for the situation which followed independence, but before June 30 some felt moved to compliment her on her handling of the situation. Thus Colin Legum commented that "The Belgians, on the whole, were quick to understand the implications of the changes that began to occur in Congo since 1946. They have shown a subtlety and flexibility that are quite remarkable" (*85*:104). On the other hand, even Belgians have expressed their doubts about the rate of speed at which the Congo moved toward independence. The Editor of the official English-language propaganda magazine of Inforcongo, the Belgian Information Service for the Congo, commented in January, 1960: "The only mistake the Belgians may be making is to expect . . . moderation and common sense from the self-appointed Congolese leaders. . . . Recent outbursts in the Congo . . . have demonstrated that political consciousness in the modern sense is not yet strong enough to override tribalism and feuds between races. Extreme forms of tribalism . . . are also inspiring some wholly unrealistic plans for cutting the Congo into pieces without calculating the economic consequences. . . . The road is now open to Congolese self-rule. But it is not until the Congo's leaders have given earnest proof of their sound intentions and have shown that they are capable of restraints and balance, that they will establish a vital reputation for credit-worthiness. The Congolese leaders will have to show their wisdom in not jeopardizing that credit-worthiness even before their present direct goal is attained" (*79*:3, 4, 5).

If some Belgians had their doubts, so did some Congolese. The Chef de Secteur based at Mitombe near where I spent the year 1959–60 was frankly afraid of the consequences of independence, and the reaction of the Congolese villagers in the area is discussed in Chapter V of this book. But Inforcongo itself gave us further clues when it reported that "News reports from Brussels indicated that most Congolese delegates at the [Round Table] conference could hardly believe what they heard when Mr. de Schryver [De Schrijver] made his historical statement [of June 30 independence]. Their first reaction was one of baffled exultation mingled with real misgivings. The present seemed a little big to take home" (5:5).

And what of the Belgians in the Congo? For the most part resigned to the events that were taking place around them, some still spoke out against independence and the speed with which it had been given. R. E. Lenain, representing perhaps an extreme voice, wrote a bitter denunciation of the Belgian government, not against independence but against the manner in which it had been given:

> That truth is that the Belgian government, whatever be its reasons, wants to rid itself of the Congo.
> That could perhaps be justified. But what is criminal on its part is its hypocritical deliverance of the Congo into disorder, anarchy and impoverishment, and to do it only to be able to wash its hands, like Pontius Pilate, of the future of the Congo.
> "Messieurs, we have occupied the Congo during three quarters of a century; that is true, but you see that in 1960 we have turned the power over to the natives.
> "If they assassinate, if they pillage, if the Congo is returned to barbarism, don't accuse us. Address yourself to the Congolese government. There is nothing more for us in this affair. We have done our duty in turning over to the Africans that which is theirs."
> So goes the language of these Messieurs.
> It is simple, facile, and cowardly. But far too facile, much too simple, and above all far too cowardly to succeed. All the same, outside of our Africans there are some worthy men in the

112

Congo, Messieurs the Ministers, and you will see it someday. (*87:12*)

Whatever be the case, and particularly in the light of subsequent events, the independence of the Congo and the speed with which it was conceived and given, as well as the difficulties under which its first government was formed, will be the subject of discussion among politicians and political scientists for decades to come. But despite their talk and analyses, the fact remains that the Congo is independent and that it is independent because that independence was granted by Belgium. Too soon, too late, done well or badly, that fact remains.

CHAPTER IV

Parties and Politicians

The multi-party system in the Congo presents a particularly confusing picture to those accustomed to thinking in simpler political terms. As of September 1, 1959, DeBacker listed thirty-one political parties in the Congo (*66*:153–57), but by January 11, 1960, this had grown to fifty-one (*72*:265–80), and by May 20, 1960, Artigue listed no fewer than 120 Congolese political organizations (*58*:115–31). The situation was made particularly confusing by a number of special factors including the fluidity of the organizations, ignorance on the part of their leaders of political movements in other parts of the Congo, ethnic diversity, and the rural-urban split.

Many parties, once created, disappeared or were absorbed into another party which, in turn, might well fuse with still a third. In some cases, as many as twenty-five political parties merged together into a single new group, but in such a situation it was often the case that a portion of party A would merge with party B, while a second portion of party A would merge with party C. This fluidity can be laid in part at least to the fact that Congolese leaders had virtually no political experience and, once having formed a party they sometimes found that after a few months it no longer represented their own desires or that their own ideas had changed and the party refused to change with them. In some instances, political leaders learned that other parties formed in other parts of the Congo were organized around similar principles and were perhaps stronger, thus dictating political fusion for self-preservation.

Another problem was the tribal organization of political groupings. Almost every party formed in the Congo had its origin in a tribal group, and since there are many tribes there were many parties as well. Local interests were paramount in early political formation and they have never ceased to be a powerful factor in politics.

Finally, there is a stringent question in Congo politics as to how much popular support any leader can command at any given time, and to a considerable extent this is a function not only of poor communications but also of differences between urban and rural areas. Almost all political parties were formed in urban centers by relatively educated Congolese, and while some parties were organized specifically to protect the interests of rural areas, they were not always successful since the urban leaders often failed to reach their rural constituencies. The urban-rural split is a real one in the Congo, and the transitory nature of the popularity of almost any leader, plus his urban problems of coralling and keeping the rural vote, has contributed heavily to the shifts, movements, appearances, and disappearances of political parties.

Because of the various problems, there is a strong question as to whether these can be called political parties at all, and equally important, whether it is really possible to speak of political platforms. In Congo politics what passed for platforms were more often simply extremely tenuous declarations of principles; thus they spoke almost invariably in general terms—"in the field of politics," "in the field of economics," "in the social and cultural sphere," or hedged further by noting that "a study group has been set up to outline a complete platform." Certainly up to mid-June of 1959 no group had presented a clear platform nor was the mass of people particularly interested in their doing so. Instead of platforms the parties were intent upon making more spectacular claims than the opposition in a race to outbid each other.

There were four major political tendencies which developed in the Congo in the short period of time since political parties appeared upon the scene. The first of these was separatism, best exemplified by the ABAKO. By separatism is meant an expressed aim of dividing the Congo in order to create new and completely independent states from the recognized Congo territory. Separatism shades almost imperceptibly into a second tendency, federalism, and in Congo politics it is often difficult to know whether a certain political party is espousing separatism or federalism. In a federal system the state is characterized by the existence of a government and a legislative power common to all the federated states, but with certain powers vested in the states themselves. Thus in a federal system, the governor of a province is the representative of the province, while in a unitary system he represents the central government. The degree to which powers are divided between the central and local governments in a federated state depends upon the definition and distribution of powers established by the constitution. (See *99*:15–22.) In the Congo situation a number of political parties espoused federalism, but in the case of the Katanga, for example, federalism often seemed to mean almost total independence. On the other hand, the ABAKO demands for separatism could just as often be seen to shade off into federalism which, again, came very close to being a demand for independence with virtually no responsibility to the central government.

A third tendency in Congo politics, exemplified primarily by the policies of Patrice Lumumba and his party, the MNC, is the establishment of a united Congo with a central government which administrates the entire territory and which makes almost no concession to federalist tendencies. One of Lumumba's rallying cries was "Congo Uni," or "United Congo," and he and his party stuck doggedly to this principle throughout the campaigns.

The fourth tendency was dictated by the principle of moderation, and the demands of representative parties for independence were in general agreement with the Belgian governmental declaration of January 13, 1959; this declaration stressed the Belgo-Congolese community and outlined no specific timetable for independence. The Interfédérale as well as the PNP and other parties supported this course although, as in so many cases, their support often tended to waver and, in some cases, to change markedly.

Finally, other political parties espoused combinations of the four tendencies noted above, combining moderation and support of Belgian policy with a call for federalism, for example, as in the case of the UC, or on the other hand, not taking any clear-cut stand except perhaps for a demand for independence. In this general category must also be included the several European parties which for the most part were against independence but which, in some cases, set forth programs that were modifications of the principal tendencies.

PRE-POLITICAL MOVEMENTS

Coinciding roughly with World War II, Belgian educational efforts in the Congo began to produce a group of young Congolese who held secondary school degrees and who, because of the displacement of Belgian personnel for war purposes, were taken into the administration and the private business world in jobs of varying responsibility. After the war, primarily in Léopoldville but in other urban centers as well, this movement to enlist the *évolués*, as they were called, became an avalanche and many young men took places of growing responsibility and began to see new possibilities in the colonial situation. Thus the Association des Anciens Elèves des Pères de Scheut (ADAPES) which, since its foundation in 1925 had remained almost completely quiescent, suddenly turned into an association of 15,000 members who organized themselves into study circles. At the same time other similar organizations were founded, among them the Union des Anciens Elèves des Frères Maristes (UNELMA), the Association des Anciens Elèves des Frères des Ecoles Chrétiennes (ASSANEF), and the Anciens Elèves des Pères Jésuites. All these associations were directed by a president, a vice-president, and a central committee, and all took as their primary aims of study the new problems being created by the emergence of the *évolués* class; their attention, too, was inevitably drawn to the problem of the political future. These *évolués,* and particularly those of Léopoldville who worked in the Belgian administration, found themselves in daily contact with Europeans, and their hopes and ambitions grew especially in the social sphere.

In 1946, a group of administration clerks formed a nascent union called the Association du Personnel Indigène du Congo Belge et du Ruanda-Urundi (APIC), a group which spread rather widely and rapidly through the provinces of the Congo. Occupying itself primarily with questions such as that of equal pay for equal work, pension questions, the treatment of Congolese workers and like matters, APIC grew rapidly in influence and began to create an awareness among its members of the necessity for a broader ideology.

At the same time, another group of *évolués* in Léopoldville founded a second organization, the Union des Intérêts Sociaux Congolais (UNISCO); its president was Eugène Kabamba, who was a government clerk. UNISCO was founded as a study group, with its principal subjects of study the total suppression of all racial discrimination, the amelioration of social conditions of Congolese in general and the defense of the rights of the *évolués* in particular.

Thus some basic pre-political institutions existed in the Congo before the first real political parties were formed. Organizations such as APIC and UNISCO gave the *évolués* a forum within which they could not only discuss their problems but see future possibilities. UNISCO itself, as we shall note later, was further instrumental in beginning the careers of at least two Congolese who were later to be in the forefront of independence movements—Joseph Kasavubu and Jean Bolikango.

118

SEPARATIST-FEDERALIST PARTIES

The ABAKO (Alliance des Bakongo)

Among the separatist movements, the ABAKO and its leader Joseph Kasavubu are the outstanding forces, but it was the so-called Mouvement de Regroupement des Populations Congolaises, the MRPC, which backed the first openly published announcement of a desire to create a completely independent Bakongo state in the Lower Congo region. This announcement was made on February 27, 1959. The leaders of the MRPC were unknown in Léopoldville, where the party was supposedly formed, and it is generally felt today that the MRPC itself was a fiction created by the ABAKO as an indirect means of attempting to make its program seem stronger than, quite possibly, it was. In any case, the Belgian news agency, Belga, released a report on the program of the MRPC which stressed the ethnic unity of the Bakongo people west of Léopoldville and pointed out the arbitrary nature of the political boundaries of that region of the Congo.

> . . . This movement aims at the regrouping of the populations of the Bakongo ethnic group and at the formation of a state which will comprise certain people of the Belgian Congo, of the Republic of Congo, of the Cabinda enclave and of Angola. In a manifesto which it is publishing, the MRPC considers the present division of the territories as arbitrary and denounces "the separatist and destructive action of the Berlin conference of 1885." It was then that the people of the Congo were divided and enfeebled and that its territory was divided among France, Belgium and Portugal. . . . Under present conditions, it is utopian to believe in the unification of the peoples of the Belgian Congo. . . . [We must] . . . regroup the great ethnic divisions into distinct states, leaving it to them to create a federation when they themselves feel the necessity to unite. (65:53)

The announcement went on to cite the various resources of the proposed independent state, to ask for Belgian co-operation in creating and maintaining it, and to assure the white population of safety and security. The MRPC was probably a fictive creation of the ABAKO, and in any case the announcement of its formation seems to have been its only action; it never reappeared on the political scene.

It was the ABAKO itself which made the strongest separatist movements, always in respect to the Bakongo people of the Lower Congo region, and the ABAKO was personified in the strong direction of its leader, Joseph Kasavubu. Shortly after World War II one of the movements of the emerging class of *évolués* was the UNISCO, formed to study various social problems. As UNISCO developed, it came to a point at which it wished to present to the Belgian administration a series of recommendations and demands for the solution of these problems. At this time, UNISCO was composed of *évolués* whose education was not higher than secondary school, and the members felt that their demands would not be heard by the government unless they could find a strong representative personality who could present and discuss them, even with the Governor General himself. Mr. Jean Bolikango, one of the founders of UNISCO and the president of another similar organization, proposed a friend for the position of UNISCO spokesman; the friend at the time was employed as a government clerk and for three years had pursued post-secondary study in theology and philosophy at the Seminary of the Missions de Scheut at Kabwe near Luluabourg. This friend was Joseph Kasavubu, and the members of UNISCO, feeling that he was the man to represent them before the government, invited him to join their association. But in order to be a member of UNISCO, it was necessary to be a director of one of the student organizations; to circumvent this difficulty Bolikango arranged for the election of Kasavubu as secretary general of ADAPES, of which Bolikango was president, and Kasavubu kept this position until 1956.

These events took place in 1946, and the first speech Kasavubu made before the membership of UNISCO showed plainly the direction his thinking had already taken. The lecture was titled "The Right of the First Occupant," and in it he followed the thesis that the Congolese, and particularly the Bakongo people, were the first occupants and therefore the owners of the Congolese soil, and that the soil thus ought to be returned to them. This was a revolutionary idea for the times, and UNISCO was apparently somewhat taken aback by the radical position of its new member. Over the years the society continued to discuss the various projects for which they had united—equal pay for equal work, participation in the administration, and so forth—but Kasavubu stuck with his thesis, expanded it, and presented it continually under new and varying forms. In 1955 he was named president of the ABAKO, and a year later resigned his position in ADAPES in order to devote himself exclusively to his new position.

The ABAKO movement had been formed in Léopoldville in 1950 by a group of Bakongo *évolués*. Since the turn of the century, the Bangala people from the Upper Congo region had begun to assume numerical ascendancy in Léopoldville. Further, they seemed quicker to take over European ways, or at least to accommodate themselves to European patterns, than the Bakongo who remained relatively hostile, and as a result Bangala-Belgian relations were closer and better than those between Bakongo and Belgians. Eventually, the Bakongo began to feel the need for organization in order to counteract the Bangala influence, and in 1950 the Bakongo *évolués*, led by Mr. Nzeza-Lanbu, formed an association. Their aim at this time was almost strictly cultural and revolved officially around the rebirth and unification of the Bakongo language.

In Chapter III we reviewed the development of the ABAKO party and Mr. Kasavubu beginning with the ABAKO Counter Manifesto of August 23, 1956, and continuing through ABAKO's part in the December, 1957, elections, Kasavubu's inaugural speech as mayor of Dendale in April, 1958, his part in the January 4–7, 1959, riots, the dissolution of the ABAKO and Kasavubu's exile in Belgium in the spring of 1958, his call for the independence of the Lower Congo on June 24,

1958, his appointment to the Executive College in February, 1960, his attempt to form a government on June 18, 1960, and his election as President of the new Congolese state on June 24, 1960. It remains, then, to present the structure of the ABAKO organization, and its political aims.

The present organization of the ABAKO as a political party took place in January of 1959, when the Bakongo population was drawn together sharply as a result of the riots in Léopoldville which produced sympathy for the imprisoned ABAKO leaders and for the victims of the riots. At this time, the ABAKO had a simple structure, derived from traditional Bakongo culture in which the basic social structure provided the foundation for a loose grouping of local units each of which retained a high degree of autonomy. The central ABAKO committee in Léopoldville accepted almost any unit which appeared to have the full support of the local populace. The ABAKO structure was comprised of two parts, the first of which was the Central Committee or ABAKO College composed of ten directors and ten legal members who were presidents of various sections in Léopoldville, and thirteen co-opted members who represented the interests of various territorial areas in the Lower Congo. The second part of the structure included the local sections of the Lower Congo: each section had at maximum a president, vice-president, secretary, treasurer, and a variable number of councilors, and existed through its acceptance by the local population and in turn, by the Central Committee. This organization, however, did not continue to serve its purpose, and by various ABAKO decrees of November 17 and December 29, 1959, and January 19, 1960, changes were made in the structure which was reorganized into three parts. The Central Committee, the first part, was cut in size to fifteen members. The second section, made up of the regional presidents, was left with a considerable degree of autonomy and this later caused confusion and scission in the party, especially during the Round Table Conference. The third part of the organization was made up of the various sections spread throughout the Lower Congo region and controlled both by the people themselves who elected officers and, to a certain extent, by the Central Committee which held the party together and formulated general policy. The principal work of the sections was to enlist members in the ABAKO and make dues collections which formed a large proportion of the central treasury.

The ABAKO published three widely read newspapers in Léopoldville and the Lower Congo, *Kongo Dia Ngunga, Notre Kongo,* and *Kongo Dieto,* all dailies. These papers were important to the ABAKO movement, and their existence was made feasible by the high literacy rate in this area of the Congo, estimated at about 37 per cent in the Lower Congo and 54 per cent in Léopoldville itself. Further, the tradition of publication in Kikongo reached back to biblical translations in the sixteenth century and missionary papers begun as early as 1896. The content of the ABAKO dailies varied but followed in general an anti-Belgian line; they served also, of course, as a news organ for the party. (See *41.*)

The platform on which the ABAKO stood is not always easy to follow, although at its core was separatism for the Lower Congo region. At times Kasavubu seemed to waver between separatism on the one hand and federalism on the other, but in either case it is clear that his conviction was that the Lower Congo should be independent. When he seemed to lean toward federalism he conceived of it only as the loosest possible form of that type of government. During Kasavubu's exile to Belgium in the spring of 1959, he and his two fellow exiles, Daniel Kanza and Simon Nzeza, were allowed liberty of movement and took the occasion to visit rather widely in the country. On each trip they took, however, they were accompanied by a representative of Inforcongo of whom one, Mr. DeBacker, has recorded his impressions which derived from long talks with the three leaders. DeBacker says:

By the end of these discussions, I arrived finally at the well-established conviction that:

The three heads of the ABAKO and particularly MM. Kasa-vubu and Kanza had but a single aim: the foundation of an independent state of the Lower Congo, free of all ties with the rest of the Belgian Congo and of the Republic of Congo, one of the regions of the old French Equatorial Africa.

That M. Kasa-vubu and none other than he would become the head of this state (at this time it was impossible to predict its form).

That he would not hesitate to use any means to arrive at this end. (65:45–6)

This program was given full expression in the declaration made June 24, 1959, by the three leaders of the ABAKO, Messrs. Kasavubu, Kanza, and Nzeza, which we have already had occasion to touch upon in Chapter III. In more detail, however, the declaration was sent to the Minister for the Congo, and it outlined the proposed new state:

. . . As of the month of January, 1960, the Province of Léopoldville will become an autonomous state which will be called the "Republic of Central Kongo." It will be a democratic and social republic, and its capital will be Léopoldville. The republic is headed by a president elected by the people, assisted by a vice president also elected by the people. The government of the republic will be composed of three distinct powers: 1) legislative; 2) executive; 3) judiciary. Legislative power will be represented in a Senate and a Chamber. Senators and Deputies will be elected through universal suffrage. Executive power will be vested in a cabinet of fifteen ministers and a Secretary of State. It will be supported by a provincial government, and a territorial and communal administration. The Cabinet will include ministers of Interior, Foreign Affairs, Justice, Health, Defense, Commerce and Industry, Youth and Sports, Education and Social Affairs, Economic Affairs, Transport and Communications, Agriculture, Waters and Forests, Finance, Public Works, Information, and Press and Work. The judiciary will include a supreme court, a court of appeals, a Tribunal . . . The provincial government will administer the five provinces of the Republic of Central Kongo, as follows: 1) the province of Kinshasha, capital Kintambo; 2) the Cataract province. capital Thysville; 3) Lower-River province, capital Boma; 4) Kwango province, capital Kikwit; 5) Kwilu province, capital Kenge.

124

. . . The Republic of Central Kongo will elect its president the 12th or 13th of December, 1959. In order to be considered eligible for election as president, the candidate must be: 1) from the Republic of Central Kongo; 2) 40 years old; 3) a person whose conduct toward the people has been irreproachable. In order to participate in the presidential election, the electors must be from the Republic of Central Kongo and 20 years of age. The right to vote is given to women as well as to men. . . .
. . . The geographic limits of the Republic of Central Kongo are: to the west, the Atlantic Ocean, Angola and the Republic of Congo (formerly French Equatorial Africa), to the east, the Kasai River; to the south, Angola; and to the north, the Kasai River, the River Congo, and the Republic of Congo. (*65:70–71*)

The response of the Minister to this ultimatum was to refuse it, as we have already seen, but the declaration represents clearly the basic position of Kasavubu and his party.

From December 24 to 27, 1959, the Kisantu Congress took place in the town of that name in the Lower Congo. This conference was called by the ABAKO in co-operation with three other parties of which we shall speak later, the MNC-Kalonji, the PSA, and the PP, and it grouped together into a new Cartel all the major parties which had separatist-federalist tendencies, except the Conakat of the Katanga. The position of the ABAKO in respect to separatism on the one hand or federalism on the other was by this time beginning to be cloudy, and indeed the Kisantu Congress was quite possibly the beginning of an ABAKO split along these two lines.

The Congress opened on a moderate tone which denied any hatred of Europeans and in which Kasavubu made a remarkably conciliatory statement toward Belgium: "It is to the Belgian people that we address ourselves and of whom we think at this moment; they are courageous and proud people, people who have never recoiled before great sacrifices in order that their rights and liberty could triumph, people profoundly Christian and good." It closed on almost equally moderate tone, but neither statement accorded precisely with the resolutions passed by the Congress. The tenth resolution, for ex-

125

ample, stated that the Congress "reiterates its position for immediate and total independence of the Congo," while others demanded the formation of an immediate provisional government, refused to recognize the right of Europeans to vote, and reaffirmed the confidence of the Congress in federalism, "the only form of government which can assure the harmonious development and the normal flowering of all the people." Thus, the ABAKO position here turned more toward federalism as opposed to separatism, although this may well have been due more to the nature of the Congress than to the personal feelings of Kasavubu.

The resolutions of the Kisantu Congress also expressed an economic stand, something rather rare in Congo political parties. Resolution 3 noted that the Congo was a basically capitalistic state and demanded that "the economy of the Congo be oriented toward the satisfactions of the needs of man and not toward individual profit," insisted on "the equitable division of the national revenue," and urged that legal measures be taken immediately to control the exportation of capital invested in the Congo. (See *1*:11–13.)

In sum, it has never been entirely clear whether the ABAKO as a party stood for separatism or federalism. It is almost certain, however, that Kasavubu himself has always favored separatism, and that in this stand he has been supported widely by the Bakongo population of the Lower Congo. In responding to political exigencies, he has from time to time altered his position toward federalism, but at the same time he has consistently used separatism as a weapon to wield against the Belgian administration and to reassure his own constituency. In any case, as has been noted, separatism and federalism in the context of Congo politics do not by any means necessarily indicate different things, and those who have supported federalism have often in actuality been striving for separatist states.

Joseph Kasavubu's date of birth has been variously described as 1910 and 1917; he was born in the Lower Congo region in the town of Tshela in the Mayombe. His primary schooling was taken at Kizu in the Catholic mission of the Pères de Scheut, and his secondary studies in a small seminary, Mbata Kiela, from 1928 to 1936. The following three years he spent studying theology and philosophy in the seminary at Kabwe near Luluabourg. Unsuccessful as a candidate for the priesthood, he returned to the Mayombe and studied for a year at Kangu; he received his teaching certificate in 1940, and taught for one year at Lemba. After a short term as clerk for the Belgian company AGRIFOR, he went to Léopoldville in 1942 where he was engaged by the Service des Finances of the Belgian Congo government and assigned to the supply division. We have already followed Mr. Kasavubu's subsequent career in some detail, but it should be added that he has made at least three trips to Belgium, and probably more. His behavior in Brussels during the Round Table Conference was puzzling, for on January 25 he left the Conference and did not return until February 10. During these fifteen days, his movements are not clearly known, but he did make at least two trips to Paris, one to Aix-la-Chapelle, and another to Liège. It is generally believed that he was received in Paris by the French Foreign Minister, and that he probably obtained legal advice from French lawyers. Returning to the Congo after the Conference, he made a trip to Elisabethville in April of 1960 where he established relations with the powerful Conakat, the federalist party of Moise Tshombe. In late April he returned to Brussels for the Economic Round Table. He was elected President of State of the Congo Republic on June 24.

Very little personal information exists concerning Mr. Kasavubu. He is married and the father of seven children. The *New York Times* (*31*) has described him as: ". . . a small, rotund man. . . . Mr. Kasavubu supports the principle of non-violence of the late Mohandas K. Gandhi. He is a bad public speaker and he reads French speeches in a halting, squeaky voice. In his own Kikongo language he is soft-spoken and produces a soothing effect on easily aroused African tempers." Colin Legum, who interviewed him in March of 1960 in Léopoldville, adds:

> He is short and squat, with mongoloid and Bantu features; he is suspicious and unforthcoming. He peers stolidly through large glasses; but this general impression of unfriendliness disappears if one succeeds in breaking down his natural reserve. He has a sly humour.
>
> He was trained by the Roman Catholics, and remains close to the Church. But he is at the same time close to the Kibanguists, the separatist church movement of the Bakongo. . . . He is a Thomist. . . . He has great political integrity. The Belgians accuse him of playing politics with Gaullist agents in Africa, and of making secret contacts with the West Germans. He has even been accused of being a Communist agent . . . (86:83)

The PP (Parti du Peuple)

Among the political parties which expressed strong support of the ABAKO was the Parti du Peuple (PP), and its President, Alphonse Nguvulu: this movement, aimed primarily toward federalism, took place after a brief flirtation with Lumumba's MNC and its goal of a united Congo. The PP was officially formed on April 26, 1959, but it grew out of a previous organization, the Action Socialiste, which was formed December 3, 1957, and which was the first official Congolese political party. Its basic approach, as we shall see, was socialist, at least in its economic proposals, but its principles followed the federalist line. Thus on June 9, 1959, the PP published a basic set of principles which it later put into action by joining the ABAKO in calling the Kisantu Congress in late December of the same year.

> In that which concerns our Congo, a worker's regime, that is to say a socialist democratic regime taking account of Congolese realities, is the only one which will not turn aside the wheel of history.
>
> What is this reality?
>
> It is a mosaic of tribes which have no sociological lines

among themselves and which live almost as strangers to one another in spite of the artificial fusion realized by the Colonizer. Each tribe still has its own personality. The tribes are characterized by a disparity in their degree of evolution. Some have changed from a tribal state to a national one in the modern sense of the word, and others remain in the tribal stage.

What should be done about it?

In order not to wound the natural susceptibilities of each region, *a government which gives some or a large degree of autonomy to each province is the only possible one at the present time. Thus, the need for federalism.*

Each province should have its autonomy in the care of a central government. The United States, the Soviet Union, India, the Nigerian Federation give us examples of a federal regime. Let those who confuse secession and federation be calm. These are two mutually exclusive ideas. On the contrary, the unity that they praise, and that we praise, can only exist in federalism. (72:95)

The pronouncement goes on to note that the Manifesto of the Action Socialiste had rejected federalism as a principle in 1958, and blamed the "error" on the influence of Belgian advisors. At the same time it is worth noting that the PP was not a professedly anti-Belgian party:

It should be noted that "independence" in the Congolese spirit in no sense means . . . the departure of whites working in the Congo. By "independence" the Congolese demand that their country benefit from the prerogatives of sovereignity in the same way as do the European, American, Asiatic and African nations whose governments are recognized by other nations. . . . In the Congolese spirit, all the Europeans who take Congolese nationality . . . will benefit from the same rights as the inhabitants of this country. . . . (66:15–16)

The PP is one of the few political parties which advanced any specific economic measures before independence. Drawing from various party publications, CRISP has put together the chief economic aims:

A distinction is made among three notions: patrimony, enjoyment and exploitation, and ownership. The means of production, land, and riches in general are the common patrimony of all. The right to the enjoyment and the exploitation of this patrimony is subordinated to the social utility and to the maximum well being of all. The ownership of riches and of means of production cannot be reserved to any individual who will use them for his own profit.

The PP called for the socialization of large holdings under a collective directorate, not only to guarantee equal distribution of profits but also to force the participation of workers in the responsibilities and decisions of the economic and social life of the country. The PP called for

giving the ownership of the land to the political entities which would be charged with exploiting them for the benefit of all;
suppression of the charters of the concessions;
development of cooperatives;
nationalisation of the exploitations of mineral products, power, and transport;
suppression of private banks in favor of a national bank;
a planned Congolese economy in a collective conception;
writing into the Constitution the fundamental ideas of an economic program. (*43*:15–16)

The program of the PP was thus avowedly socialistic. The party had some difficulty in capturing widespread support both because it was considered to be strongly influenced, if not secretly led, by Belgians, and because its program was at certain points probably too subtle for the majority of the electorate. It gained some stature, however, by joining with the ABAKO in a Cartel which took strong positions at the Round Table Conference in Brussels.

Its leader, Alphonse Nguvulu, was appointed a member of Premier Lumumba's first cabinet in the capacity of Secretary of State for Economic Co-ordination and Planning. He was born at Vista, in the Lower Congo, on September 19, 1922, and worked as a chief clerk in the Office of Secondary Technical Schooling for the Belgian government. He participated in the Round Table Conference, and when Mr. Kasavubu disappeared from that meeting, he took over as President of the

Cartel; he also participated in the Economic Round Table conference. A founding member of Lumumba's MNC, Nguvulu resigned from his post in that party in order to devote himself to the PP. In April 1960, he attended the Communist Party Congress at Liège in Belgium, but insisted that he was there only as a disinterested observer.

The PSA (*Parti Solidaire Africain*)

Another political party which strongly supported the policies of the ABAKO was the Parti Solidaire Africain (PSA), and indeed, it has often been suggested that the PSA was simply a sectional movement of the ABAKO in the Kwango and Kwilu regions of the Léopoldville Province. The PSA apparently grew out of a grouping of former students of the Vicarate of the Kwango-Kwilu, and began its activities by proclaiming itself for a united Congo in June of 1959. However, it moved rather rapidly into the ABAKO camp, though its original "platform" had called for various social reforms without much reference to the future political organization of the Congo. By September 3, 1959, however, it had sent to the Minister of the Congo a strongly federalist, if not separatist, plan which divided the country into six republics. The PSA was one of the founding members of the Kisantu Congress, and from this point forward stood solidly with the ABAKO and supported the plan for an independent Republic of the Lower Congo.

In general, the PSA seems to reflect the socialist tendencies of its leaders and one, Sylvain Kama, has been quoted as saying that "the PSA intends to realize a socialist economy in order to raise the standard of living of the masses, promote agricultural enterprises and small business, change the salary structure, favor the acquisition of better housing . . . We wish a state in which the work of all will contribute to the wellbeing of all" (*43*:17).

Relatively little is known of the President of the PSA, Antoine Gizenga, who was appointed Vice Premier in the first government of the Congo. While he attended the Round Table Conference in Brussels, he was seldom in attendance at the sessions, and it has been suggested that during this time he made a rather extended visit to Prague. It has also been reported that he has visited in Guinea and in Moscow, and that the PSA is a "Marxist" party.

One of the frequent spokesmen for the PSA has been Cléophas Kamitatu who held the position of President of the PSA for the Léopoldville Province. He was born October 10, 1931, played an important part at the Kisantu Congress, and was elected second Vice-President of the Cartel which resulted. He took part in the Round Table Conference as the chief spokesman for the PSA in the absence of Gizenga. Two additional members of the PSA were appointed to Lumumba's first government, but information concerning them is unavailable: they are Mr. J. Masena, who was appointed Minister of Labor, and Mr. Pierre Mulele, who was the Minister of National Education and Fine Arts.

FEDERALIST PARTIES

The parties discussed to this point represent a fusion of ideas concerning separatist and federalist tendencies, with a probable emphasis on the former as espoused particularly by the ABAKO. The ABAKO and Conakat, the party of the Katanga under the leadership of Moïse Tshombe, have often been discussed together, but at least two major differences of opinion separate the two groups. In the first place Conakat, at least before independence, was strongly in favor of a federalist system, although some overtones of separatism were evident— the difference here is therefore one of emphasis. A sharper separation, however, is found in Conakat's support of a Belgo-Congolese community and close co-operation with Belgians both in the Katanga and in Belgium. Such a position was never taken by the ABAKO.

*Conakat (Confederation des Associations du Katanga)
and Allied Parties*

In the December, 1957, communal elections in Elisabethville there were no political parties, and the elections were
won primarily by individuals from the Kasaï Province. According to Moïse Tshombe, Conakat was formed after the elections because of the victories of strangers to the Province:
"the Katanga should be run by Katanga people." Under the
banner of the new party were grouped most of the tribal associations of the Katanga; a second party, the Balubakat was
also founded and until shortly before independence kept a
gingerly alliance with Conakat. Since just before independence, however, the two parties, and more specifically, the leaders of the two parties, have been at sword's points. A third
party in Elisabethville has also played some part in Conakat;
this is a European group, Union Katangaise, headed by Mr.
Achille Gavage. Finally, Ucol-Katanga is a European party
made up of colonials whose primary aim is the assurance of
the continued presence of Europeans in the Katanga.

Since September, 1957, Ucol-Katanga has urged massive
European immigration into the province as well as internal
autonomy; these two points form the major platform of the
party. In respect to racial policy, Mr. Gavage, who in addition to being head of the Union Katangaise, is also president
of the political commission of UCOL, has praised the *apartheid* regime in the Union of South Africa. The UK has received a grant of some 50,000 francs (1,000 dollars) from
Mr. Guillaume, president of the CSK, and its organ has been
the daily paper, *L'Essor du Congo.* The UK has never been
popular with the African population in the Katanga, and although it attempted to affiliate itself with Conakat in 1959, the
marriage was never completely successful.

Following the Governmental Declaration of January 13,
1959, Conakat came out firmly in favor of total and loyal col-

laboration with the Europeans in the framework of an independent but federalist state. This attitude drew the hostility of other Congolese parties and Conakat has long been accused of collaboration with the Belgians, which is in fact true. Hostility was also directed early toward Conakat on the basis of supposition that it would not hesitate to leave the Congo and form its own independent state in collaboration with Belgium; this, too, has since proven to be a well-founded suspicion. But the two ideas of federalism and co-operation with Belgium have remained central in the Conakat program.

As in all pronouncements and programs supporting federalism, there is more than a hint of separatism, and thus during the Round Table Conference, a group of Conakat delegates made public a telegram which read: "The Round Table is useless. The people of the Katanga judge that the only solution is the independence of the Katanga. Let us form immediately a Katangan government." Another telegram addressed by thirty-two Europeans to Mr. Tshombe at the Round Table, read: "If there is a stalemate at the Round Table, we stand behind you for a future independent Katanga" (*42:4*). On the other hand, Tshombe himself is quoted as declaring at a press conference in Léopoldville on December 11, 1959, that it was the Belgian administration and metropolitan government which had misinterpreted his federalist position as a separatist movement. But if there is some question as to federalism or separatism, there has never been any question of the relationship proposed by Conakat between Congolese and Belgians, and thus in January, 1960, "Conakat wishes a Belgo-Congolese community, which will constitute the institutional cadre in the framework of which the member states of this community will discuss and rule on the questions of common interest. The Congo has the highest interest in remaining associated with Belgium. The person of His Majesty the King of the Belgians can happily represent the symbol of the Association between the two countries" (*42:4*).

The political platform of Conakat was enunciated at the time that Moïse Tshombe was named President.

> The total decentralization of powers in order to prepare the future "federated states" before the proclamation of independence.
> The independence of the Congo in order and calm as soon as possible.
> A federal system, uniting the large Congolese provinces and Belgium in the framework of a Belgo-Congolese community, each constituent part retaining its internal autonomy.
> Growth of the productivity of the rural regions by the adoption of a well-studied plan of action aiming to obtain the modernization of equipment at the disposition of the farmers.
> Development of access roads in order to allow outlying regions to better participate in the economic life.
> Development of education in all possible ways in the interior, and above all agricultural and secondary education.
> Extension of the system of governmental credit to the middle classes of the centers and in the interior.
> Expansion of the formula: equal pay for equal work.
> Frank and sincere collaboration between Blacks and Whites in order to pursue together the value of this country for the benefit of its two collectivities.
> Respect for laws established by traditional authorities. (*66:66*)

In late November of 1959, DeBacker summed up the position of Conakat as follows:

> Conakat . . . demands the creation of a federal state within the framework of which the province of Katanga would be directed and administered by authentic Katangan citizens to the exclusion of all members of other races or tribes and would have the right to separate itself from the rest of the Congo if the defense of its Katangan interests made such secession necessary. The establishment of a Belgo-Katangaise community would also be envisaged. (*67:26*)

This general summation represents the position held by Conakat up to independence. It remains only to be added that Conakat has apparently received the thorough backing of the Union Minière, and since independence, of almost all Belgians and other Europeans in the Katanga.

Moïse Tshombe, Conakat's president, was born November 10, 1919, at Musumba near Kapanga in the Katanga; his ethnic origin is Lunda. His family is wealthy, holding plantations, hotels, and retail stores, and Tshombe himself is a business man and accountant. He finished primary and secondary school and studied by correspondence to be an accountant; he is reported to know English and, if so, is one of the very few Congolese leaders who does. He has been a member of the Provincial Council of Katanga from 1951 to 1953, and a member of the Governmental Council and the Territorial Council of Sandoa since 1957. He traveled to Brussels in December, 1959, to engage in preliminary talks with the Belgian government before the Round Table, and emerged as the real leader of Conakat at the Round Table Conference. Tshombe also participated in the Economic Round Table where he was elected vice-president of the conference, and shortly thereafter made a short trip to the United States in May, 1960, at the invitation of its government. In speaking with Mr. Tshombe, one gets the impression of a pleasant, soft-spoken, and highly reasonable and intelligent person whose outlook is basically cautious and whose actions are taken only after deliberation. It seems clear that he relies heavily upon Belgian advisers, but that at the same time probably makes his own decisions. Under Tshombe's leadership, Conakat has counted a great deal on the support of his own ethnic affiliation, the Lunda.

Two further members of Conakat, for whom no information is available, became members of Lumumba's first government: Mr. Robert Yava who was named Minister of Economic Affairs, and Mr. Albert Nyembo who was appointed State Secretary for National Defense.

Balubakat (*Association des Baluba du Katanga*)

The same questions that appear whenever federalism and separatism are discussed apply to the Balubakat, the chief opposition party in the Katanga under the direction of Mr. Jason Sendwe. As is usual in Congo politics, the Balubakat follows an ethnic line, receiving its main support from the Baluba people of the Katanga. Balubakat split off from Conakat toward the end of November, 1959, and has since remained in opposition to it. The program of Balubakat has never been made clear and detailed, but Sendwe has laid down the main point in saying that, "Separatism must be fought against, because it will bring the Congo to suicide. . . . This is why we wish a united Congo with a central government, composed of six federated provinces each of which has a large degree of autonomy" (*42*:6). Late in December, 1959, the Balubakat formed a cartel with Fedeka and Atcar in opposition to Conakat; the cartel was formed upon the basis of a union of Baluba peoples in both Katanga and Kasaï Provinces, and also included some of the Chokwe people. Fedeka is a small political party formed under the presidency of Isaac Kalonji and stressing Baluba affiliations, while Atcar is directed by Ambroise Muhunga and seeks to unite the Chokwe of the Congo, Angola and Rhodesia. Of the two major groups, Conakat on the one hand has always leaned more strongly toward federalism and toward separatism and autonomy, while the cartel led by Balubakat has embraced the federal idea but with emphasis upon a central government to hold the six federated provinces together.

Mr. Jason Sendwe, leader of Balubakat, was born in 1917 and has been a medical assistant and Methodist pastor. He was bourgomaster of the Albert commune of Elisabethville, President of the Balubakat and of the cartel, and the head of the cartel's delegation to the Round Table Conference. He is a Muluba, born in Kabongo where he took his primary schooling at a Methodist mission school. He followed this with four years of normal and bible school at the Methodist mission of Kanene and five years of a medical assistant's course at Yankusu near Stanleyville and at Elisabethville; finally, he took

137

six years of study as a medical assistant in Léopoldville. He is married and the father of eight children; beginning as a Methodist pastor and teacher, he later took a job in the Belgian administration in 1942. He took part in both Round Table Conferences and made a short trip to the United States in May of 1960. In the first Congolese government he was named tentatively as Commissioner of State, or "Governor" of the Katanga Province but, needless to say, has been unable to fulfill that function since independence.

In the new government, Isaac Kalonji of the Fedeka was tentatively named as Commissioner of State in the Kasaï Province. Kalonji has been a communal councilor of the Albert commune in Elisabethville and was a representative of the Katanga cartel at the Round Table Conference. In 1956 he was named a member of the Provincial Council of the Katanga. Mr. Rémy Mwamba of the Balubakat, was named in the first government as Minister of Justice. Mr. Mwamba was born in 1921 and completed six years of primary school, four years of secondary school, and two further years of study. He was a member of the Executive College which advised the Governor General and is said to be a specialist in agricultural affairs. He is a co-founder of the Balubakat and took part in the Round Table Conference as a member of the cartel.

PARTIES IN SUPPORT OF A STRONG CENTRAL GOVERNMENT

MNC (*Mouvement National Congolais*)

To this point we have been concerned with those political parties which followed two of the principal political movements in the pre-independent Congo, separatism and federalism, and it has been pointed out how thin the line often was between the two ideas. A third tendency in Congo politics was that toward a united Congo with a strong central government, and this movement was espoused most firmly and consistently, and with the most publicity, by Patrice Lumumba and his MNC party, the Mouvement National Congolais.

The MNC had its origin in the Motion handed to M. Petillon, then the Minister of the Belgian Congo, on August 26, 1958. The Motion was apparently an outgrowth of De Gaulle's speech in Brazzaville two days earlier; it was signed by a number of leaders, including Lumumba, who later became important in Congo politics, and its objective was the independence of the Congo couched in terms of the rejection of federalism in favor of a strong central government. On October 10, 1958, almost all the signers of this Motion formed what was called a "provisionary committee" under the name of the Mouvement National Congolais, which had as its aim the inclusion of Congolese ideas and personnel in the Study Group slated to arrive in the Congo ten days later. It was Lumumba who sent notice of the creation of the committee to the press agency Belga, and in so doing he designated himself President of the MNC. There is some question as to whether he took this position upon himself with the consent of his cofounders, and how a "provisionary committee" could be dignified by the office of a President, but in any case it was done and the MNC was born with Lumumba as its first President. It is important to note two further points concerning the formation of the MNC. The first is that apparently under the urging of Lumumba, personalities from highly diverse political parties joined in the formation of the committee: Mr. Diomi, one of the lieutenants of Kasavubu and the ABAKO; Messrs. Nguvulu and Adoula, President and Vice-President respectively of the Socialist Action party; Mr. Joseph Ileo, Editor of the *Conscience Africaine* and probably author of the first Manifesto of 1956; and Mr. Antoine Ngwenza, Secretary General of the Bangala. The second point is that, again apparently under the suggestion of Lumumba, the committee was to be considered temporary only: after the immediate problem of liaison with the Belgian Study Group was solved, it was to

139

be dissolved with its members returning to their separate political parties. The party, of course, was never dissolved, though as we shall see it suffered serious splits later on, nor was Lumumba ever ousted as President.

From this point forward, the MNC grew steadily in strength, but it was not until after Lumumba's attendance at the Accra Conference in December of 1958 that any basic principles were stated for the party. At this time Mr. Lumumba found himself completely in accord with the resolutions of the Accra Conference, but he also laid down a "program" for the MNC:

> The Mouvement National Congolais, of completely African origin, has for its fundamental aim the liberation of the Congolese people from the colonial regime and the accession of the Congolese to independence.
>
> We base our action on the Universal Declaration of the Rights of Man—rights guaranteed to all the citizens of the world by the Charter of the United Nations—and consider that the Congo, as a human society, has the right to accede to the ranks of free peoples.
>
> We wish to bid farewell to the old regime, this subjugating regime which deprives our nationals of the enjoyment of political rights granted to all humans and to all free citizens.
>
> We want our country, our fine country, to reflect another face, the face of happy people released from anxiety, fear, and all colonial domination.
>
> It would be a great shame for the inhabitants of this country —and above all for the Belgian administration—if, in this time when the universal conscience condemns the domination of one people by another, the Congo were to remain under the regime of a colonial empire.
>
> The work of colonialization undertaken by Belgium in the Congo must be limited in time and space. In our view, these limits have been largely realized. . . .
>
> We do not exclude the possibility that after having obtained our independence, a confident, fruitful and durable collaboration can be established between the Congo and Belgium and between the black and white inhabitants of this country. The Belgians, like all other foreign inhabitants, will continue to reside in the Congo. . . . (64:40)

140

We have already cited other pertinent portions of this speech, including the specific objective of the MNC ". . . to unite and organize the Congolese masses in the struggle for the amelioration of their lot, the liquidation of the colonial regime and its exploitation of man by man."

The period following this declaration by Mr. Lumumba was filled with fast-moving events, including the Léopoldville riots of January 4–7, 1959, and the subsequent arrest and deportation of the three ABAKO leaders. This period developed into one of political trouble for Lumumba, for he suddenly found himself almost alone in the Congo, with a considerable number of emerging political leaders firmly ensconced in Brussels engaged in talks with the Belgian government. Messrs. Kasavubu, Kanza, and Nzeza were, of course, being politely detained, but the Minister had also invited about a dozen other Congolese leaders to spend three weeks in Belgium. Among them were three leaders of the Interfédérale, three of the PUC, and the President of the Bangala, Mr. Jean Bolikango. Confronted with the political realities involved in the face-to-face meetings of these leaders with the Belgian government, Mr. Lumumba was forced to take some sort of action.

In the meantime, on March 31, 1959, on the occasion of the installation of the permanent office of the MNC in the commune of Kinshasa, Léopoldville, Lumumba had declared himself and the MNC in basic agreement with the Governmental Declaration of January 13, saying that "in respect to the position of the MNC vis-à-vis the Governmental Declaration, the MNC declares itself in basic agreement, but the document must be considered only as the beginning of talks and negotiations" (65:31). At this point Lumumba had just returned from an International week held in Ibadan, Nigeria.

The next event was the Luluabourg Congress held April

7–12, 1959, from which Lumumba departed for Brussels before its closing. The Motions of the Congress have been reproduced by DeBacker.

First Motion: The following political parties: Union Congolaise, Mouvement national congolais, Parti démocrate congolais, Parti de l'Unité congolaise, Parti du progrès national congolais, Union progressiste congolaise, (UPECO), as well as the Union Économique congolais (Uneco) and the Mouvement national pour la protection des milieux ruraux, gathered in congress at Luluabourg, state that it will be the responsibility of the government which the Congress demands be installed in January, 1961, to determine on what date the Congo will accede to its total independence.

Second motion: The same parties pledge themselves to defend the geographic unity of the Congo, reserve to themselves the right to examine after independence the possibility of entering into a larger community, and demand the convocation of a national linguistic commission.

Third motion: The same political parties express the desire that the traditional chiefs, unless elected, be made members of the Councils only by a special statute . . . guaranteeing stability and defining their attributions.

Fourth motion: The same political parties recognize the services rendered by the tribal associations in the framework of their traditional cultures and mutual aid, but contest their right to make themselves into political parties. They demand a legal disposition taken in this matter.

Fifth motion: The same parties, deliberating on the electoral process, express the desire:

1) to see installed as the electoral process universal direct suffrage on the scale of communes and territories, suffrage on the second degree on the provincial level, and direct universal suffrage on the level of the General Council.

2) to see installed as the system of voting, a vote by list, but with preferential vote.

3) for the representation of voices: to see installed proportional representation.

4) Woman's voting: demand the qualification of voters without distinction of sex.

5) Minimum age: to be a voter: 18 years without distinction as to sex. To be eligible: 25 years without distinction as to sex.

Sixth motion: The political parties enumerated above address the following motion to the Minister of the Congo and Ruanda-Urundi: Having pronounced itself on the problem of national

unity and having marked its agreement on this subject, having
stated that the linguistic problem is of a nature to cause an
obstacle to this spirit of national unity, having understood, moreover, that a linguistic commission is now functioning at Usumbura, support the initiative of this commission and to make it
more efficient and official demand the urgent constitution of a
national linguistic commission which will be made up of six
members, one from each province.

Here are the wishes expressed by the economic commission of
the Congress:

1) The economic commission urges that the political parties
of the Congress state that the respect of goods including those
originating from foreign investment as well as those of local
enterprise, is a firm principle.

2) It wishes to see the Government not block private Congolese initiative in the commercial and financial domains.

3) In order to encourage private initiative it is suggested
that a credit organization be founded to aid small artisans, merchants, farmers, and the middle classes. The capital for this
organization would be contributed by the Congolese themselves . . .

Such an organization would make low interest loans to the
middle classes and to those whose resources are low. It should
be created on a national and non-regional scale. Although the
parties themselves should not intervene in the constitution of
this organization, they should encourage their members to participate in it. (*65:24–5*)

The first of the motions listed here was apparently urged on
the Congress by Mr. Lumumba. It did not receive the support
of all the parties, and a much more cautious statement was issued independently the next day.

Before the end of the Congress, Mr. Lumumba had left for
Conakry, Guinea, in order to participate in a meeting of the
Permanent Council of the Pan African Congress of which he
had become a member during his visit to Accra. At the end of
April, 1959, he continued on to Brussels where he declared to
newsmen at the airport that he did not wish to make a statement until he had consulted his "good friend" Jean Bolikango, which he did that evening with the intention of asking
Bolikango to take a directorship of the MNC; Bolikango re-

fused to make a final decision. In Brussels, Lumumba also apparently sought to reach a private agreement with Kasavubu, and made a number of flattering public statements: "I am convinced that the administration has launched an anti-Bakongo campaign," Mr. Kasavubu is the man "who has had the courage to start the struggle against colonialism" (*65*:35). It seems clear that during this period Lumumba was seriously engaged in attempting to form alliances with other Congolese leaders in order to strengthen his own party.

While in Brussels, too, Lumumba took the occasion to launch a number of intemperate attacks on Belgium, citing punitive expeditions, deportation of slaves to the New World, the destruction of Negro African art, the exploitation of the Congolese by Belgium, and so forth. But he also granted certain advantages that had accrued to the Congo through Belgian occupation including the suppression of certain customs, social and human progress, the introduction of education, the development of sanitation, and the development of agriculture.

The MNC, however, still had no real program or platform and this had been emphasized through questions posed to Mr. Lumumba by Belgian journalists to which he had had to reply in the negative or at best with circumlocution. Accordingly, on May 6, 1959, a program was published in various newspapers; it began with a general statement which called attention to economic and social problems and again denounced the colonial regime for its injustices. It continued:

A. Political
1. The fundamental aim of the MNC is the liberation of the Congolese people from the colonial regime and the installation of an independent democratic state.
2. The MNC defends the fundamental liberties guaranteed by the Universal Declaration of the Rights of Man: individual liberty, freedom of association, of meeting, of formation of groups, of opinion, and of the press.
3. The MNC will struggle with all its power to guarantee the unity of the country and the relations among all its inhabitants.

144

It will combat all maneuvers toward balkanization as well as all discrimination based on ethnic affiliation or race. . . .

B. Economic

1. The MNC demands respect for the human individual without distinction of race, sex, or religion, and condemns the exploitation of man by man.

2. The establishment of an economic regime based on the satisfaction of the needs of man, notably by equal distribution of the Congolese national revenue.

3. Installation of a single work code and of equal salaries which will equalize minimal legal salaries throughout the nation.

4. The exploitation of the great riches of the country for the raising of the standard of living of the Congolese community.

5. Revision of the regime of land and other monopolies.

6. In view of their development, the granting of generous assistance to the middle classes. . . . and African cooperatives. Reevaluation of agricultural products.

7. Revision of the fiscal regime in order to redivide the public charges according to a progressive system. Fiscal penalty for enterprises which maintain costly services outside the limits of our national frontiers with the aid of a portion of the Congo's national revenue.

8. Abolition of certain privileges held by firms, which must be made up by the government.

9. Respect of reasonable rights of capital which is invested in the Congo to the degree that it contributes to the raising of the standard of living of the Congolese community.

The MNC recognizes the right of capital investment to a reasonable profit.

C. Social

1. Installation of a system of social security guaranteeing the individual's welfare from the cradle to the grave:

—Full employment. Immediate assistance to the unemployed. The MNC condemns violently the passivity of the government which consists in weighing down the poor classes with unemployment.

—Familial allocations which are decent without consideration of the social rank of the head of the family. All children being equal, they must be allowed to benefit from equal protection and support.

—A system of pensions and sickness benefits more favorable to old workers. Amelioration of too rigorous conditions for grants for sickness allocations while incomes are insignificant.

—A system of awards for damages resulting from accidents while at work and professional illnesses without discrimination of any sort.

2. The MNC considers the cost of health services to be a public national responsibility. The receipt of medical care must not be subordinated to considerations of the economic well-being of the ill.

3. The MNC binds itself to a program which will make the Congolese masses owners of decent and inexpensive housing.

4. In education, the development of free primary, secondary, technical and superior education. Obligatory school attendance. Suppression of all measures which limit schooling on the basis of economic considerations or philosophic opinion; freedom of parents for education of their choice.

5. Support of youth organizations and the intensification of the education of youth.

6. Promotion of the African woman.

7. Protection of Congolese arts and cultures and respect for ethnic customs and conceptions so long as these do not restrict liberty and the advancement of the human individual. (65:39–41)

This MNC document was published in Léopoldville while Lumumba was still in Belgium and although it called for the formation of a Congolese government in January, 1961, five days later in a Brussels press conference Lumumba called for the formation of a Congolese government in 1959. Meanwhile the organization of the MNC was proceeding and all the African communes in Léopoldville were provided with MNC sections headed by a president, vice president, secretary general, and a committee of direction. Returning from Brussels, Lumumba visited Stanleyville and Coquilhatville where he made further organizational moves both in the cities and in the countryside. In the course of these visits, attacks on the Belgian government were stepped up in intensity, and the Minister and the Governor General who were touring the Congo at the time were met with placards reading "The year '59, last colonial government," "No more Colonial Ministers, no more Governor Generals," "The Congo of Boula Matari and of colonists is dead. If they won't understand it, we will die with them."

We have already noted in Chapter III the next step in the MNC's political evolution: the audience granted eight political parties by the Minister in Léopoldville on June 24, 1959. The memorandum submitted to the Minister called for the immediate implementation of individual liberties, the creation of supervisory commissions to oversee the coming elections, and universal suffrage; it also proposed a definite timetable for independence, in which the demand for the formation of a Congolese government was set at January, 1961. On the following day Lumumba, acting on his own and in spite of the fact that he had signed the petition of June 24, pressed further demands which called for the formation of a provisional government in June, 1960.

On July 1, 1959, on the occasion of a general assembly organized by the MNC, Lumumba opened the proceedings by asking for five minutes of silence "in the memory of the Congolese victims of colonialism who fell on January 4, 1959." His following address was a bitter attack against the colonialists, and he took a theme which was to become the rallying cry for the MNC—"Immediate Independence." In closing his address he said, "Down with colonialism, down with the Belgo-Congolese community, down with the politics of intimidation, down with the saboteurs of the Congo and of national independence, long live immediate independence!" A week later, on July 13, he added:

> The Belgian government, in promising independence to the Congo wishes to achieve it not through the aspirations and wishes of the Congolese people, but according to its own aims.
> And what are these aims? To put in power white colonialists and black colonialists; to set up a puppet government in the framework of which the old colonial administration will continue to pull the strings thanks to the marionettes which it will have placed in power. The regime will thus not be changed, only the actors. . . . (*66:*81)

The Split in the MNC

Due in part to the increasing violence of Mr. Lumumba's speeches as well as to differences of opinion which had been developing fairly steadily between him and others in the MNC, a real split in the MNC began to develop in July of 1960. The dissenting faction was led by Mr. Joseph Ileo. On July 16 Mr. Ileo published a document for the Central Committee of the MNC in which certain reorganizational measures were taken and certain individuals appointed to specific posts. The next day Lumumba replied with a short document charging that Mr. Ileo's memorandum was false, that organizational revision of the MNC had not been authorized, and that the new appointments were invalid. Ileo's reply was to castigate Lumumba for statements which Ileo said were not in accord with the Central Committee's views, and to claim as official organ of the MNC an Elisabethville paper rather than Lumumba's own *Indépendance,* published in Stanleyville. There followed a considerable series of charges and countercharges which resulted, finally, in making the split permanent. Much has been said of the "rightist" half of the MNC, led at this point by Ileo, and the "leftist" half, led by Lumumba, but caution should be taken in using such terms. For the Westerner they are convenient and popularly understood labels, but to apply them to the MNC is to apply Western labels to Congolese politics, and the labels are not always apt. Much more proper would be the use of the terms "extreme," which Mr. Lumumba certainly was and is, and "less extreme" which Mr. Ileo certainly was.

The MNC-Kalonji

At this point it is necessary to introduce the name of Mr. Albert Kalonji, a Muluba of Kasaï Province origin. Mr. Kalonji had been a member since 1957 of the Provincial Council of the Kasaï, and was invited to Brussels to work at the Pavilion of Missions during the World Exposition in the summer of

1958. In Brussels he took part in the creation of a political party, the Mouvement pour le Progrès National Congolais, and he returned to the Kasaï after the Exposition as the local head of this party; shortly thereafter he resigned his position to join the MNC. When the scission of the MNC took place, Kalonji followed the less extreme portion under the direction of Mr. Ileo, but gradually this wing of the MNC began to take on his name and has since come to be known as the MNC-Kalonji as opposed to the MNC-Lumumba.

This rise to power took place largely as a result of the Baluba-Bena Lulua struggles which developed in June of 1959 in Luluabourg. On June 29 the so-called Dequenne report was stolen from the government offices, copied, and replaced in the files. It was then published, but often quoted out of context and in pieces by the Congolese press which frequently presented it as representative of the official government position. That the report was favorable to the Bena Lulua is undeniable, but at the same time had its content not been twisted, causing many misinterpretations, there probably would not have been what has since come to be called "the Kolonji affair." On July 31 a tract was published concerning the Dequenne report and the attitude of the administration, and as a result of this publication and of a violent public meeting, Messrs. Kalonji, Nyembwe, and Evariste Kalonji were arrested on August 3 on the ground of inciting racial hatred. Mr. Albert Kalonji's political popularity dates from the time of this arrest. Although Kalonji and Lumumba had broken off relations with each other, Lumumba took the opportunity to come to Luluabourg to protest the arrest and to attempt to obtain Kalonji's release, while Messrs. Ileo and Ngalula went to Brussels to plead the same cause.

Kalonji's detention was fixed at three months, but in the meantime the Provincial Council of which he was a member, was scheduled to meet. On the eve of this meeting, one of the Congolese members informed the press that the African members would abstain, but the remainder of the Council overrode this decision and the Council did, in fact, meet. Mr. Kalonji was finally released before his three-month term was finished, but after the meetings of the Provincial Council. By this time his popularity had been vastly strengthened, and in the elections of December, 1959, in the commune of Ndesha at Luluabourg he scored a substantial popular victory, receiving 4,836 votes out of 7,919 cast.

In the meantime, Kalonji had repaid Lumumba's favor by going to Stanleyville when Lumumba was arrested in November of 1959 to attempt to gain his release; but he had also entered into political arrangements with the ABAKO. Although he had begun by supporting the concept of a united Congo, Kalonji moved fairly rapidly toward support of a federal system, and at one point declared himself in favor of an independent Kasaï. As his relations with the ABAKO were strengthened, he took part in the Kisantu Congress in December of 1959, aligned the MNC-Kalonji with the ABAKO Cartel, and was elected the Cartel's First Vice-President. At the Round Table Conference, he took part as a member of the ABAKO Cartel, but as the talks ended, he and Lumumba were once again reconciled. The Central Committee of the MNC-Lumumba, however, was wary of this personal reconciliation and in March of 1960 it went on record as refusing to reunite the two divisions of the party without further proof that Kalonji had dropped his federalist tendencies and returned to the united Congo fold. By March, 1960, Lumumba was again denouncing Kalonji as having been "responsible for the incidents which bloodied the Kasaï." The near accord was broken, and the two parts of the MNC definitely and irrevocably established. (See *58*:41–5; *66*:125–29.)

The MNC-Kalonji had held a conference in Elisabethville from October 31 to November 3, 1959, and on the final day the following resolutions were voted:

1. The hour of independence approaches. It is more than ever necessary to be united. Old rivalries encouraged by the colonizers must cease. It is only in the uniting of all its peoples that the Congo will be a strong and prosperous country.

2. Conscious of its responsibilities toward the nation, the MNC intends to make its work constructive. It will marshall its total energies toward the struggle for the complete emancipation of the Congo as well as toward the solution of political, social and economic problems which will assist the country toward a better future.

3. The MNC is scornful of the attitude of certain demagogues who place their personal interests before the interests of the country and who, in a program of low propaganda, do not hesitate to make falacious promises to the people which they know are unrealizable.

The MNC condemns energetically these irresponsible people whose inconsidered acts put the future Congolese leaders in a delicate and difficult position.

4. The MNC desires to enlighten the people loyally and objectively and to draw their attention to the fact that Independence will not solve all the grave problems which face the Congo at the moment.

The attainment of Independence in freeing the Congo from the colonial yoke, in bringing liberty to its inhabitants, in giving them back their dignity, will only be the first step toward the realization of a happy Congo.

5. For the good of the nation and its people, it is indispensable that all the people go to work and support the necessary sacrifices in union and fraternity.

6. The MNC does not take an exclusive position against anyone. It extends its fraternal hand to all the political parties without exception in the struggle for the common ideal: the attainment of immediate independence for the Congo. (66:23–4)

Mr. Albert Kalonji was born June 6, 1929, at Hemptinne in the Kasaï Province. He is married and the father of four children. His schooling was with the Brothers of Charity at Lusambo and he obtained a diploma as an agricultural assistant after five years of study at Kisantu with the agricultural unit established by the University of Louvain. In 1958 he indicated his intention of studying at the University of Louvain in Belgium, but was apparently dissuaded by Mr.

Lumumba. While working for the administration he followed a bookkeeping course by correspondence, later became an accountant in a Luluabourg firm, and still later opened his own accounting firm. He has been associated with a number of newspapers. He has been described as "intelligent but impulsive, moderate but quick tempered . . . facile at making friends, but less facile at keeping them." At times in the past his speeches have been frankly and openly anti-white. He attended the Round Table Conference, and shortly thereafter made a short visit in May of 1960 to the United States at the invitation of the American government.

Mr. Joseph Ileo whose actions caused the split in the MNC, was born in 1922 in Léopoldville and followed secondary school courses in philosophy and sociology. In 1951 he was employed in the office of African Cities. He was Editor-in-Chief of *Conscience Africaine,* and probably chief author of the first Manifesto published in that paper. He is considered to be a political moderate and one of the deepest, most original, and wisest of the Congolese politicians. At the Round Table Conference he was a representative of the ABAKO Cartel, specifically of the MNC-Kalonji. He was not named to the first government.

The MNC-Lumumba

At almost the same time that the MNC-Kalonji was holding its meeting in Elisabethville, the MNC-Lumumba met in congress in Stanleyville. As a prelude to this meeting, which took place from the twenty-seventh to the thirty-first of October, 1959, Lumumba sent a telegram to the Minister demanding immediate negotiations and the postponement of the December elections; the Minister's reply was predictably negative, and partly as a response, the Congress voted the following resolutions:

> The Congress judges, that as a result of the deliberate refusal of Belgium to accede to the political aspirations clearly expressed

by the Congolese, Belgium has violated the Charter of the United Nations of which it is a co-signer, notably article 73, paragraph B.

The National Congress, supported by the popular masses, which have decided to gain their immediate independence:

Decides not to participate in the anti-democratic and anti-national elections prepared by the Belgian government in the sole aim to perpetuate the colonial regime in the Congo by artificial means;

Reaffirms the will of the Congolese people to enjoy without delay the prerogatives of their sovereignty;

Rejects the pretension of considering the Congo as a colony when the Congo was recognized in 1885 as an Independent State by the international powers and when this independence is celebrated each July 1; . . .

Condemns the subversive propaganda spread in concert by the Administration and certain colonists whose end is to sabotage national independence;

To vote in December is to vote against Independence. Better to die than to continue to support the regime of subjection.

The National Congress:

Launches this day its plan of positive action for the immediate liberation of the Congo;

Addresses a strong fraternal appeal to all the oppressed people of the Congo to mobilize themselves to put an end to Belgian domination. (*67*:22–3)

We have already noted that as an aftermath of this Congress an upheaval took place which resulted in the arrest of Mr. Lumumba on the grounds of his inciting to riot; in January, he was sentenced to six months in prison. An Associated Press report on November 1 gives some details of the rioting:

. . . The Belgian Ministry of the Congo said the Africans fired an African social center and a number of other buildings which burned down.

Belgian local authorities had banned the meeting, which followed the MNC congress in Stanleyville.

Police first tried to break up the meeting but were rapidly overwhelmed by rioters. Police then called out the Force Publique . . .

Rioters attacked troops and police with stones, spears and arrows. Troops first used tear-gas grenades but after some soldiers and policemen fell injured, officers gave orders to fire,

apparently to rescue their injured men, including a Belgian officer with a spear wound in the chest.

Riots also occurred at the Stanleyville prison Friday where
African prisoners attacked European prisoners with bricks.

Police used tear-gas grenades to rescue the European prisoners, whose cells were encircled by the rioters. . . .

Store windows were broken in various parts of Stanleyville
and northeastern Congo. Thirty houses belonging to the Stanleyville brewery were damaged. . . . Numerous cars were
stoned.

Lumumba's response to the charges against him and to his
incarceration was to publish a pamphlet while in jail dis-
claiming all responsibility: "I am not, directly or indirectly,
responsible for the incidents at Stanleyville. The entire population of Stanleyville will testify to this innocence" (*89:27*).
The pamphlet also refuted government charges one by one and
attacked the Administration. While Lumumba languished in
jail, various protests were entered by his supporters concerning his arrest and an MNC-Lumumba Congress took place in
November at Bukavu. After his sentence was pronounced, Lumumba was transferred to Jadotville prison in the Katanga,
for the authorities considered it prudent that he not remain in
Stanleyville. However, two days later, on January 25, he was
provisionally freed to attend the Round Table Conference. At
the Conference, where he arrived dramatically showing hand-
cuff scars on his wrists, Lumumba took active part, and on his
return he put in considerable time in strengthening the MNC
in local areas.

Patrice Lumumba was born July 2, 1925 at Katako-Kombe
in the Sankuru District of Kasaï Province; his ethnic origin is
Batetela, and his education is of primary school only. In
1954 he became a postal clerk in Stanleyville and a year
later was made President of the APIC (Association du Personnel Indigène du Congo Belge et du Ruanda-Urundi). On
July 1, 1956, he was arrested in Stanleyville, and charged
with the embezzlement of a substantial sum of money in connection with his work with postal money orders. While the sum

154

of the embezzlement is the subject of numerous different citations, most authors place it at 126,000 francs or 2,520 dollars. He was arraigned, judged guilty, and condemned to two
years in prison, but the sentence was later reduced on appeal
of June 13, 1957, to 18 months, and still later to 12 months.
It is both interesting and significant to note that during his imprisonment the *évolués* of Stanleyville gathered together to
pay back the sum embezzled and to care for Lumumba's family. In 1957, Lumumba left Stanleyville for Léopoldville
where he was engaged in a local brewery; he became its commercial director in August, 1958, but resigned in 1959 to occupy himself exclusively with political matters. In 1956 he
traveled to Brussels on a study voyage with a number of
other Congolese, and in 1958 he was President in Léopoldville of the Association of the Batetela and vice-president of
a study group. In Stanleyville he was President of the Cercle
des Évolués, and President of the Friendship group of the
post office. He was the Director of *Indépendance,* the journal
of his wing of the MNC, and collaborated in the direction of
several other papers. Colin Legum, on the basis of a personal
interview apparently in March, 1960, and thus before independence, characterized Lumumba as

> . . . a tall rake of a man, with a tiny, narrow head and a
> chinful of beard, "especially grown for independence." His man-
> ner is lively and vital; his smile is light and quick and frequent;
> his movements are rather like those of a praying mantis. His
> tongue is silver; he talks rapidly and ceaselessly. But his easy,
> pleasant manner is deceptive; Lumumba is earnest and tough
> and capable, if the need should arise, of being ruthless. His hero
> is Dr. Kwame Nkrumah; his model is Ghana.
> . . . He is a republican and a reformer. . . . His outlook is
> firmly Western. . . . Ideas spill out, easily and well marshalled.
> He is a visionary and a realist. Also, he is a fly politician.
> (*86*:84–5)

The MNC, then, began as a provisional committee and was
turned into a political party by Lumumba who, on his own
initiative, took over what at the time was a non-existent presi-

dency. Lumumba and the MNC held steadfastly to a position of a united Congo and carried on their activities under a slogan of immediate independence. The split in the party produced the MNC-Kalonji which followed a federalist position in unity with the ABAKO. The MNC, and particularly the Lumumba wing, was and is one of the most important political parties in the Congo, while its splinter group headed by Kalonji has, since independence, provided it with one of its most difficult problems.

In Lumumba's first government eleven members of the MNC-Lumumba were named to various posts. Among them was Georges Grenfell, appointed as a member of the Council of Ministers of State. Mr. Grenfell was bourgomaster of the commune of Mangobo at Stanleyville, and an ex-medical assistant. He was a co-founder of the MPNC at Brussels where he took part in the Exposition in the summer of 1958. Mr. Aloïs Kabangi, named Minister of Economic Co-ordination and Planning, was the President of the Mouvement pour l'Unité Basonge created at Kabinda in the Kasaï in March, 1960. He was a member of the founding committee of UNIPOCONGO, and was a clerk in the Belgian administration until appointed attaché to the cabinet of the governor of the Kasaï Province in September, 1959. In February, 1959, he was a member of the Belgian delegation to a CCTA meeting in Monrovia, Liberia. Mr. Antoine Kiwewa, appointed Secretary of State for Foreign Commerce, was an MNC-Lumumba delegate to the Economic Conference in Brussels; he worked as a clerk in the Office of Foreign Commerce in Stanleyville, and was Secretary-General for the MNC-Lumumba in the Eastern Province. Mr. Maximilien Liongo, named Secretary of State for Justice, was clerk and recorder for the tribunal of the District of Léopoldville, President of APIC, and a communal councilor of Kinshasa in Léopoldville. He was one of the signers of the Memorandum presented to the Minister after the visit of Charles de Gaulle to Brazzaville in August of

156

1958, and was a member of the temporary committee of the MNC. Mr. Alexandre Mahamba, appointed Minister of Lands, was a delegate of the Executive College to the Economic Round Table in Brussels, and a member of various committees at those meetings.

Mr. Joseph Mbuyi, named Minister of the Middle Classes was born August 12, 1929, at Mikalaye near Luluabourg. He was an early member of the MNC, followed Lumumba at the time of the scission, became Secretary of the National Committee of the MNC-Lumumba, and was one of its delegates at the Round Table Conference. Mr. Joseph Mobutu, appointed Secretary to the Presidency, was born at Lisala, October 14, 1930, served seven years in the Force Publique and followed courses at Luluabourg in the Force Publique School; he finished his secondary school studies in Coquilhatville. He left the Force Publique in 1956 and became a journalist, contributing to various papers and later becoming the Editor of *Actualités Africaines.* He was at the Brussels Exposition as a representative of the press and remained in Brussels for a year at Inforcongo. He was a delegate of the MNC-Lumumba to the Economic Conference, and was a member of the local MNC committee at Bandalunga near Léopoldville. Mr. Alphonse Songolo, Minister of Communications, was the bourgomaster of Kabondo, Stanleyville. He was arrested for subversive activities in December, 1959, but later released. There is no available information on Mr. Chrystophe Gbenye, Minister of the Interior; Mr. Joseph Lutula, Minister of Agriculture; and Mr. Maurice Mpolo, Minister of Youth and Sports.

PARTIES OF MODERATE TENDENCIES

The Bangala Parties

We have spoken to this point of the political parties which favored separatism, federalism, and a united Congo. These were the three major stands taken by the Congolese politically, but there were other parties which showed perhaps some of the same tendencies but which were, for the most part, under a determined program of moderation.

Interfédérale-PUC (*Parti de l'Unité Congolaise*)

Among the parties of generally moderate tendencies is the tangled skein of organizations centering around the Bangala federations of Léopoldville. We have previously noted that Léopoldville was the scene of a number of pre-political groupings, such as the APIC, UNISCO, ADAPES, and others, and that one of the most active participants, especially in the latter two was Mr. Jean Bolikango who, indeed, introduced Kasavubu into the UNISCO and thus was one of his earliest sponsors. Léopoldville was also the scene of political struggles between the Bakongo people of the Lower Congo region on the one hand, and the Bangala of the Upper Congo on the other. In the December, 1957, elections at Léopoldville, the Bakongo scored a smashing triumph over the Bangala.

The people of the Upper Congo region had for a considerable time held a numerical majority in Léopoldville, but their political organization at the time of the December, 1957, elections was almost non-existent. While a Bangala Federation had been created under the presidency of Mr. Bolikango, its organization was weak and its membership small; further, the strength of the Bangala was seriously divided by the existence of at least eight different small organizations in Léopoldville, most of which counted some Bangala in their membership. It was this division of forces as opposed to the high degree of organization among the Bakongo that carried the elections of December, 1957, for the ABAKO.

Realizing the importance of this lack of organization on the part of the Bangala and other groups in Léopoldville, Mr. Bolikango immediately after the elections organized a group called Interfédérale, of which he was made President. The Interfédérale joined together almost all the associations of Upper Congo people which existed at that time in Léopold-

158

ville: the Bangala Federation, the Bassonge Federation, the Kwango-Kwilu Federation, the Kasaï Federation, the Bateke Federation, the Mongo Federation (Fédération des Ressortissants de l'Equateur), the Batetela Federation (of which Lumumba was President at the time), the Kivu-Maniema Federation, and several smaller groups. From a numerical point of view, Interfédérale thus represented approximately 50 per cent of the Congolese population of Léopoldville, but division within the ranks based on ethnic origins continued, and the Interfédérale was considerably weaker than its opponent, the ABAKO. As a party of moderation Interfédérale was also plagued by rumors that it was merely a front for the Belgians, and that it had received millions of francs from the Belgian administration "to sabotage the independence of the country." Interfédérale lacked any clear-cut program, and also had trouble with its system of rotating the presidency rapidly among the heads of the eight major groups out of which it had been formed. Almost its only declaration on the subject of independence was made in January, 1959, during the course of a meeting of the presidents with the Minister:

> This delegation has given to the Minister of the Belgian Congo and Ruanda-Urundi the assurance of its complete support of the new politics as defined by the governmental declaration [of January 13, 1959]: it promised the Minister its full cooperation in the course of the execution of the declaration. At the moment Interfédérale has begun a program of study of the feelings of the different ethnic groups which it represents and to this end has sent delegations to all the regions of the Congo. (*64:47*)

It is evident that this brief declaration in no way constitutes a platform and further, that the adherence of Interfédérale to the governmental delaration made it the object of further suspicion in respect to its relationship to the Belgian administration. Thus, the Interfédérale launched a new political party called the Parti de l'Unité Congolaise (PUC) on January 27, 1959. In announcing the formation of the PUC, Interfédérale expressed its annoyance at some of the charges concerning the

Interfédérale role vis-à-vis the Belgian administration, which had been leveled against it and against those unnamed parties which officially spurned European co-operation but secretly used European councilors. It also spoke of the PUC as a "vast political movement which will defend the ideas of tolerance, equality, justice and co-operation among the people of different races . . ." Interfédérale and the PUC remained two distinct entities, the former to study cultural and social problems, and the latter to pursue political aims.

1. Build a strong, democratic and independent "Congolese nation" through the union of all the peoples of the Belgian Congo and with respect for traditional organizations.

2. Develop an African personality drawing from Bantu values and Western civilization.

3. Guarantee to the people of the Congolese Nation all the democratic liberties, equality before the law and in the Institutions, respect for the individual whatever be his race, religion and opinions.

4. Develop the standard of living of rural and urban populations by the constant growth and best distribution of the national revenue, through the study and application of a healthy and national economic policy assuring full employment and security. Through a climate of stability guaranteeing investments and attracting new Belgian and Western capital. Through the development of a strong and well organized middle class. Through an Association with Belgium.

5. Demand for the Congolese nation the role of leader which will come to it through its unity, its central position, its size, its riches, in the building of the Africa of tomorrow and through its association with Europe, to guarantee stability in the world.

6. Participate with Belgium, the free African nations and the friendly nations, in the maintenance of peace in the world and in the development of prosperity.

7. In the immediate future, that is before January 1, 1960— creation of the Congolese nationality; struggle against all the forces of division menacing the unity of the Congo; abolition of all racial discrimination both in official and private places; cooperation toward social peace in extolling a program of salaries adapted to the needs of employees and workers . . . ; reestablishment of a climate of confidence necessary to the next democratic elections and to the economic development of the country.

160

> Also, the PUC launches an appeal to all the inhabitants of the country, Batekes, Bangala, Bakongo, Kasæiens, Kwangolais . . . Europeans, etc. . . . to join together and construct a united, prosperous, free and independent Congo. (*64:48b*)

The division of responsibilities between Interfédérale and the PUC was more or less a fiction, and slowly they appeared to grow apart with Interfédérale presenting a rather detailed program to the Belgian government on April 20, 1959, which discussed political, economic, and social problems at some length. (See *65:53–8.*) Further troubles emerged from the lack of a strong president; although Mr. Bolikango appeared to be the outstanding leader, it was Mr. Jacques Mbilo, president of Interfédérale at the time, who seemed to take the lead and who, on June 29, 1959, reaffirmed the generally moderate stand of Interfédérale (See *66:93–4.*) It was Mr. Mbilo, too, who was apparently responsible for a sudden change in the politics of Interfédérale on August 12, 1959. On that day he had written a letter to Mr. Bolikango, who was in Belgium at the time, pointing out that Interfédérale's moderate stands were making the party appear ridiculous and suggesting that it was losing the respect of the Congolese. Apparently he decided to act on his own initiative: speaking for Interfédérale and not mentioning the PUC which by this time had become an almost dead issue, he published a new program in the newspaper *Actualités Africaines*. This program reaffirmed the need for unity in the Congo, and concentrated its attack on demands for economic reform. But its major shift in policy was its abandonment of the Governmental Declaration and a demand for:

> Immediately, Interfédérale wishes:
> 1. a Congolese government;
> 2. the creation of the Congolese nation;
> 3. the abolition of all racial discrimination;
> 4. the effective and not timorous Africanization of governmental structure as well as adequate increases in salaries;
> 5. continuing effort in social and medical organization;

6. the development of primary, normal, technical, and university education, taking account of the real needs of the country.
7. respect of traditional institutions of the Congo which are compatible with the installation of a healthy democracy;
8. the growth of revenues of the Congolese peasants. (*66*:130–32)

UNICO (Union pour les Intérêts du Peuple Congolais)
Exactly one month later, the PUC-Interfédérale was absorbed into a new political party, UNICO, which announced its formation on September 12, 1959. The origin of this movement is somewhat obscure, but it seems to have been formed through the initiative of Mr. Jean-Pierre Dericoyard who, on May 1, 1959, had been the founder of the PTC (Parti Travailliste Congolaise). The UNICO absorbed, then, the PUC-Interfédéral, as well as the PTC and six other parties, including PDC (Parti Démocrate Congolaise), founded in February, 1959; the MPNC (Mouvement pour le Progrès National Congolais) founded in October, 1958; the PIL (Parti de l'Indépendance et de la Liberté), founded in July, 1959, by Mr. Antoine Bolamba who later became the first Secretary of Information and Cultural Affairs; the UPCO (Union Progressiste Congolaise) founded in October, 1958, and later fused with the MLN, headed by Mr. Antoine Tshimanga whose sympathies are quite probably closest to the Communist line of any Congolese politician; and the Union Congolaise, founded at Elisabethville in December, 1957. The result of this fusion was the liquidation of the individual parties and the grouping together of almost all the political organizations in Léopoldville, with the exception of the ABAKO and its satellite PSA, the MNC, the PP, and one labor union. Thus almost all the ethnic groups in Léopoldville, with the exception of the Bakongo, were finally allied in a political movement which, because of its political stand on a united Congo, appeared to pose a real threat to the MNC-Lumumba.

162

PNP (*Parti National du Progrès*)

Two further steps in the development of this long political line remain to be discussed. The first of these took place at a conference at Coquilhatville in the Equator Province, November 11–16, 1959, when all the parties under UNICO, plus nineteen others, formed themselves into a new party, the PNP. All the groups in the new party were of moderate tendencies, and the PNP itself opted primarily for independence within the framework of the governmental declaration of January 13, 1959, and the augmentation of this declaration by Minister DeSchrijver on October 16, 1959. PNP further emphasized the strong desirability of a united Congo and set itself firmly against any federalist or separatist tendencies. (See *58*:124.)

PUNA (*Parti de l'Unité Nationale*)

The final movement takes us back once again to Mr. Bolikango who, on January 20, 1960, formed a new party, the Front de l'Unité Bangala (FUB). In March, 1960, the FUB changed its status, uniting at least five smaller parties, and became PUNA (Parti de l'Unité Nationale). PUNA is primarily a party of two ethnic groupings, the Bangala and the Mongo, and its program includes the following points: a united Congo in opposition to the federalism of ABAKO and Conakat, a considerable provincial decentralization, and the maintenance of collaboration with Belgium.

This movement of the Bangala parties gives perhaps the clearest picture of the ephemeral nature of Congolese political movements, and the bewildered reader may well be grateful here for a recapitulation of its development. UNISCO developed partly into the Bangala Federation, which in turn became the Interfédérale. Interfédérale itself created a supposed political party, the PUC, and thus the organization came to be known as PUC-Interfédérale. This was later absorbed into UNICO, a fusion of some eight major political parties, but this is turn was absorbed into the PNP, a coalition of parties holding moderate platforms. Mr. Bolikango, the real creator of the entire series, finally formed another party, the FUB, which in turn shortly thereafter turned into PUNA. Both the PNP and PUNA continued as distinct entities at least up to the time of independence. It is equally interesting to note that the platform of this line of parties was at first extremely moderate, later took a sudden turn toward a much more belligerent program, and finally, in the PNP and PUNA returned for the most part to its original conservative stand.

Mr. Jean Bolikango was born in 1909 in Léopoldville to a family from Lisala in the Equator Province which had established itself in the city in 1903. He completed primary and secondary schooling with the Catholic Pères de Scheut in Léopoldville, and taught for the same organization from 1926 until 1958. In 1958, he resigned to become head of public relations for the Pavilion of Missions at the Brussels Exposition, and this work prompted him to continue his studies in this field. He was taken into the Office of Information and Public Relations for the Belgian Congo and Ruanda-Urundi (Inforcongo) where he studied press, radio, television, movie, and mass education techniques. In August, 1959, he was appointed Assistant Commissioner of Information, the highest position occupied by a Congolese at that time. Legum describes him as a "tall, broad, proud and handsome man; a strong Catholic, . . . The main political influence in his life has been M. Leopold Senghor. But he also finds it possible to admire Mr. Houphouet-Boigny, . . . 'for his wisdom and calmness.' To his own people Bolikango is sometimes known as The Sage, and sometimes as The Moses. . . . His aim is independence and unity" (*86*:86–7). In his work for Inforcongo, Bolikango made a comparative study of the information services of the countries south of the Sahara, created a documentation of the political personalities of the

Congo, spoke widely before diverse audiences, and assisted in Bantu language courses at the University of Ghent. He is the author of a novel, *Mondjeni-Mobe (The Guys)*, which won a literary prize at the International Fair of Ghent. He has come out strongly for a union of African states, and has addressed letters to Nkrumah and to United States authorities protesting the assumption that Kasavubu and Lumumba speak for all Congolese. He was one of the councilors for the group that produced the first Manifesto, and he has long been regarded by Belgian authorities as a thoughtful and highly intelligent person. He was arrested by Premier Lumumba on September 2, 1960, for an alleged plot against the lives of Lumumba and Kasavubu as well as for the alleged advocacy of a separate state in the Equator Province; his release from prison by rebellious anti-Lumumba forces, took place September 6.

Mr. Antoine-Roger Bolamba, named in the first Congolese government as Secretary of Information and Cultural Affairs, was born in Coquilhatville and is of the Mongo ethnic group. He was President of one of the early pre-political groups, the ASSANEF (Association des Anciens Elèves des Frères des Ecoles Chrétiennes), and later Vice-President of the PIL. He has been Editor in Chief of the paper, *La Voix du Congolais*, attaché to the cabinet from September, 1956, to October, 1957, and Vice-President of the Mouvement Cultural Belgo-Congolais. He took part in the Round Table discussions and made a short journey to West Germany in April–May, 1960, at the invitation of the Bonn Government.

Mr. Paul Bolya, named a Minister of State and member of the Council of Ministers in the first government, was born October 10, 1924, at Bengala in the Equator Province. After his primary schooling, he studied three years at the Catholic Mission of the Fathers of the Sacred Heart, two years at the School of Medical Assistants at Coquilhatville, and four years at the School for Medical Assistants in Léopoldville; he received his diploma as a Medical Assistant in 1948. He was sent for a short period to the Institute of Tropical Medicine at Anvers, and became a teacher of medical assistants at the Léopoldville school in 1959. Mr. Bolya was at the Brussels Exposition in 1958, and later became the President of the PNP as well as a member of the Léopoldville Provincial Council and the Léopoldville City Council. He participated in the Round Table discussions, and was a member of the Executive College attached to the Governor General where he was chiefly occupied with the Ten-Year Plan, medical services, and the Geographic Institute.

Mr. Albert Delvaux, appointed Resident Minister in Belgium charged with Belgian-Congolese relations, was born May 8, 1918, at Kapanga in the Katanga. He later became the National Secretary of the PNP, President of the Union Kwangolaise pour l'Indépendance et la Liberté (LUKA), and President of the Kwangolese Federation at Léopoldville. He was a member of the PNP delegation to the Round Table Conference.

Mr. Jacques Lumbala, named Secretary of State to the Presidency, was the Chef du Secteur of Pania Mutombo, Kasaï Province, and later became the secretary of the political commission of the congress which formed the PNP. He was a PNP delegate to the Economic Round Table. In January, 1960, he was arrested for inciting racial hatred, but released almost immediately.

Mr. Antoine Ngwenza, appointed Minister of Social Affairs in the first Congolese government, was born in 1919, was a student at the Missions of the Catholic Fathers de Scheut, and was later National Secretary of the PUNA. He was a co-signer of the Memorandum of 16 in August, 1958, and followed Lumumba and the MNC until shortly after the split when he joined the PUNA.

Mr. Jean-Pierre Dericoyard, the founder of the PTC which later fused with the PNP, was not named to a post in the first

166

government. He was born in 1914, and is of the Azande tribe; he finished his secondary schooling with the Mariste Brothers, and was an administration clerk for six years before setting himself up in business in 1949. Mr. Dericoyard was also one of the founders of UNICO, but it was under his urging that the PTC initiated the idea of the Round Table Conference. Mr. Dericoyard was a member of a number of groups which stressed Belgian-Congolese co-operation.

OTHER POLITICAL PARTIES

To this point we have discussed the four major tendencies among the political parties of the Congo: separatism, federalism, a united Congo, and moderation. These various tendencies represent the only "platforms" in Congo politics, and we have already seen that as platforms they were often partial and inconsistent. There remain, however, a few major parties whose platforms either changed markedly or were never clear-cut, as well as a few of the European parties in the Congo.

UC (*Union Congolaise*)

One of the parties whose policies changed somewhat during the course of their existence was the Union Congolaise (UC), founded in Elisabethville in December, 1957, under the aegis of a Belgian lawyer, Mr. Antoine Rubbens. From its beginning the UC stressed the concept of a united Congo, but it was in its attitude toward Belgium that its policies changed. Thus on October 10, 1958, the president of UC, Mr. Gabriel Kitenge, issued a statement in which he called for the co-operation of all people, and stressed co-operation with the whites " . . . because I do not see how we can succeed without recourse to the experience, techniques, and capital of the whites." However, the program of the UC changed gradually to that of demands for immediate independence, and by July, 1959, Mr. Kitenge denounced the whites ". . . who, under the pretext of guarantees, sabotage the work of Belgium in the Congo." The UC aligned itself for a while with the MNC, but in the end returned to its relatively moderate policy and joined the PNP, though parts of it remained independent, particularly the organization at Stanleyville.

CEREA (*Centre de Regroupement African*)

CEREA was founded in Bukavu on August 23, 1958, but its platform was never very clearly stated, and in its later existence it was racked with dissension. At the beginning it declared itself for a united Congo and based its organization on the Universal Declaration of the Rights of Man of the United Nations. The party was headed by three leaders, Messrs. Bisukiro, Kashamura, and Weregemere, and it was during the Round Table Conference that these leaders split. Mr. Weregemere was late in reaching the Conference, and on his arrival he found that Messrs. Bisukiro and Kashamura had chosen Mr. Terfve, a previous Communist Deputy in the Belgian Parliament, as their advisor, and had declared the CEREA in favor of the federalist stand of the ABAKO. Mr. Weregemere thereupon split the party and formed his own aisle, although the Central Committee later decided in favor of the more radical wing. Mr. Weregemere's group seems not to have gained much influence, while that of Bisukiro and Kashamura finally allied itself with the MNC-Lumumba.

Mr. Marcel Bisukiro, who was named Minister of External Commerce in the first government, was born in 1929 near Rutshuru in the Kivu, and was employed by various commercial firms. He was named President of CEREA, and won a seat in the communal elections at Kadutu (Bukavu) in December, 1959. He was a delegate of CEREA to the Round Table Conference, and was later named Vice-President of the ABAKO Cartel at the conference after Mr. Kasavubu departed. He is the Commercial Director of *La Vérité*, organ of the CEREA.

Mr. Anicet Kashamura was named Minister of Information

and Cultural Affairs in the first Congolese government. Born December 17, 1928, at Kalehe in the Kivu Province, he was first employed at the Comité National du Kivu, then at the government research organization, IRSAC, and from 1950 to 1956 he served as an accountant in various government offices. Mr. Kashamura was a member of the Executive College attached to the Governor General where he represented Kivu Province and occupied himself with questions pertaining to the Force Publique, information and labor. He was a member of the CEREA delegation to the Round Table Conference, during which he made a voyage to East Berlin and to Prague. Interviewed on his return, he first denied that he had visited these areas, but later said that while he had visited Prague, ". . . I was only there for a few hours and it was so cold that I never left my hotel room" (*58:57*). He later added that the trip was for his own benefit and had no political significance. Nevertheless, he has been quoted as saying that "Once our government is recognized by the Soviet Union we can break all our previous promises" (*58:58*). Mr. Kashamura took part in the Conference of Positive Action at Accra in April, 1960, and took the occasion to visit in Nigeria, Togo, Dahomey, the Gabon, and the Cameroons.

The European parties which appeared in the Congo are of relatively little interest here since there is no evidence that they were normally of direct influence on Congolese politicians or the political development of the Congo. Among them are the Union Katangaise, founded at Elisabethville, which we have already mentioned in connection with the Conakat; the PEAC (Parti Economique et Agraire Congolais), founded in June 1959, at Stanleyville by a Belgian, Mr. Charles Bonté, and which later joined forces with the PNP; and the PDMN (Parti pour la Défense des Milieux Ruraux), founded at Kabinda in May of 1959, and which later disappeared. All these parties were basically interracial.

On the other hand, the Fédacol (Fédération Congolaise

des Classes Moyennes), which grew out of various European movements dating as far back as 1949, was a party primarily for Europeans and espousing European viewpoints. As of January 1, 1959, it listed 2,595 members and its program was built around the defense of the rights of Europeans. There is evidence to indicate that some elements of Fédacol were strongly attached to the apartheid policy of South Africa though this extremist position does not represent Fédacol as a whole. (See *37:9.*)

The Rassemblement Congolais, founded in Bukavu in January, 1959, was also an organization of Europeans, in this case formed in opposition to CEREA. Its program proposed internal autonomy for the Congo in a Belgo-Congolese federation, and its "frank and sincere adhesion to the superior ideas of European civilization." (See *64:42.*) The unilaterally white parties were, for the most part, dedicated to the preservation of the white communities in the Congo and, by their very nature, to gradual political development and close Belgian-Congolese co-operation.

It remains only to list whatever information is available for other members of the first Congolese government who either belonged to no political party or whose party was minor. Mr. Justin-Marie Bomboko, named Minister of Foreign Affairs, was born in 1928 in Bolombo, Equator Province. After his primary schooling, he completed his secondary education at the Mission of the Fathers of the Sacred Heart at Bamanya (Coquilhatville), and was later a student for six years in the administration section of Lovanium-Kisantu. From 1952 to 1955 he was a clerk in the provincial administration at Coquilhatville. He has been a student at the Free University of Brussels, Editor in Chief of the journal *Mbandaka* in Coquilhatville, one of the directors of Interfédérale, and the editor, if not author, of a number of Interfédérale tracts. During the early rioting in the Lower Congo after Independence Mr. Bomboko emerged as a calm leader, and his later actions as

170

Minister of Foreign Affairs have shown his considerable abilities.

Mr. Alphonse Ilunga, Minister of Public Works, was born in the Kasaï in 1931. He is of the Bena Lulua tribe, and an accountant. Elected from Luluabourg in the December, 1959, elections, Mr. Ilunga is a nominal member of the PNP while conserving his local autonomy in the Union Congolaise-Kasaï. He was a PNP delegate at the Round Table Conference and has taken a strong stand for unity and against federalism.

Mr. Thomas Kanza, Minister to the United Nations, is the son of Daniel Kanza. The first Congolese university graduate, he received his degree in economics from the University of Louvain in 1956; he has since done post-graduate study at the College of Bruges, and has received a scholarship to study at Harvard University. After his studies he worked for the European Common Market, but resigned in March, 1960, to take part in Congolese politics. He is the author of at least two pamphlets and one short book.

Mr. Alphonse Nguvulu, Secretary of State for Economic Co-ordination and Planning, is the President of the PP (Parti du Peuple), and was a delegate of that party at the Round Table Conference and at the Economic Round Table. Mr. Nguvulu has occupied himself primarily with economic affairs; at the Round Table Conference he presented the Belgian government with demands for information concerning the public debt, the assumption by Belgium of part, at least, of that debt, and the rejection of the proposed adhesion of the Congo to the European Common Market. It was Mr. Nguvulu who suggested the necessity of the Economic Round Table. He was the President of the Action Socialiste before the creation of the PP, is a Mukongo, and was born September 19, 1922. He was a co-signer of the Memorandum of 16, and was one of the founders of the MNC from which he later resigned. In April, 1960, he took part in the Congress of the Belgian Communist Party, but insisted that he was there only as an observer.

Mr. Hubert Sangara, provisionally named as the Commissioner of State for the Kivu Province in the first government, held a seat on the Kivu Provincial Council in 1958 and 1959; he was also an administrator of Sabena, the Belgian airlines system. At the Round Table Conference he represented the ARP (Alliance Rurale Progressiste).

Mr. Christophe Muzungu, provisionally named as the Commissioner of State for the Eastern Province, is virtually unknown. Of Basongye origin, he was Lumumba's Secretary of the MNC at Léopoldville and in that capacity traveled fairly extensively throughout the Congo. Mr. Raphael Batshikama, Secretary of State for the Interior, is known only as an ABAKO member; Mr. André Genge, a Member of the Council of Ministers, is known only as a member of the PUNA party; Mr. Gregoire Kamanga, named Minister of Public Health, was the President of COAKA (Coalition Kasaïenne). Mr. Kisolokele, a Member of the Council of Ministers, is known only as an ABAKO member; Mr. Rudahindwa, Minister of Mines, is known only as a member of the ARP (Alliance Rurale Progressiste).

The following members of the first government constituted by Mr. Lumumba remain completely unknown to the present writer; Mr. Tamusu Fumu, named provisionally as Commissioner of State for the Equator Province; Mr. Sylvain Kama, named provisionally as the Commissioner of State for Léopoldville Province; Mr. André Mandi, named Secretary of State for Foreign Affairs; Mr. Pascal Nkayi, Minister of Finance; and Mr. André Tshibangu, Secretary of State for Finance.

172

CHAPTER V

Two Local Views

LUPUPA

The village of Lupupa lies in the Kabinda District of the easternmost portion of the Kasaï Province, and it was here that I spent the better part of a year, from August of 1959 to June of 1960, pursuing a program of anthropological research. During this time the villagers spoke their minds freely about independence, the Belgians, and the future as they envisaged it, and their state of knowledge is probably typical of the millions of people who live in the Congo bush.

Lupupa is a pretty village set on a gently sloping open savannah which is covered with grass that grows higher than a man's head and is dotted with occasional trees. Its population was about 260 people, average village size in the area, and the people are the Bala, a clan of the Basongye. Lupupa has two sister villages, Kampata, which is about a mile and a half to the west, and Makola, some three miles to the east, and the people of the three villages call themselves the Bapupa. Twenty-five miles to the east is the nearest Belgian administration post, the town of Tshofa, with a population, during the time I was there, of eleven Belgian adults and their children and some three thousand Congolese. The Belgian population included a doctor and his wife, an agricultural officer and his wife, the administrator, and six Belgian Catholic missionaries. Some fifty miles to the west was the Westcott Presbyterian Mission, an English mission staffed by perhaps ten or fifteen British and Scotch missionaries. Finally, fifty miles to the east was the territorial headquarters of Sentery, and 160 miles to the southwest, the district headquarters of Kabinda, each with a European population of between 100 and 150 people.

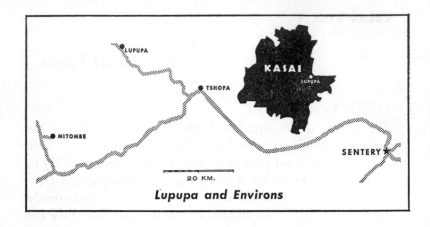

Lupupa and Environs

The Catholic mission in Tshofa had established a primary school in Lupupa which was taught by an African monitor and included the first three grades. Some children went on to the mission school in Tshofa for three further grades, but only one adult in Lupupa had had more than six years of schooling. During our residence in Lupupa, a Catholic father came from Tshofa once to say Mass; this was the first time a Mass had been said in the village in ten months, though the mission claimed a total of forty-one converts to Catholicism.

Outside influences played only a very small part in Lupupa affairs. The Belgian administrator rarely visited the village, and while the doctor passed through once a month on his way to his outstation in Ngandu, some twenty miles to the north, his visits in Lupupa were never professional, and his patients went to Tshofa for medical assistance. The mission Sisters came once or twice a month to weigh and measure the children. The most frequent visitor was the agricultural officer who came on an average of once a week and spent considerable time in the fields, inspecting, instructing, and checking the planting quotas.

The heaviest outside influences on Lupupa came from the

174

single battery-operated radio in the village, from the travels of the local young men, and from the visits of outsiders to the village. The radio was owned by my interpreter, a young man of high intelligence and, for Lupupa, considerable worldliness. He listened to the news programs each morning and evening, and for each broadcast his house was filled with ten to twenty young men for whom he translated the French into Kisongye.

The Lupupans were hardy travelers. There was a constant coming and going to Kampata and Makola and frequent journeys to more distant points. Most of the longer trips were undertaken for economic reasons. In April, for example, two men set out for Lubefu 150 miles to the northwest, and came back via Kibombo, 200 miles to the Northeast; the purpose of the trip was to buy meat to be sold in Lupupa. Several members of the village were occupied as makers of raffia baskets and platters and traveled as far east as Bukavu and as far south as Elisabethville to sell their wares. And a constant stream of travelers came through Lupupa: I remember many people from outlying areas who were taking their sick to Tshofa or Ngandu, campaigning politicians, itinerant musicians plying their trade, an itinerant photographer who carried all his equipment with him on his bicycle, the Chef de Secteur who came and went with great frequency, and many others.

Despite these outside influences, Lupupa has remained basically an isolated bush village. It would not do to say that life in Lupupa has remained unchanged over long periods of time, however, for it has changed and changed dramatically, especially in the past seventy years since the Arab slave wars swept over that part of the country. But the village is only tangentially tied to the rest of the country and has only a remote connection to the world economy. Although cotton is raised as a cash crop, its production was controlled by the Belgian agricultural officer and its sale by the Belgian cotton combine: there was little awareness and no understanding of a world market as it affected the village. Indeed, Lupupa represents an almost classic picture of a self-contained community: it depends on local products for its subsistence, on local or at most territorial organization for its legal support, on itself for political control. The people are little concerned with the outside world, and know almost nothing about it. The stories of other parts of Africa and even of the Near East and of parts of Europe which were brought back by soldiers in the two world wars have affected the village only casually, and the descriptions given by such travelers remain more tales of distant places than actualities of the world.

Perhaps the clearest picture of the relations of Lupupa to the world is to be found in the world view of the people. The earth is conceptualized as a round, flat platter; if one approaches the edge (although the distance is too great to conceive of this as a real possibility) and is not careful, he will tumble off and into a limitless sea beyond which is only the unknown. In the exact center of this platter is Lupupa and, by extension, the Congo, while somewhere around the rim are placed America, Belgium, and Portugal. These three countries, it is evident, figure in the world scene because they are the only ones known—America because there had been American visitors there, Portugal because of the presence in Tshofa of a Portuguese trader, and Belgium for obvious reasons. The English and Scotch of the Westcott Mission did not figure in the picture, possibly simply because it was not clear to the Lupupans what countries the missionaries represented.

The most sophisticated person in the village knew that this picture of the world was untrue, and told us so. He had learned the truth in school, he said, and the world, far from being a flat platter, was in reality a flat triangle, with Lupupa in the center, and Belgium, Portugal, and America at the various angles of the figure.

It cannot be assumed from this brief description of the

world view that the people of Lupupa are stupid. Quite to the contrary, they are alert and intelligent with considerable skill in human relations and in organizing and running their own affairs. If we may use the word with its intended meaning, the people of Lupupa can only be called "ignorant," ignorant of the outside world and ignorant of their relation to it. There has been no opportunity for them to visualize the world as it is, and little opportunity for them to learn about it. Within their own sphere, they are far better versed than I; outside of it, there is simply no realization of possibilities. An inflatable globe was at first a puzzle, then a partial revelation, then a "fact" (because their American said so) but a fact quite out of context and thus only skeptically accepted.

If the world view is almost nonexistent, knowledge of the Congo is not much broader. Few people have visited faraway places in the country, with the exception of Elisabethville, Bukavu, and occasionally Léopoldville, and the distant places remain almost legendary to the Lupupans. In short, the world, so far as Lupupa is concerned, consists of the world they know: Lupupa, its sister villages, the villages around them, the Basongye in a far less definite fashion, some facts, ideas, and attitudes about neighboring tribes, and an extremely limited idea of the Congo itself. All things, then, relate to Lupupa and have importance only in that relation. This is not so surprising for we all encounter the same feeling in our own communities.

Independence was conceived as something with which the young men were concerned, and the older people were not vitally interested. When they spoke of it, it was with a certain diffidence and even boredom; the problem was simply not theirs to solve and they preferred to give their attention to other matters. At the same time, they could, and occasionally did, speak eloquently: "We consider ourselves at the disposition of Europeans up to this time. Now we are like slaves of the Belgians. If someone will come who will free us, he will be our chief, and I will thank Efile Mukulu (God)."

But eloquence is no substitute for information, and it was information that was lacking in Lupupa. During the time I was in residence in the village—and this was the time that almost the entire "political development" of the Congo took place—not a single Belgian administrator ever came to explain what independence would mean. Indeed, late in April the Territorial Agent at Tshofa was transferred to another post and was not replaced; thus, during what was perhaps the most crucial time before independence, there was no Belgian administration within a radius of approximately seventy-five miles to aid and assist the people. True, the Chef de Secteur did his best in his frequent trips through the area, but his knowledge was hardly superior to that of the villagers, and his actions often tended to confuse rather than to clarify the situation.

It is no wonder that the people were almost totally bewildered by the events taking place around them and by the part they were expected to play in them. Thus the most outrageously naïve expectations grew up in Lupupa. One villager, whom we will call Old S, said: "When independence comes, I'll go on cultivating. Probably things will be better, but it is hard to know what will happen. There won't be anyone to tell me what to do. I can do what I want." He continued to express his almost certain feeling that there would be no taxes to be paid after June 30. MP, another villager, said flatly: "After independence there will be no taxes. Everyone will have plenty to eat, lots of clothes, cars to drive. Everything will be wonderful." Economic questions as they affected the Congo were simply a puzzle, and thus the president of one of the political parties in Tshofa, when pressed as to the source of funds to run the government after independence, told me that the problem was a simple one since it was only a question of having more franc notes printed. Even sophisticated A felt that as soon as independence was declared, money would be readily forthcoming, and some months before the date was busily preparing a letter and its carbon copies to be sent to Lumumba, Kasavubu, Kalonji, and two or three others, asking for immediate disbursement of funds so that he could study in an American university—A had had six years of grade school education.

Stories of this sort were, of course, by no means confined to Lupupa, and Belgians were fond of recounting instances of Congolese who asked for money from a bank in which they had no deposits and about which, indeed, they had no understanding whatsoever. Possibly the most widespread story, heard in Lupupa too, was that of the Congolese who purportedly asked a Belgian, "What is independence? Will it come in a package? When will it come? May I unwrap it right away?"

The tragedy of these stories and attitudes is that their naïveté represents almost the limit of thinking about what independence would bring. And even more, it is the tragedy that the people, the supposed voting electorate, could be led into independence with such an incredibly poor idea of what was happening to them.

In general, the attitude toward Europeans varied, but quite systematically, from individual to individual. The doctor in Tshofa, whose relations with the Congolese were excellent, was a highly respected man, and the people in the area served by his hospital were anxious and even insistent that he should remain. This was partly because of his own personality, but primarily it was because he was a doctor, and the only doctor in the area, and thus someone who constantly did "good" for the people. On the other hand, the agricultural officer was disliked, quite probably not so much for the person he was as for the job which was his to do and which automatically cast him in the role of villain. Similar attitudes were held toward the few other Europeans in the area—much depended upon their jobs and the kind of relations these jobs forced them to have with the Congolese. But individuals were also judged on their merits, and thus one Belgian was thoroughly disliked because of his personal attitude: "Do you think he will shake hands with me on the street? Do you think he will even say 'hello' to me when we pass?"

Bitterness toward such Belgians certainly existed, and many people expressed themselves strongly on the subject: "Why will they not shake hands with me on the street? Because my skin is black they think I am dirty but I use the same kind of soap that they do." "We want all Europeans to leave this country. They are rich and we are poor." "Why is the price of cotton only 5.85 francs? It is because the Belgians do not want to give us any money. They want to keep it all for themselves." Occasionally these feelings were carried to illogical extremes as in the case of a young man in Kampata who railed violently against all *whites,* saying that they should be forced to leave the Congo immediately and that only if this happened could any country, including America, be a friend of the Congolese. In the next breath he urged the necessity of financial aid from America for the Congo, but even on pointed questioning he did not see the difficulty of his double-edged view which demanded help on the one hand and spurned friendship on the other.

It the attitude toward Europeans was basically bitter but varied somewhat depending on the individual, the attitude toward other Congolese was probably even more sharply defined. Strangers to Lupupa were usually viewed with suspicion and latent hostility, although hospitality was almost always offered to them. Lupupa and the surrounding countryside strongly supported Lumumba and the Mouvement National Congolais, primarily, I think, because Lumumba represented the best-known politician whose origin was closest to the area. Kalonji, on the other hand, was severely disliked because he represented the Baluba wing of the MNC. Kasavubu received little consideration because his tribal origin and residence were almost completely strange to Lupupa, and in this respect he was as foreign as an American.

This attitude toward strangers developed to such a point that after one of the few political meetings attended by people from Lupupa, in May of 1960, one of the returning village dignitaries called a special and secret meeting to inform the people that "We have been told in Mitombe by our leaders that strangers are a bad thing. We do not want strangers in our village. We do not want to have strangers coming here."

Thus one of the responses to independence was an increase in the isolation felt by the villagers and an increase in their fear of and hostility toward strangers. Indeed, perhaps the biggest single effect on Lupupa was the proposal of a new and enlarged village site which would combine the villages of Lupupa, Kampata, Makola, and one other smaller and more or less tangential village. This suggestion was first made in October, 1959, for reasons which need not concern us here but which involved questions of malignant magic. However, as time went on and the idea was more fully discussed, the prime reason for the move came to be independence and the consolidation of the four villages into a single, much larger unit, in order to provide protection for its residents. The people were never completely sure what they needed protection from, but the undercurrent of opinion was that after independence there might be fighting and that specifically the generally "treacherous" Baluba were likely to attack. When I left Lupupa in June, 1960, a new village site had been laid out and agreement had been reached among the four villages concerned; defense was thus one of the prime considerations fostered by the coming independence, and the unity of the Congo as a new nation was made more remote instead of more real.

Another response engendered by independence in Lupupa was the furthering of a nascent and developing split between the younger and older generations. It has already been noted that the old people felt independence was something for the young, and that the young agreed in principle with this feeling. The old people were more or less content to live with the status quo whereas the young people, already chafing in a normal generational conflict over the local political power held by the old, were anxious to make changes. While to the best of my knowledge independence as such was never cited by either side as a specific sore point or means of power manipulation in the conflict, it was always present, and the fact that independence would surely change some things in the local political and social systems gave the youngsters the courage to press their complaints and to assert their power. Independence was equated with youth, not only because it was something the young would do but also because it was felt that it would probably be the young who would take the political offices both in the "national" government and in the traditional local government. By the time I left Lupupa, the village was hopelessly split down the middle even to the extent of separate treasuries for the young and old. Traditional government was, for the moment at least, almost nonexistent, for the young men had succeeded in ousting the three most important political dignitaries and had replaced only one of them with one of their own number. Thus again, one of the effects of independence was not the strengthening of the village and its organization, but the contrary, a weakening of local government and local human relations.

The heart of a Western democratic political system is the voter and the ballot he casts, and it was this system of political choice that Belgium attempted in a pathetically short space of time to introduce to Lupupa and the Congo. In Lupupa it was poorly understood. While the traditional political system had been democratic, it had not called for casting the ballot but had relied instead on majority rule based on town meetings. In brief, Lupupa was traditionally headed by a chief whose selection came about partly because of traditional lines of succession. Below the chief were ranged six political dignitaries, or notables, who constituted the ruling council of the village. They made judgments in most legal cases, were responsible for any decisions affecting the village, and were expected to set standards of probity of conduct for the people. Below these dignitaries were four substitute notables who attended all meetings but never spoke officially; they were candidates in training and their function was to learn the job of being a notable and to be prepared to step into the position of any dignitary who was removed from office. Still lower in the political organization was the division of the village into four quarters each of which was headed by a leader whose primary jobs were to keep the peace in his section of the village, judge minor disputes on a family level, and channel the more important matters to higher authority. Thus Lupupa had a highly functional system of political organization which provided for emergency, and which funneled matters of village importance to higher and higher levels of authority and responsibility.

Beneath this pyramidal structure, however, and the most important part of it, were the people themselves who held the absolute right to depose, replace, or nominate any functionary in the system. This was accomplished through meetings of all the people at which pressing matters were discussed and agreements as to action reached. A concensus of opinion was considered desirable, and a simple majority of one was not sufficient to cause action. This power of the people extended further to the vetoing of actions taken by the council of notables, and even to the deposition of the hereditary chief, should such action be considered desirable. And action could be initiated by any individual.

What has been described here is an essentially democratic system which functioned much as did our New England town meetings. But it is important to note once again that voting as a procedure never played a part in the system. We Americans do not always realize the complexity of voting, nor the extensive education we receive in how to exercise our rights in using it. From the time we are children in kindergarten we use the vote, elect our class officers in high school, vote for the most popular person in our class, ballot in mock political conventions in our universities, and thus when the time comes for the assumption of our legal political ballot we are at least relatively well prepared to assume our responsibilities.

But consider the people of Lupupa. They had no practice whatsoever in the sheer mechanics of voting. They were not instructed in any way in what voting meant, for whom they were voting, why some candidates were on the ballot and others were not, how the democratic process can include voting against rather than voting for, and how, though defeated in one election, a person can be elected in the next. Given the situation, it is remarkable how quickly they grasped the system. By the time of the second elections in Lupupa, some understood the principle of voting against a candidate, some understood that cases would arise in which they would have to decide to vote for the lesser of two considered evils. Even as early as the first campaign, political bribery actually took place as local candidates came through Lupupa offering up to eighty cents in return for a vote. But such relative political sophistication was not widespread, and for the most part the process of voting remained a mystery in Lupupa. When a registration table was set up in Lupupa on the fifth of October, 1959, almost no one registered. The table remained in Lupupa for one day, and the Congolese in charge did nothing to pursue his duties, but rather simply waited for anyone who might chance upon his shaded table. Even the sophisticated sometimes flatly refused to register; A, for example, simply said that it was not worth the trouble, that he did not understand clearly why the table was there, and that he was not going to vote in any case. He did not vote.

In these elections, held in December of 1959, registration

was restricted to male Congolese over twenty-one years of age with six months' residence in the territory, and not under prison sentence at the time of the election. The voting was for territorial councilors who were to act as advisers to the administration (in Sentery, fifty miles away). The implication, of course, was that they would form the nucleus of the first Congolese local government, and thus the election was of considerable importance. Polling places were set up at various villages in the Bala area, but the districts were arranged on the basis of Belgian administrative sections called *chefferies*. The upshot of this arrangement was that although there was a polling place in the village of Lutobo, twelve and one-half miles by road and something less by trail from Lupupa, it was in another *chefferie;* the Lupupans then, were forced to vote in Mitombe, fifty miles by road and perhaps thirty-five by trail.

Filing for candidacy was announced at a meeting of the notables of the region in October, but the announcement of this meeting was not widely heralded or explained, and as a result no notable from Lupupa attended. The result was that there were no Lupupa candidates, nor were there candidates from neighboring villages which had suffered the same confusion.

The voting record of Lupupa was not high. To the best of my knowledge, five eligible males at most made the long journey on foot or on bicycle to Mitombe and, upon finding there were no local candidates listed, some if not all of them failed to vote. Faced with an almost complete lack of understanding of the voting system, a clean miss on the filing for candidacy, a polling place thirty-five miles away, as well as other obstacles, how could the figure have been high? What American would, these days at least, persevere in the face of such obstacles?

In the second set of elections in May, 1960, Lupupa's voting record was considerably higher as some thirty men went to the polls in Mitombe. This marked jump in voting indicates primarily the increase in determination of the Lupupans who, although they were about equally unaware of what they were voting for in May as in December, at least were beginning on their own to decide that elections might be important and that their own participation was desirable. In both elections, the vote in this area of the Kasaï varied widely from village to village. Thus in Kampongo, some fifteen miles to the north, the turnout was exactly 100 per cent of the eligibles, while in Ngandu the figure ranged somewhere around 5 per cent. This huge discrepancy is explained by the fact that a Kampongo man was one of the candidates; the people in Ngandu grumbled vigorously and showed their almost completely local orientation by staying away from the polls because no candidate was posted from their village.

It has already been remarked that the MNC-Lumumba was the most powerful party, if not the almost unanimous choice of the voters in Lupupa, and that this enthusiasm came not so much from the MNC platform as from the fact that Lumumba represented the most "local" of the national candidates. Lumumba, however, was still considered an outsider, as indeed he was from the standpoint of Lupupa and the Basongye in general, and a local political party of the Basongye was formed in January of 1960. This pattern was repeated over and over in the Congo as the people, viewing politics and political organization from the purely local standpoint, organized to emphasize local interests. The Mouvement de l'Unité Basonge [*sic*] was originated by an agricultural officer and a veterinarian, both Basongye, in Sentery, the territorial headquarters. It was greeted with prompt and high enthusiasm by the people of the area, and in Lupupa it was introduced by the Chef de Secteur on the following basis: "The Congolese have returned from the Round Table talks in Brussels. There were Baluba, Bakongo, Ruandaise, people from Stanleyville and from Bukavu, all with their different languages. But there were no Basongye there. Our people were forgotten. Here in our part of the country we have nothing. They say that at Léopoldville there is much money; at Luluabourg there are diamonds [*sic*]. But the Basongye have nothing. So we must unite." Again the purely local nature of this appeal deserves to be pointed out. The MUB was to be supported strictly because the Basongye had been left out of high government negotiations, and because of the implied connection between formation of a local political party and the acquisition of wealth equal to that enjoyed by other areas of the Congo.

The aims of the organization were apparently honest and, to a considerable extent, farsighted. Thus the Chef de Secteur announced that certain sums of money were to be contributed "so that we can have an account at the bank. We will use the money to pay Europeans to come and help us. We are forgotten; we need money so that we can have doctors and other Europeans come and help us." Each adult male was urged to give one dollar as a flat contribution to the party, plus twenty cents a month for himself, ten cents for each of his wives, and six cents for each of his children. The initial contribution was to go to a general MUB fund in the town of Kabinda. The distribution of the monthly sums was somewhat less clear, but the general understanding was that part of it would go to the party coffers, and part would return to the villages. Within a few weeks fifty-six out of seventy cards given to Lupupa had been taken up by means of the initial flat contribution, and the village was strongly behind the idea. Part of the monies collected went toward the purchase of several automobiles for the business use of the party, and by the time I left the area, rather elaborate plans had been made to provide social centers and new individual housing in certain villages. The MUB aligned itself immediately with the MNC-Lumumba, and its leaders began to take part in some regional political affairs; these affairs, however, were unknown in

Lupupa, and the people there took no active part whatsoever in the organization or direction of the party.

The MNC meanwhile was sending its organizers through the territory to sell membership cards to the electorate and nominally "to inform the people" as well. In October of 1959, the organizers who came to Lupupa announced that MNC membership would cost 60 francs or $1.20; however, membership taken out in 1960 would cost $4.00, and for the laggards who waited until 1961, membership cost would double to $8.00. There were many stories in Lupupa concerning MNC membership: that the MNC card would be the new identity card, that it would exempt people from taxes, that the lack of a card would bring heavy future penalties. In spite of these rumors, not more than five to ten people bought memberships. The MNC failed in Lupupa, though it had the emotional support of the people, because it appealed to no local pride or problems. Its regional support and national platform of a united Congo had almost no influence on Lupupans.

Other individuals came to Lupupa bringing word of the rest of the Congo and its political stirrings, and one in particular represented viewpoints with which those Lupupans who heard him were in accord. Let us call this man M, a young man of about twenty-five, extremely intelligent and quick, a Musongye by birth, and at that time in a position extremely close to Patrice Lumumba; after independence, he was appointed to a position in the Lumumba government. In the course of a trip on MNC business he called on me in Lupupa on the afternoon of May 25. We spoke of many of the Congo's problems in a lengthy discussion and I shall report his views in no special order here. Early in the conversation he fell to boasting about the efficiency of the MNC undercover activities; he said that the MNC had a "file" on every administrator and agent in the Congo and that it had already marked those whom it wished to eject from the country and those whom it wished to have stay. This, of course, was before it was known that Lumumba and the MNC would form the first Congo government. When I asked how he felt he could persuade the "desirables" to stay and work with the independent Congo, he simply turned the question aside unanswered. Perhaps more exactly, his response was unbounded confidence that such desirables *would* stay. This attitude was widespread in the Congo. Few plans were ever made by Congolese for a program after June 30, but with an intense self-confidence it was simply taken for granted that the world would come to the Congo and that, without any effort on the part of the Congolese, help in all its forms would be available. Thus M was justified in his attitude, at least so far as he was concerned, because the supreme naïveté, the tremendous localization of thought, and the inheritance of paternalism were his as much as any man's: his veneer of sophistication was so thin as to allow him little room for thought.

Although he would deny it, everything for M was black and white, both figuratively and literally, and thus all Belgians, if not all white-skinned people, were bad, and all Africans, namely the Congolese, were good, and oppressed by colonialism. All the troubles in the Congo at that time, among which the most pressing local problem was the Bena Lulua-Baluba conflict in Luluabourg, were caused by Belgians. No sins on the part of the Congolese were admitted, nor was any good on the part of the Belgians. Furthermore, in his logic all troubles, for example those in Luluabourg, would stop at the stroke of midnight on independence day, quite literally. If we accept his premise that all problems were being caused by Belgians, then we must accept his conclusion, but we now know, of course, that his premise was only tragically naïve and that independence brought only further outbreaks in that troubled city.

M was full of generalizations of this sort: "All whites are armed to the teeth," he said, and I was unable to convince him of the truth of the fact that I personally carried no arms whatsoever save for a machete. Another generalization which again he would strenuously deny, was that everything Western is good and everything Congolese bad, in the sphere, at least, of material culture. When I suggested that perhaps there were things in Congolese life to be valued too, I was hotly accused of being "like all the other Europeans who want the Congo people to stay as they are, who want to deny us the good things of the West." I amplified my remarks to say that I personally felt there was much value in Congo art, and the response was: "Oh, of course we would not forget that. After independence we will have a factory to make masks and we will sell them in America!"

Another subject discussed was cotton, which is Lupupa's cash crop. Citing the price always at 5 francs per kilogram, where in actuality it was 5.85 francs in 1959 and, in the face of a world market drop was *raised* to 6 francs in 1960, he castigated the Belgians saying that the price was unfair and that they were, in effect, stealing the cotton from the people of Lupupa. "Look at these poor people. Up at six in the morning and working in the fields until six at night; they suffer terribly." The fact of the matter is that, quite aside from his misquotations concerning price, almost no one in Lupupa ever worked in the fields from six in the morning until six at night and, in the sense that he was using the word, no one suffered. But these generalizations represented for him a crystallized idea which he used to convince others, and of which he had certainly convinced himself.

I would not suggest for a moment that all his ideas were wrong or that he was a deliberate liar, or that there was not some truth in his charges, but I cite the conversation to illustrate his appalling generalizations, his twisting of words, his naïveté and his expediency. I am convinced that he could not, as an ardent nationalist, allow himself the luxury of conceding anything to the other side. All Belgians, if not all whites, are bad; all rival political parties are unspeakable; Lumumba is virtue personified; all Congolese are hard-working slaves to the colonial system; and all would be rosy and calm the day independence dawned.

I asked what the United States could do to help the Congo, and although he was not at all concise we finally reduced his thoughts to three propositions: (1) cash "to put all the people to work." This, he felt, would have to be given as a gift "because in our position we could not guarantee to repay a loan"; (2) private capital, in the form of investment "in factories"; (3) American professors to teach English in the universities "so that we can learn English and send our ambassadors all over the world."

These views expressed by M were far more sophisticated than those held by the people of Lupupa, but as views of a Musongye who had "made good" in the outside world and who was obviously in a position of importance, the Lupupans accepted them eagerly. My own arguments and questions were for the most part put aside, and M gave to Lupupa some sense of their position in Congo politics. Although I would not suggest that they immediately began to regard themselves as "sufferers in the cotton fields," the germ of this idea, as well as others, was quite possibly planted by this outsider.

But these broader problems were not the typical ones of Lupupa. On one mid-April night I was visited by a delegation of about seventy-five men from the three sister villages, who announced that they wished to talk over the problems of independence. Their questions were frank: (1) Why was the doctor leaving the hospital in Tshofa? (2) What were they to do after independence without white people to help them, and with the Baluba arming themselves for war? (3) What kind of help was it that they were seeking?

These are not simple questions to answer despite their deceptively simple appearance. It was not difficult to say, of course, that the doctor was leaving because he had served his three-year term and was due for a six-month vacation. But

191

this answer was not really satisfactory for, with their inward-centered view of life, it was not really conceivable to them that he would prefer, even for a six-month vacation, the company of his own people in Belgium to the company of the Basongye. As for the second question, there is nothing to answer to people who are convinced that they are about to be attacked, and I could only murmur words about America and how it prepared itself against the possibility of attack but had a tradition of not attacking first. The Lupupans were polite, but my words were not what they had hoped for. What they wanted were the names of the American firms that would send them rifles. The answers to the third question, complicated and lengthy on my part I am afraid, are not important here; what is important is the question.

I wrote in my journal that night, April 19, 1960: "Two things bother me: First, it seems so hopeless to talk to them for they visualize independence as something only for themselves, not for the country as a whole, and although one tries to stress a unified Congo he cannot get far with it. Second, it is useless and somewhat specious to talk of peace in a country which is pretty clearly heading for war—what they want is not reassurance and brave talk of peace, but guns."

How typical the people of Lupupa are cannot be said with complete assurance, but it seems more than likely that their plight represented that of at least 80 per cent of the people in the Congo: the vast groups of the bush whose understanding and education was far below that of the relatively few Congolese who had migrated to the cities. At the basis of their difficulty lay an inward-looking attitude which led them to see themselves and only themselves as the central aspect of all problems: their expectations for independence were that all things would be done for them by others. On a national scale, the feeling was multiplied, and independence everywhere was conceived in individual terms on the one hand, and

as bringing the unlimited assistance of outsiders regardless
of any actions of the Congolese on the other. Influences from
the outside that might have changed this provincial outlook
were present but minimal and, as in the case of M, not always to the good.

Further, the people of Lupupa were left almost totally uninformed by the Belgian administration. No Belgian agent
ever came to talk to them about the requirements of independence, or about the mechanics of achieving it. Rather, the
administration relied exclusively on calling representatives
of the village to the local administrative post—messages did
not get delivered, apparently no check was made on attendance, and the notables themselves did not understand clearly
what they were told in the infrequent sessions if, indeed, they
bothered to attend at all. But the lack of information went
further than a simple void of knowledge concerning the mechanics and meaning of independence; it reached out to the
world as well, and so Lupupans can hardly be blamed for
seeing these events in a purely local frame of reference—
they had no other.

Independence, as a matter of fact, tended to trouble rather
than help Lupupa in that it strengthened its traditional isolation and contributed strongly to a split between generations
which, by the time I left, had thoroughly wrecked the traditional political system. Still Lupupa met its new problems
with courage and determination despite its limitations: the
people *did* learn to vote, they did walk thirty-five miles to do
so, they did join a political party which was formed on the
basis of self-help for the Basongye. And they can justly take
credit for these things.

But localism and isolation were their chief problems, and
the people of Lupupa in June of 1960 were only barely coming to recognize them as such. Why should independence have
meant anything to them save for the vaguest of hopes and
generalizations? That it meant freedom was clear, but free-

dom except as a bright star shining from a great distance, and except as a desirable ideal, meant nothing in the concrete realities of the times.

STANLEYVILLE

Stanleyville, the third largest city of the Congo, is located some 2,000 miles up the Congo River from Léopoldville, one-half degree north of the equator in the central equatorial forest. It was Stanley who in 1877 discovered the Falls that now bear his name and that mark the end of the longest navigable stretch of the Congo River. Stanleyville is a transportation center of great importance to the area it serves, but it has never reached the size or sophistication of Elisabethville or Léopoldville.

In 1959 Stanleyville's population was estimated at between 50,000 and 80,000 Congolese and 5,000 Europeans, with the Congolese representing some sixteen different tribes of which the Lokele were the largest single group; three-quarters of the African population came from the hinterlands of the Stanleyville district. The European population consisted of government employees, by far the largest single group and usually Belgian; colonials (*colons*) who owned land, ran plantations, and were also primarily Belgian; and merchants, who were Belgian, Portuguese, Greek, French, and Indian. The city was organized into four communes and one zone annex: three of the communes, Mangobo, Kabondo, and Lubunga were exclusively Congolese, while the commune of Stanleyville was primarily European although a few African families moved into it in 1959. The zone annex included the Wagenia, the Arabized peoples, and the remainder of the outskirts of Stanleyville.

The dominant Christian group was the Roman Catholic Church which conducted two racially mixed schools for children, one for boys and one for girls. The Protestant British Mission Service and the Salvation Army were also established in the area. There was a government-run lay school for children which provided the first twelve grades. Two French newspapers were available, as well as two weekly newspapers in Kingwana, the local dialect of Kiswahili. Many Congolese owned radios.

The Africans in Stanleyville were very much aware of the whites, for they were in a position to watch them constantly, and the differences in the two ways of life were not only apparent but a continual source of irritation. The European lived in a beautiful home, had a car, had servants to do his wife's work, and had Congolese nurses for his children. He always had plenty to eat and drink, and he had many clothes for himself and his family. He was always the boss and always in a position to order the African. He seemed to be able to obtain money whenever he needed it simply by using checks and the bank. And when he wanted to buy things he did not have to pay but could write an I O U.

All Congolese were not this naïve, of course. The *évolué* may have had a good job and may have raised his standard of living to remarkable heights compared to other Congolese, but his standard of living never seemed to approach that of the European. This was a constant source of frustration, bitterness, and resentment, and even if the African could have a house of brick instead of a mud hut, a bicycle so that he could ride instead of walking, a radio, clothing for his family and himself, and usually food enough, he could seldom quite master his sense of inferiority and resentment, and he could never seem to catch up with what the European had.

There is a certain amount of tribalism in a city such as Stanleyville, but in the native communes there were no distinct areas occupied by specific tribes. Even the attachment to Lumumba, which so marked Stanleyville, was not based upon ethnic origin, for Lumumba is a member of the Batetela tribe and there were few Batetela in the city. The root of the troubles and difficulties which plagued Stanleyville was basically racial rather than tribal and once under way, it developed almost immediately into a vicious racial struggle of black against white.

The greatest political impact upon Stanleyville was provided by Patrice Lumumba, for this was where he began his political career as the modest president of a local club. His arrest for embezzlement made him a widely known figure, and by the time he returned to Stanleyville in October, 1959, he had traveled a good deal, presumably learned a good deal, and had formulated the political program which would carry him to victory. His speeches were centered around two major points: immediate independence, and "drive out the European." In stressing them he did what no one had dared do before: he told the people what they wanted to hear, that the whites were the cause of all their troubles, and that once they were free and the Europeans had left, life would be perfect. Independence in Stanleyville meant freedom from the European yoke, less work or no work at all, more money, no taxes, and freedom to share the houses, cars, and women of the whites.

Lumumba arrived with great fanfare for the October, 1959, convention of the MNC: he drove through the communes in his white convertible and drew wild demonstrations of support, particularly from the women for whom he had great personal appeal. In his speeches, he used the tactic of speaking first in French and then in Kingwana, but in the latter version adding inflammatory and insulting remarks about the Belgians. Within a few days tempers ran high and liquor flowed freely; independence was a heady topic, and rioting began. Anger was first directed toward the things that represented the enemy, the social centers, public buildings, and within a short time the European section of the city. Uprisings and incidents continued in the communes for two days, but the European city was sealed off by the Force Publique, and an armored division including nine tanks was brought in from the outside. The tanks frightened the Africans and word began to spread that the Belgians were going to kill everyone caught on the streets. Road blocks and barbed wire entanglements were set up and remained for two weeks; a curfew was imposed, and the rioting died away.

Lumumba was charged with being responsible for inciting to riot, and a warrant was issued for his arrest, but he went into hiding, moving from place to place, protected by Congolese followers and also assisted by two Europeans who were sympathetic to his cause. The Europeans were eventually arrested and jailed, but their ultimate fate is obscure; it was rumored that they were deported. Lumumba was also eventually caught and jailed, but not before considerable difficulty, for as the police closed in on a hiding place, he was apparently warned by means of the talking drums; dozens of drums were reported confiscated during the course of the search.

It was said that a full colonel was sent to make the final arrest, for the Belgians were extremely anxious that nothing should go wrong. Lumumba was thoroughly disliked by most of the Europeans, and it was feared that a less responsible officer might shoot on sight. In jail he was apparently well treated and spent his time writing; he was given "European" accommodations and food. After his arrest, the town was filled with rumors, and it was said among the Congolese that the police had shot at him several times but that the bullets could not harm him. Crowds gathered outside the prison each day in hopes of either seeing him or hearing something about him. It seems clear that he was able to keep in touch with the MNC, for new directives were issued almost daily.

The MNC had of course been very active in Stanleyville; membership cards were sold for 60 francs ($1.20), and possession of the card was said to guarantee privileges after independence. The opposition party in Stanleyville, the PNP, was not strong, and the MNC took every opportunity to ridicule and denounce it; its leader, Paul Bolya, was called a "European boot licker" and a "Traitor to the Congo." These tactics were successful, for no one had much patience with moderation.

The newspapers were full of the December, 1959, elections which took place during Lumumba's detention, and each day the new candidates for office received recognition. The literate Congolese read the papers avidly, and it became a source of prestige to be seen carrying a newspaper. Many Belgians poked fun at the Congolese for this, and indeed, it was often a ridiculous and pathetic sight to see illiterate Congolese carrying newspapers like all the others. But the more the Congolese succeeded in acting and sounding like Europeans, the more they were derided by some of the white population. One might hear conversations on the street between two Congolese:

"Good day, M. Kabea!"

"Ah, good day, M. Yakusu. And how is Madame, your wife?"

"Very well, thank you. And yours?"

A simple conversation, normal in any culture, and yet in many cases, Belgians would react with deep anger: "Imagine their nerve acting as if they were civilized. They don't even know they are just out of the trees. Just monkeys."

Not all Belgians were this vehement, of course; there were many who had a genuine concern and affection for the Congolese, and there were some who were diplomatic enough not to show their scorn so openly. But there is something inherent in the paternalistic approach which conveys the idea that charges, no matter how much they learn, are never quite acceptable. A child stays a child, and a parent stays a parent, and there seemed in Stanleyville to be little or no meeting ground. Both parties were aware of this, and it was a constant source of distrust, misunderstanding, and friction.

In considerable contrast to the situation in Lupupa, the Belgian government made a substantial effort in Stanleyville to prepare the Congolese for self-government, but there was never enough time. The elected Congolese bourgomasters were installed in their respective areas with a European adviser; a town council was appointed of representative Congolese and Europeans, and the government administrators held lectures concerning the electoral procedure. When the elections did take place in December of 1959, the MNC gained a smashing victory. Although Lumumba had originally ordered a boycott of the elections, he changed his mind and word came from his prison that everyone was to vote. Nowhere was participation less than 60 per cent, and in some places it reached 80 per cent. The MNC won seventeen out of eighteen seats at issue. Election day produced no incidents and the voting was orderly in all parts of the city: residents lined up, patiently awaited their turn, cast their vote, and left. Europeans took no part in this election.

A week before the elections, King Baudouin made his sudden decision to tour the Congo, and Stanleyville was chosen as the first city on his itinerary. Local authorities received the news via Radio Congo Belge only the night before his arrival, and the town was thrown into an uproar. Schools were let out early and the children brought to the airport in special busses; the turnout was enormous. It soon became clear that the crowd was filled with MNC supporters, many with black arm bands to show they were in mourning for Lumumba who was still in prison. Banners reading "Vive Lumumba" and "Indépendance Immédiate" appeared. Rumors flew through the crowd that Baudouin would step off the plane and declare independence. When he did arrive, the crowd was at a fever pitch, shouting in cadence "In-dé-pen-dance." The King came out of the plane, smiled, saluted the Belgian flag and made his way down the steps; at that moment the crowd broke through the police guard and surged toward him. Immediately a platoon of soldiers formed a ring around the King with fixed bayonets and, instead of greeting the dignitaries and reviewing the troops, he was whisked into his car and taken to the Governor's mansion.

Immediately after his departure, the mood of the crowd turned against the whites, and as they tried to make their way to their cars to leave the area, unpleasant incidents began to take place. Angry words were spoken, insults passed, pushing begun. As the cars drove away, stones and mud were thrown, and they were surrounded by Congolese who banged on them and rocked them. Since the King's departure had taken the bulk of the forces of order there were not enough police and soldiers present to keep the peace. It was a tense moment, and the danger was probably greater in Stanleyville at this time than it had been even during the previous October's riots, for the administration had been prepared and forewarned at that time, while the troubles at the King's arrival had not been anticipated. The only reason that the occasion was not disastrous was that, as was so often the case, the Africans were not organized and did not realize that they had the upper hand.

As the crowd broke up around the airport, the rumor spread that Baudouin was going to release Lumumba, and the majority started for the prison. The roads leading into the city were thick with people, and the angry mob continued to menace European cars. The crowd gathered again in front of the prison, but by this time word of what was happening had reached the Force Publique officers, and jeeps filled with soldiers and their white officers, still in their dress whites with ribbons, medals, and swords, arrived on the scene. They began to disperse the crowd, and tension again mounted. Belgian officers ran back the crowd with drawn swords; reinforcements appeared, and noise grenades were thrown. The crowd broke and ran toward the African sections of the city, smashing windows and generally engaging in vandalism on the way.

From the time of the elections, a cold war was declared in Stanleyville between the Africans, whose courage and audac-

ity had grown, and the Europeans, who were finding themselves in a more and more difficult situation. Stones flew whenever the occasion presented itself, logs were left across the
roads on the outskirts of town, and boards with the nails stick-
ing up were thrown into the streets. Those who stopped to re-
move the obstacles were showered with stones. Almost all
Europeans began carrying arms, and both men and women
took 9mm revolvers with them whenever they left their
homes. There was a wave of housebreaking and pilfering.
Purses were snatched as women walked down the streets even
in broad daylight. The post office was systematically robbed
of stamps and correspondence. The MNC was said to be setting up a file of undesirables in town; Europeans would be
sent back to Belgium after independence, and undesirable
Congolese were threatened with death after the Belgians had
left.

Lumumba was finally brought to trial in January of 1960,
charged with having incited a riot, but the trial was a fiasco.
The prosecution's case collapsed as witnesses suddenly lost
their memories, and statements taken at the time of the riot
were renounced. In spite of this, Lumumba was sentenced to
six months in prison. In February he was transferred to Jadotville because of the continual stir caused by his presence in
Stanleyville, and a few days later he was flown to Brussels
for the Round Table Conference. Independence was declared for June 30, 1960.

In Stanleyville, the announcement of the independence date
contributed heavily to the constant turmoil. Rumors ran
wild, some so persistently that the administration was forced
to publish public notices denouncing them. One such rumor
was that the coming May elections would not be secret, and
thus that the MNC would know who had voted for and against
it and would take reprisals. For some time, word went around
that the Europeans were planning to kill all the Congolese by
the simple expedient of poisoning the beer supply, and most

people stopped buying beer. Later the story changed to the effect that the Europeans had failed in their effort to buy off the breweries, and that they were planning to poison the local water supply instead.

Another result of the setting of a date for independence was the emergence of Congolese opportunists who busied themselves with the redistribution of European goods. European houses were sold to more naïve Congolese for 2,000 francs (40 dollars), and another 1,000 francs bought the car and perhaps the European's wife as well. There were stories concerning Congolese who knocked on European doors and asked to see the house which was to be theirs after independence. At one point a Congolese newspaper published an article in which it was stated that black and white would be equal after independence and that while there had in the past been mulatto children of black mothers and white fathers, now there would be mulatto children of black fathers and white mothers; the European population was outraged. Another published article suggested that since King Baudouin was as yet unmarried, it would be a fine thing if he were to choose a Congolese bride; again the Europeans were horrified.

As tensions continued to mount, European social life became more and more restricted; people were unwilling to leave their children with African "boys" in the evening, and the bars and restaurants were almost deserted. A local restaurant advertised that as part of its New Year's Eve celebration, the attached hotel would supply European-supervised baby sitters. In the streets and markets, misunderstandings flared into bitter arguments. The Congolese were never really sure that the Belgians would indeed grant independence, even after the date had been set. The Europeans, on their side, were extremely uneasy about their own status after independence, for a program of basic guarantees was never spelled out for them. Political leaders made vague statements about co-operation but in many cases talked out of both sides of their mouths, and the Belgian government was equally unclear as to what its intentions were toward civil servants. As a result, houses were stripped of everything of value and all movable properties sent back to Belgium. Excess money was transferred to European banks. Final examinations in the schools were moved up to an earlier date so that children and their mothers could return to Belgium before June 30. Airline flights were booked solid and extra planes were put on to handle the crowds. Few stayed whose work did not absolutely require it.

Thus in Stanleyville tensions increased as one event piled upon another—the convention riots, Lumumba's arrest, the King's visit, the elections, Lumumba's trial, his freedom, the Round Table Conference, and the setting of an independence date all made their contributions. As businesses failed or closed and as Europeans departed, more and more Congolese found themselves unemployed. In turn more and more people began to roam the streets and discontent led to incidents. All the past and present woes were blamed on the Europeans. "When independence comes, we will rule everything." How? Lumumba will see to it.

The contrasts in these two local views—of Lupupa on the one hand and Stanleyville on the other—are clear. In Lupupa, there was no European population, and the result was that the difficulties of the coming independence became difficulties for the Congolese themselves, while in Stanleyville, they developed quickly into problems of a racial nature as the Congolese came to understand their future domination of the Europeans. And the two local views point up again a central problem which confronts us in understanding the Congo— that of the basic and essential differences between rural and urban areas. What happened in Lupupa was not what happened in Stanleyville, and what happened in Stanleyville could not have happened in Lupupa, for the situations were markedly different. The Congo has two faces, and one reflects the softness of naïveté while the other shows the hardness of racial conflict and the tragic situation of the marginal man.

CHAPTER VI

Since Independence

History demands perspective, and in the future we shall be able to look back on the events which followed the independence of the Congo and see more clearly what happened. We shall be able to divide the events into phases, to see the differing lines of development, and to give to each development its proper evaluation in relation to the others. But as the history of the independent Congo develops, and as these words are being written, events are blurred, actions unexplained, the importance of separate developments often unknown. In this chapter we shall simply undertake to chronicle those recent events which seem the most important, the day by day developments which we have seen as problems, actions, forces, and counter forces appear on the scene, unroll in high drama, and vanish again.

June 30–July 3. The first four days of independence were declared a national holiday in the Congo, and for the most part they passed in tranquillity. Jack Mendelsohn, Jr., has described the situation in Léopoldville:

> When the great moment of independence came . . . to this nation . . . the surface atmosphere was so calm it seemed as if most of Léopoldville was unaware of the history being made. The crowds for the various festivities in the inner city were comparatively small and orderly. Cordons of helmeted Congolese troops, still under the command of Belgian officers, were completely in control of all ceremonial areas. Everything, except the hotels and cafes, was shut down. When King Baudouin flew into Léopoldville on the afternoon of June 29 and was driven with top Congolese leaders along the four-lane Albert Boulevard, spectators were relatively few and undemonstrative. . . . In a field just outside Matete there were a scattering of hastily constructed African bush huts, thrown up by "country cousins" of

> the city tribesmen, summoned for the expected fighting. The huts were deserted, and it was obvious the troops intended to keep them so. As one Congolese official said, "There will be no Belgian paternalism in our suppression of these tribal scraps. The Belgians couldn't afford to be too harsh for fear everyone would gang up on them. We have no such inhibitions and we have no intention of letting these crazy tribal differences upset our plan." (*93:6–7*)

In Elisabethville, where I spent the period before, during, and after independence, all was equally calm. On June 30, there was a poorly attended meeting at which Belgian officials politely marked the day and turned over the power to the Congolese, and at which Congolese officials just as politely expressed their warm sentiments toward Belgium, and received the power. African crowds in the center of the city were larger than usual, but completely calm. One bar which was ordinarily patronized by Europeans was crowded with Africans in a somewhat noisy display of high spirits; it was evident that many were spending their money ostentatiously and that their financial resources would not last much past the holiday period. In the evenings, the city square in front of the post office was the scene of organized entertainment in a temporary outdoor pavilion. The relatively small crowds, mostly African with Europeans tending to stand around the outer edges, were noisily appreciative of the all-African entertainment provided by an emcee and various rock and roll singing and dancing groups. Driving through almost all the African communes, I saw no troubles, though the crowds in the streets were heavy in some places; for the most part, both Congolese and Belgians seemed to be staying home.

Almost all the Europeans in the Congo at this time were apprehensive if not alarmed; though many of us felt that some troubles and minor incidents were bound to occur, a general racial struggle was not foreseen. Looking back on that period now with the perspective of time, perhaps we should have seen what was to come, for there were small and tenta-

206

tive indications that all was not well. Yet these early indications were so small that they seemed to be only a part of the expected minor incidents and not a portent of the complete collapse of the Congo. One of them was Lumumba's speech delivered before the King and the assembled dignitaries of the world on June 30 in which he spoke with extreme contempt and, in Western eyes, rudely and unwisely, of the history of the Belgians in the Congo and, vindictively, of the changes which would be made. The speech did nothing to calm what now seems to have been an already restive populace; indeed, it was almost a call to arms, and its tone was intensely nationalistic.*

Difficulties also began to emerge in Léopoldville where, on the night of July 1, Bayaka and Bangala began skirmishing with Bakongo, and Baluba with Bena Lulua. Houses were burned and some small public buildings sacked, and by Saturday evening, July 2, thirty-six had been wounded, some seriously. Sunday, July 3, forty-three more were wounded, of which eleven had to be hospitalized, several hundred persons had been arrested of whom ninety-three were sentenced to prison for various infractions of the law, and a curfew was imposed, six o'clock for the closing of bars, and eight o'clock on the streets.

Since the preceding Wednesday, June 29, OTRACO, the major shipping firm in the Congo, had been closed by a strike of workers who demanded an increase in certain fringe benefits. On July 5, two passenger trains carrying 600 Congolese travelers and a few Europeans were dispatched from Léopoldville to Matadi; they were able to depart because of the efforts of the European personnel, but all commercial traffic remained blocked.

In the meantime, on July 1, Lumumba had cabled the United Nations requesting membership, stating that the Congo

* See Appendix IV.

"accepts without reservation the obligations stipulated in the Charter of the U.N. and undertakes to abide by the same in absolute good faith." On July 3, he announced a general amnesty for prisoners, although it was never implemented. Indeed, the general situation seemed reasonably calm; the incidents were small and local and did not involve Europeans. But the expolsion was to come.

July 4: The first non-tribal difficulties occurred in Coquilhatville where workers for private and government operations announced a strike for higher wages specifically because election promises had not yet been fulfilled. Crowds gathered before the offices and houses of the members of the provincial government, and a two o'clock curfew was imposed. Later in the day, new crowds gathered, arrows were shot at the soldiers who had been mobilized to keep order, and the troops opened fire—nine were killed, and an undetermined number wounded.

July 5: In Léopoldville, the OTRACO strike continued. In Coquilhatville, the strikers had not all returned to work, and it was discovered that the discontent arose on the one hand from electoral promises which had assured the workers that their salaries would immediately jump from 700 francs (14 dollars) a month to as much as 15,000 francs (300 dollars) a month, and on the other from the large increases which had, in fact, been voted by the members of the new government to themselves. Calm was re-established, but it was an uneasy calm. In Luluabourg, fighting continued between Baluba and Bena Lulua, and it was estimated that two hundred houses had been burned, three residents killed and at least twelve very seriously wounded; a six o'clock curfew was established.

In Léopoldville, the first rumblings of the revolt of the Force Publique appeared. During the afternoon and throughout the night soldiers began to refuse to obey their Belgian officers at Camp Léopold II in Léopoldville, and at Camp Hardy in Thysville.

July 6: The revolt of the Force Publique was under way in earnest, with the troops demanding the resignation of General Janssens, the Belgian Commander of the Force, the firing of the white officers who were advisers to Lumumba's cabinet, and the rapid replacement of white officers by Congolese. At 7:30 that evening, Mr. Lumumba promised that Congolese would be promoted, and Mr. Bomboko, Minister of Foreign Affairs, announced the firing of General Janssens. Most important, however, Messrs. Lumumba and Kashamura attributed the responsibility for the troubles to the Belgian officers and other "enemies of our independence." At this point, the first wave of panic swept over the European population; although Belgian officials remained generally calm, military forces in Belgium were placed on a state of alert. Lumumba and Kasavubu left Léopoldville for Thysville to quiet the troops; the Belgian officers at Camp Hardy were reported to have taken refuge on two hilltops inside the camp with their families and about 200 loyal troops. A radio message by Lumumba asking the rebels to lay down their arms and promising that pay raises and promotions would be forthcoming failed to improve the situation.

July 7: The situation remained somewhat confused in the Lower Congo with conflicting reports that on the one hand the Belgian officers had regained control, and on the other, that Camp Hardy especially, was in the hands of the mutineers. The Belgian foreign office announced that measures had been taken, in co-operation with the Congolese government, to protect the lives and goods of white residents in the Congo, but the exodus of refugees began. At Stanleyville, the Force Publique, demanding higher pay and quick promotions, joined in the general mutiny, and at the same time, there was a prison break which resulted in the freedom of most of the prisoners in the central prison.

Ndjili airport in Léopoldville was in the hands of the mutineers, and this left a single escape route from Léopoldville to Brazzaville across the Congo River. At two in the morning, Lumumba visited the Belgian Ambassador to denounce a plot against his person; no measures of co-operation were decided upon between the two governments. In New York the United Nations Security Council unanimously recommended to the General Assembly the Congo's admission to membership in the U.N.

July 8: Marked by extreme panic, thousands of Europeans fled from Léopoldville, but with the Force Publique now in command of the city, the exodus was stopped after an estimated three thousand to four thousand had escaped to Brazzaville. Armed troops patrolled the city, and all stores and offices were closed. In Brussels, the Prime Minister announced that two companies of Belgian troops of about three hundred men each would leave for bases in Kamina and Kitona; about two thousand to three thousand Belgian troops were reported already on duty in the Congo. Tension eased somewhat when Lumumba announced that he had reached agreement with the rebels to dismiss all white officers and form a purely Congolese army; he also reported an attempt on his own life by an unnamed "group of Europeans." Some of the mutineers suggested that Lumumba resign to be replaced by Albert Kalonji. After guests at the two major Léopoldville hotels had been forced into the streets, the Foreign Minister, Justin Bomboko, arrived on the scene and helped to restore order. The American Ambassador refused entrance to the Embassy to a group of soldiers.

July 9: Passage across the river to Brazzaville was still closed; Sabena announced the cancellation of all regular flights in order to organize an airlift from the Congo. Two Europeans, a Belgian administrator and a Portuguese settler, were killed as they tried to escape from Katanga Province by riverboat; two others were killed at Goma in Kivu Province. In the Katanga, Moïse Tshombe threatened to call on help from Rhodesia if Belgian troops did not intervene quickly in the situation. Carloads of refugees fled Elisabethville as truckloads of mutinous troops began arriving in that city during the night of the ninth. Seven Europeans, including an Italian consular agent, were killed. Troubles in Matadi reached the crisis point with refugees attempting to escape by riverboat but being forced at gunpoint to return. Two United States Globemasters arrived in Léopoldville from Tripoli to evacuate United States personnel, and all American women and children were reported to have left.

July 10: Belgian forces intervened in the situation in Elisabethville at 5:40 A.M., and order was quickly restored. The Belgian government decided to take unilateral action and dropped paratroops in various parts of the Congo. New trouble broke out in Luluabourg where Force Publique mutineers attacked whites; three Europeans were killed and one seriously wounded. In Stanleyville, troops mutinied, invaded the airfield, and prevented a planeload of refugees from leaving; they disarmed their Belgian officers and took over control. Léopoldville was reported calm, but postmen went on strike demanding that all positions held by Belgians in the postal system be turned over to Congolese. Kasavubu and Lumumba were reported to be on the way to Luluabourg and Stanleyville by plane to attempt to quiet the disturbances there. Former Sergeant Victor Lundula was named General of the Army and Joseph Mobutu Chief of Staff. Refugees fled from Elisabethville, from uprisings in Goma, and from Léopoldville, Matadi, Stanleyville, Luluabourg, and other areas. American Kasaï missionaries assisted in the evacuation of American missionaries from that area. Portuguese were reported evacuated to Angola; Italy was reported to be assisting Italian personnel to leave; the two American Globemasters removed American personnel. Congolese troops were reported marching on Elisabethville.

July 11: In Elisabethville, the situation was reported under control, but further outbreaks occurred in Jadotville,

211

Albertville, and Kolwezi in the Katanga. Stanleyville was besieged by Africans who were pouring into town from outlying areas and searching for arms. More than 3,000 were reported to have fled Elisabethville where 300 American missionaries were awaiting transportation; about 200 American missionaries awaited planes in Luluabourg, and 49 Americans reached Accra. In Brussels an angry crowd of 4,000 people demonstrated against "cowardice" by the Belgian government in the Congo. Mr. Moïse Tshombe declared secession of the Katanga from the Congo and accused the central government of trying to establish "a ruinous and communist state," adding that it had deliberately established a reign of terror. He announced the continuation of economic ties with Belgium and asked for more Belgian troops. The Union Minière shut down its copper and cobalt operations in the Katanga. It was estimated that 15,000 whites had fled to neighboring territories. The Congolese government requested the United States to send troops to the Congo to help restore order; Ambassador Clare Timberlake was reported to have agreed in principle, and American troops in Germany were alerted for possible movement. At the United Nations, Secretary General Dag Hammarskjold returned from Geneva to study proposals for U.N. technical assistance to the Congo to overcome "the present transitional difficulties as may be forthcoming." In the Congo, Lumumba was reported on his way to Elisabethville.

July 12: Lumumba and Kasavubu were denied permission to land at Elisabethville airport, and the secession of the Katanga was thus sealed. In Washington, Press Secretary Haggerty reported that President Eisenhower and Secretary of State Herter had denied the Congo request for United States troops, because it was their feeling that "it would be better for the Congo" if troops were not sent there "from any of the large western nations." In New York, the Secretary General met with U.N. diplomats from nine independent African states to discuss the Congo crisis. From Léopoldville, Lumumba and

Kasavubu sent a cable to the United Nations, requesting of the Secretary General the "urgent dispatch" of U.N. military assistance and calling the dispatch of Belgian troops to the Congo "an act of aggression." They requested military aid "to protect the national territory of the Congo against the present external aggression which is a threat to international peace." The United States view was that "The United Nations has now before it an official appeal for assistance from the Congo government, and the United States believes that any assistance to the government of the Congo should be thru the United Nations and not by any unilateral action of any one country, the United States included." The American aircraft carrier, *Wasp,* was reported cruising toward the Congo. In Matadi Belgian troops were making a strategic retreat, but in Léopoldville the airport was cleared of Congo army troops by Belgian paratroops in a brisk machine gun and hand grenade skirmish of forty-eight minutes in which one Congolese soldier was reported killed, and one Congolese soldier and three Belgian civilians wounded. Following the fire fight, Belgian troops moved into Léopoldville where they were reported taking control of the road to the airport.

July 13: Lumumba and Kasavubu in a joint communiqué, ordered all Belgian troops to return to their camps, on the basis of the treaty signed with Belgium on June 29. The order was specifically applied to Léopoldville where it was demanded that Belgian troops evacuate the airfield within two hours—it was ignored. The escape route to Brazzaville was reopened, with Belgian troops patrolling the streets of Léopoldville. Mutinous forces were reported in control of Thysville, and at Matadi Belgians were surrounded and unable to flee. A second message to the United Nations said that if U.N. military forces were not sent to the Congo without delay, Lumumba and Kasavubu would be obliged "to appeal to the Bandung Treaty Powers." A Security Council meeting was called in New York and the Secretary General said that the presence of Belgian troops in the Congo was "a source of internal and potentially also of international tension." Late in the evening, Tunisia introduced a resolution to the Security Council appealing to Belgium to withdraw its forces and authorizing the Secretary General to organize a military operation to restore order in the Congo. The Soviet Union and Poland delayed proceedings for almost an hour by insisting that a Congolese representative sit in the meetings. Earlier in the day Russia accused the United States and other Western powers of helping Belgium undertake "direct military intervention" against the Congo; the statement was handed to envoys of the United States, Belgium, Britain, West Germany and France. The statement said, in part:

> The colonialists' intervention in the Congo provides new proof of how certain powers, in the first place the United States, continue to march along the road of aggression and provocation. . . . The Soviet government warns of the grave responsibilities borne by the leading circles of the Western powers for unleashing armed aggression in the Congo, and demands that it should immediately be stopped. . . . By using its armed forces for military operations on the territory of the Congo and by sending, despite the protests of its government, new forces within the frontiers of the Congo, Belgium is committing a crude violation both of the territorial inviolability and the political independence of the Congo; . . . (*98*:10:1–8)

In Léopoldville, some stores and factories were reported opened, but in Luluabourg evacuation of refugees was in full swing.

July 14: The Security Council adjourned at 3:22 A.M. after approving the Tunisian resolution, with China, France, and the United Kingdom abstaining. The full text of the Tunisian resolution reads,

> The Security Council, Considering the report of the Secretary-General on a request for United Nations action in relation to the Republic of the Congo; Considering the request for military assistance addressed to the Secretary-General by the President and the Prime Minister of the Republic of the Congo; Calls

upon the Government of Belgium to withdraw their troops from the territory of the Republic of the Congo; decides to authorize the Secretary-General to take the necessary steps, in consultation with the Government of the Republic of the Congo, to provide the Government with such military assistance as may be necessary, until, through the efforts of the Congolese Government with the technical assistance of the United Nations, the national security forces may be able, in the opinion of the Government, to meet fully their tasks; Requests the Secretary-General to report to the Security Council as appropriate. *(13:8)*

The Belgian Ambassador to the United Nations, Walter Loridan, promised that Belgian forces would leave the Congo as soon as the United Nations force could take over and establish order. After the Security Council meeting had closed, Hammarskjold spent the rest of the night cabling requests to the independent African nations for forces to go to the Congo. He also dispatched a group of ten Canadian and Scandinavian officers from the U.N. truce organization in Palestine to the Congo to prepare to receive the U.N. troops. Troops were slated to be drawn only from countries other than the great powers and primarily from African nations. Observers of the U.N. actions were reported to have said that the meeting showed new proof that the U.N. could act quickly in an emergency, and that the new countries of Africa would lean heavily on the U.N. in their early years.

In the meantime, Lumumba was reported to have received assurances from Red Chinese Premier Chou En-lai that Peiping would send help if asked. He was also said to have sent a message to Russian Premier Khrushchev urging him to follow the situation closely since the Congo might need Russian military intervention if Belgian aggression were not stopped. Raymond Scheyven, in charge of the Congo's financial and economic affairs, said the Belgian government did not consider its military bases in the Congo affected by the Security Council action, and Auguste de Schrijver, Minister for the Congo, told newsmen in Brussels that after United Nations troops had restored order, Belgian troops would remain in their Congo bases. The Belgian government reported that the Congo had broken off diplomatic relations, and Foreign Minister Pierre Wigny denounced "the Communist influence" in the Congo, while Premier Eyskens said, "As far as the record is complete, it can be stated that the mutiny of the Force Publique was not a matter of chance. It seemed to be a provoked and prepared uprising. Countries like ours that feel repugnant to use certain measures can easily be made the victim in this way."

In Léopoldville an uneasy peace reigned as Congolese troops roamed through the city shooting, looting, and burning cars; the outbreak was attributed to the deaths of two Congolese soldiers in the previous day's fighting. A representative of Ghana took part in a cabinet meeting and promised Ghanaian troops, apparently unilaterally. Rebel troops were reported massing in Camp Léopold, and Matadi was still under a state of siege. Kasavubu and Lumumba returned to the capital and were met by a Belgian honor guard which Lumumba angrily refused. Thysville was reported to be still controlled by mutineers who were holding hostages, including women and children. In the Katanga, secession was ratified by the legislature, and order was reported restored. Belgian paratroops took over Jadotville, and the Katanga government reported that it would not accept U.N. forces in its territory.

July 15: The first United Nations troops arrived in the Congo, represented by Major General Henry Alexander, British commander of Ghana's army and a small detachment of Ghanaian troops. The commander of the U.N. forces, Major General Carl Carlsson von Horn of Sweden, left Jerusalem with eleven military advisers, five radio technicians, and five security guards. The first elements of a Tunisian army force of 600 men left Tunis for Léopoldville in U.S. Hercules C-130 transports. Ralph Bunche, who had been stationed in Léopoldville by the United Nations on Independence Day, reported that 2,400 troops from Ghana, Tunisia, Morocco, Guinea,

216

and Mali were expected within a few days. The problem of feeding the urban areas of the Congo was becoming acute, and the United States began an airlift, "Operation Safari," which provided 1,800 tons of foodstuffs, including flour, dried beef, rice, and powdered milk from bases in France and Germany. Khrushchev made a blunt statement to the Congo government in which he said Russia was ready to act "if those states which are carrying on direct aggression against the Congo do not stop their criminal measures." The United States, in an equally blunt reply, labeled Khrushchev's remarks "intemperate, misleading and irresponsible" and said "This is yet another example of the current Soviet attempt to inflame the international atmosphere." The State Department continued: "We are gratified that the United Nations has moved despite soviet delaying tactics to take constructive and effective action directed toward meeting the request of the Congo Republic for assistance. Like the independent African states, the United States is supporting fully the United Nations efforts to help the people of the Congo." In a separate statement, the Belgian government replied to the Russian note saying, "The Belgian government rejects without further comment and with contempt the offensive arguments of the soviet government." It was reported by the Belgian government that some 25,000 white residents had fled the Congo.

July 16: More than 600 Tunisians as well as 40 Ghanaians and 150 Moroccans arrived during the day in United States planes. General Von Horn reached Léopoldville, and 140,000 pounds of flour were turned over to Ralph Bunche through the American embassy. Belgian troops were flown to Kikwit to control an uprising there, and in Brussels the Belgian government announced the recall of its ambassador to Moscow. Lumumba charged the Belgians with a number of abuses, including another plot to kill him and Kasavubu, the killing of two Congolese at Coquilhatville thus causing unrest in that city, and the promotion of the Katanga seces-

217

sion. In respect to his request to Russia, he said, "We are not communist just because we have appealed to Moscow and will prove this shortly. We are African nationalists." In Elisabethville, Moïse Tshombe announced that he had had feelers from the Kivu and Kasaï Provinces, as well as Ruanda-Urundi, to join him in a federation opposed to Lumumba's government, but the United Arab Republic was the first to refuse recognition of the independence of the Katanga because it "believed secession would weaken the Congo union." Lumumba's ultimatum that Belgian troops leave the Congo by 6:00 A.M. on this date was ignored. Lumumba flew to Stanleyville.

July 17: Two planes, one a Belgian helicopter and the other a Belgian air force spotter plane, were reported shot down by mutineers in the Lower Congo. Moroccan troops were ordered to take over the port city of Matadi in which Belgian troops had previously been defeated. The Congolese government issued an ultimatum to the United Nations to clear all Belgian troops from the Congo within seventy-two hours; if the Belgians failed to meet the deadline, the government would call "Soviet Russian troops" into the Congo to deal with the situation. The Soviet Union requested a second series of Security Council meetings for July 19 to discuss the Congo situation, and the Belgian government requested the U.N. to form a commission of inquiry into the atrocities committed by Congolese troops. Meanwhile a Polish ship was reported steaming toward the Congo with 300 tons of arms and ammunition for the Congolese government, and the Belgian government announced that it would consider it an act of war if the Polish ship were allowed to discharge its cargo. Polish sources denied that the freighter was carrying munitions. In Elisabethville, Tshombe called for a federation of anti-communist African nations and denounced Lumumba as pro-communist. The newly appointed General Victor Lundula was detained in Jadotville and then expelled

218

from Katanga. U.N. troops began fanning out over the Congo, particularly to Stanleyville and to the Lower Congo area.

July 18: Ralph Bunche rejected the Congolese ultimatum and threat to call in Soviet troops, saying that the U.N. is "not in the habit of accepting ultimatums." The Congolese Senate voted unanimous approval for a resolution "rejecting energetically any eventual intervention by the Soviet Union in Congolese internal affairs," but reaffirmed its demand for an immediate departure of Belgian troops. The Secretary General of the United Nations made the first report on the implementation of the Security Council resolution, and indicated that 3,500 troops had arrived in the Congo from four African countries. Belgian foreign ministry officials denied the report of the Polish arms ship headed for Matadi and pointed out that in any case it would be unable to land at Matadi since the harbor was presumably silted. A Moscow report said Russian planes were taking off from Moscow airport to start a Congo airlift. There were unconfirmed reports, later proved false, that some Moroccan troops had been killed at Thysville. The Katanga sent an ultimatum to the U.N. demanding a decision on recognition of its independence within forty-eight hours. Belgium reaffirmed its decision that its troops would stay in the Congo as long as needed. At United Nations headquarters a secret meeting of members of the African bloc unanimously opposed the Congo threat to call in Russian troops and sent Tunisian Ambassador Mongi Slim to give this word to Soviet Deputy Foreign Minister V. V. Kuznetsov. Members of the bloc were reportedly upset at Lumumba's actions and felt that he had "lost his head." United Nations forces, it was announced, were slated to reach a total of 10,000 within the next few days, and Hammarskjold announced plans to visit the Congo himself about July 23. The first Belgian units were reported to have left Léopoldville on July 17.

July 19: The Congolese threat to call in Russian troops reportedly was ended by the agreement to withdraw Belgian troops from Léopoldville, and Lumumba said that "the question of the ultimatum no longer arises. The withdrawal of Belgian forces has been agreed," but, he added, "if the U.N. does not know how to give satisfaction to our demands we will be obliged to call in other nations to fight the aggressors"; he did not name the "other nations." Belgium and the U.N. agreed on a four-day withdrawal of Belgian troops from Léopoldville, starting July 20. Canada, Italy, Burma, and Ireland confirmed reports that their troops would join the U.N. forces, and Bunche reported: "The United Nations is now in a position to assure that there will be arriving this week sufficiently strong elements of the U.N. force from European as well as African countries to insure order and protect the entire population, European as well as African." Moroccan troops were reported in charge of Thysville, and Stanleyville was under U.N. control, but Belgian troops controlled Coquilhatville and Banningville. An American missionary, Dr. Bernard Jackson, on his arrival in Chicago said that he believed communists had engineered much of the rioting in the Congo.

July 20: A Belgian Air Force transport plane crashed near Goma in the Congo killing 34 Belgian soldiers and injuring seven others. In Léopoldville, the cabinet of the Congo decided to appeal immediately not only for Soviet help but also for that of any other Afro-Asian country including Red China. However, Lumumba said that in view of the Security Council meeting scheduled for 8:00 P.M. he would wait until evening to send the request. He added that he would not hesitate to "make a pact with the devil himself" to achieve immediate departure of the Belgians. In the Congolese Parliament, Lumumba faced a vote of censure for his "communist-leaning dictatorial demands and ultimatums." In Léopoldville, the threat of famine was reported severe with

220

70,000 unemployed. Because of Belgian troop withdrawals in Léopoldville, the U.N. meetings opened in an optimistic atmosphere. The Security Council met at the request of the Secretary General, and Thomas Kanza, the Congo's Minister to the U.N., and Pierre Wigny, the Foreign Minister of Belgium were in attendance. Mr. Hammarskjold reported that the U.N. force consisted of twelve African and two European battalions, "the biggest single effort under U.N. colors, organized and directed by the U.N. itself." He asked that there be no "hesitation because we are at a turn of the road where our attitude will be decisive, not only for the future of this Organization but also for the future of Africa; and Africa may well in present circumstances mean the world." He also reported that the U.N. force had reached a strength of ten thousand men. In Léopoldville, a reporter asked Lumumba what his position would be if the Security Council opposed Russian intervention in the Congo, and he is said to have replied: "It would be proof that there is a capitalist plot against the Congo." In Elisabethville, Foreign Minister Justin Bomboko was arrested when his plane landed there.

July 21: At the meetings of the Security Council, Ambassador Lodge of the United States announced that "with other United Nations members, we will do whatever may be necessary to prevent the intrusion of any forces not requested by the Secretary-General." Kuznetzov of Russia said "Hands off the Congo. If aggression continues, the necessity will naturally appear to take more effective measures, both along United Nations lines and along lines followed by peace-loving states." Hammarskjold confirmed that he had told Katanga's Premier that the U.N. was acting "in reference to the Republic of the Congo as an entity," and thus in effect refused Katanga's bid for recognition as an independent state. Two Russians flew into Elisabethville and were immediately taken into custody and later deported, and Russian planes joined in the U.N. airlift carrying United Nations troops, sugar, and some Russian diplomats from Accra to Léopoldville. Three companies of Swedish troops reached Léopoldville. Three Belgian leaders, including the former provincial governor and the former mayor of Stanleyville, were accused of plotting against the Congolese state and were given four hours to leave the country. Stanleyville was reported to be completely chaotic. In Léopoldville, it was reported that Lumumba had decided to fly to New York to attend the Security Council meetings, and in Washington Christian Herter said he believed the Russians were bluffing in threatening to send troops to the Congo.

In the United Nations, Belgian Foreign Minister Pierre Wigny delivered a highly emotional speech detailing some of the atrocities committed against Belgians in the Congo. Addressing himself to Thomas Kanza, he asked:

> Mr. Kanza, do you believe that if we had prepared any plots or any aggressions we would have been capable of being such traitors so without honor with respect to our women, our daughters, our granddaughters, as to leave them in such a hell? I do not say that the Congolese people participated in all this. The Congolese people as a whole—I honor them just as you have paid homage to the Belgian people, for which I thank you—stayed apart from all these horrors. But the fact is that a mutinous group was not under your control, and that your government did nothing and has not been able to do anything to regain control over them. (*70:2:3–4*)

Thomas Kanza replied, in part:

> The Congolese Government is prepared to recognize that abuses have been committed. . . . I would be the last to deny that there were specific events, but if I went into a recital of all the atrocities committed by the Belgians against the Congolese it would not be an edifying thing to do. . . . Mr. Kasavubu and our prime minister were insulted. They were spat upon when they landed at the airport. . . . We are very young in international affairs, but the first example given to us by Belgium is that when you sign a treaty you should try to violate it. (*70:2:3–4*)

Wigny continued, in another context:

It would have been better . . . to recognize also, first of all, that frightful things have happened, frightful things which, naturally, have caused the departure of all the Belgians who trustingly remained among you.

Our intervention . . . is not an aggression. Nor is it an act of madness. It is an action justified not by our hostility towards a people whom we love and to whom we have just granted independence, nor by hostility on the part of the Congolese people toward us, but by the fact that the Congolese Government—certain of its members, and perhaps one of them alone—was incapable of re-establishing order.

In these justified, necessary interventions we have always done everything to limit them to the maximum possible extent. . . . Our present position is this. We sent troops. They intervened strictly because of our sacred duty to protect the lives and the honor of our fellow citizens. The action of our troops was always limited to these specific objectives. As soon as the U.N. troops arrive in sufficient numbers, so that their Commander is able to assume full responsibility for the re-establishment of public order, then, and to that extent, we are prepared to withdraw. Members of the Security Council would not expect the representative of a civilized nation to admit of a gap, an interval, in which massacre may start again. All that we ask is that safety be reassured. As soon as the attacks cease, we shall withdraw.

These are recollections which are terrible, but a country acquires greatness by its sufferings and a country does not build its future only by remembering the past. (*13:9*)

Kanza made four requests of the United Nations:

There are four points which the Congolese Government has instructed me to present to the Council. (1) An end would have to be put to the aggressive action of the Belgian troops in the Congo. . . . (2) The evacuation as soon as possible of these Belgian troops from our national territory. . . . (3) Asks you not to permit a certain recognition to an independent Katanga. . . . (4) General technical assistance. . . . (*13:9*)

July 22: The United Nations unanimously approved a resolution which had been submitted earlier by Ceylon and Tunisia:

The Security Council, Having considered the first report by the Secretary-General on the implementation of Security Council Resolution S/4387 of 14 July 1960; Appreciating the work of the Secretary-General and the support so readily and so speedily given to him by all Member States invited by him to give assistance; Noting that as stated by the Secretary-General the arrival of the troops of the U.N. Force in Léopoldville has already had a salutary effect; Recognizing that an urgent need still exists to continue and to increase such efforts; Considering that the complete restoration of law and order in the Republic of the Congo would effectively contribute to the maintenance of international peace and security; Recognizing that the Security Council recommended the admission of the Republic of the Congo to membership in the U.N. as a unit; Calls upon the Government of Belgium to implement speedily the Security Council resolution of 14 July 1960, on the withdrawal of their troops and authorizes the Secretary-General to take all necessary action to this effect; Requests all States to refrain from any action which might tend to impede the restoration of law and order, from any action which might undermine the territorial integrity and the political independence of the Republic of the Congo; Commends the Secretary-General for the prompt action he has taken to carry out Resolution S/4387 of the Security Council and his first report; Invites the Specialized Agencies of the U.N. to tender to the Secretary-General such assistance as he may require; Requests the Secretary-General to report further to the Security Council as appropriate. (*13:9*)

In Léopoldville, Lumumba hailed the resolution and said that "there is no further need for soviet intervention"; he was also pleased that the resolution referred to the Congo as a unit, and said this meant that the independence of the Katanga "will never be recognized because Katanga forms part of the Congo. This news has greatly gladdened us. The international organization has rendered justice . . ." It was also announced that the Congo government had signed a financial agreement in the sum of two billion dollars with Mr. Edgar Detwiler who was described as an American business man. Mr. Detwiler said that his firm, made up of bankers, industrialists, and economists from the United States, Britain, Canada, France, and other Western countries, would supply management and technical training to the Congolese government. Lumumba emphasized that the agreement was purely private and had no political strings attached.

Meanwhile, near Kolwezi some two hundred miles west of Elisabethville, sixteen Congolese and two Belgians were killed in heavy fighting in which rocket-firing planes were used to quell a new revolt by some two hundred and fifty mutineers, of whom two hundred were said to have been taken prisoner. In Elisabethville itself, Tshombe warned that if U.N. forces tried to enter the Katanga it would be "dangerous," and that his own forces would attack the U.N. troops "if necessary." Premier Lumumba left Léopoldville for Accra in a plane loaned by the Ghanaian government. It was reported that President Kwame Nkrumah in a two-hour conference tried to dissuade Lumumba from continuing to New York; however, Lumumba accompanied by Mr. Detwiler, continued on to London, where he spent the night.

July 23: Hammarskjold announced that Belgian troops had completed the evacuation of Léopoldville, that 6,000 U.N. troops were now in the Congo, and that the total was expected to reach 12,140 within a week. The nations contributing to the force and the totals each pledged were: Ethiopia 1,800; Ghana 2,100; Guinea 1,200; Ireland 680; Liberia 225; Mali 800; Morocco 2,500; Sweden 635; and Tunisia 2,200. Congolese representatives conferred with Hammarskjold to arrange for meetings with Lumumba, who was scheduled to arrive in the evening. In a conference at the London airport, Lumumba denied that he was a communist, and said that he would not use force to recover the Katanga. "We are against violence. We are sure that if the simple problem of removing Belgian troops can be resolved, the whole problem will be solved." Belgian troops were reported pulling back to the bases of Kamina and Kitona, and Moroccan troops were scheduled to take over at Boma. An advance brigade of Tunisian troops was sent to Luluabourg. The Congo Finance Minister flew to Stanleyville to pick up eight million dollars for the central treasury, and was attacked by Congolese soldiers. Mr. Tshombe in Elisabethville proposed a United

States of the Congo and said he would willingly work for the central government if they would agree to his proposal.

July 24: About 1,100 Tunisian troops took over Luluabourg and persuaded 3,000 Congolese troops to lay down their arms, and at the same time Moroccan troops took over without incident in the Lower Congo towns of Boma and Tshela. The first contingent of troops from Guinea arrived in Léopoldville, and the railroad and pipeline between Matadi and Léopoldville were reported in working order. The Belgian Health Ministry warned of the possibility of epidemic in the Congo and the Red Cross appealed for medical teams to be sent into the country. Mr. Detwiler reported that his contract would have to be ratified by the Congolese Parliament, but that he expected no difficulty; he added that he had won the contract despite "fantastic" pressure from "unfriendly nations," and added with no little self-confidence: "Unfortunately the state department could not compete at a speed equal to soviet Russia, so they gave us their moral support and good wishes, and I'm glad to say we reached an agreement. I explained to the state department that if we lost the resources of the Congo it would be one of the most tragic things to happen to the free world."

Lumumba spent two and a half hours in talks with Hammarskjold and later told newsmen he was "very optimistic." He reiterated his confidence in the United Nations, and said he hoped to appear personally before the U.N. "to inform international public opinion" about conditions in the Congo. On his arrival at Idlewild Airport he said "We extend our compliments and friendship to President Eisenhower and we also thank the American people for all they have done for the emancipation of the African people." Some hours later he held a secret two-hour conference with Soviet Deputy Kuznetsov and the Soviet permanent delegate to the United Nations, Mr. Sobolev. In an interview granted to Simon Malley, Lumumba noted that "the great sin of Belgium was in not preparing us for independence, by prohibiting any political expression or organization by Africans." He continued:

> Let the real blame be put upon those who forbade all my fellow citizens to leave the national territory until 1952 . . . and even then, rare were those who received the necessary exit visas. . . . I can never forget the atrocities and humiliations we suffered throughout the duration of Belgian colonial rule. . . .

In describing his country's foreign policy, Lumumba added:

> First of all, neutrality, that is, strict non-alignment between the two blocs but also our attitude will depend upon the real demonstration of sympathy and aid by each nation.

And in respect to the United Nations, he said:

> We put all our confidence in the United Nations and in the task which they now undertake in the Congo according to the latest resolution calling for the total evacuation of Belgian troops from the whole of Congo territory and the respect of its territorial integrity. (*90:1–2*)

At the same time Russian sources were charging that "American magnates stand behind the Belgian aggressors" in the Congo: "American millionaires participate in robbing the people of the Congo . . . The Rockefellers do not want to let such riches as Katanga province out of their hands." Party Chairman Mao Tse-tung, President Liu Shao-chi and Premier Chou En-lai were reported to have met with a group from the Congo in Peking.

July 25: In New York Lumumba and Hammarskjold continued their talks at lunch with members of the Security Council, and Lumumba later held further talks with delegates of the Asian-African group. In the Congo, Belgian paratroopers were dropped at Tshikapa to protect Europeans threatened by Kasaï warriors.

July 26: It was reported that to this date 32,178 refugees from the Congo had landed at Brussels airport since July 9. United Nations strength was reported at approximately seventy-five hundred men. The U.N. mission announced that it was pushing a crash program of medical and financial assistance, while the treasury and currency situation was reported so precarious that it appeared many August 1 payrolls could not be met; the long term outlook for replenishing government revenues was gloomy with the economy largely paralyzed. The United States announced that it had airlifted as part of the U.N. operation more than 2.6 million tons of supplies and 6,330 troops to the Congo. The carrier *Wasp* was pumping aviation fuel at Accra to supply the airlift. A spokesman for the Congo government said that the Detwiler financial agreement was not valid because Finance Minister Pascal Nkayi had not been consulted about the pact. Nkayi added that "if in the next few weeks Belgian and foreign technicians are not back at their posts or United Nations technicians do not replace them soon, the mass of workers will be plunged into unemployment and poverty." The problem of health controls appeared again, and an urgent appeal was made to the World Health Organization for a team of doctors for the Kasaï Province.

July 27: Hammarskjold arrived in Brussels for talks with Belgian officials on the military and economic conditions in the Congo, and Lumumba arrived in Washington where he held talks with Herter in the afternoon. In a speech at the airport in Washington, Lumumba asked for United States aid and, after conferring with Herter, said that he had been assured of such aid but through the United Nations. In Belgium Hammarskjold said that he believed Belgian troops should be pulled completely out of the Congo, but Belgian sources reported that Belgian interpretation of the Security Council resolutions was that the troops should only pull back to the Belgian bases in the Congo.

July 28: Hammarskjold arrived in Léopoldville. In Brussels the Belgian Minister of Justice, Mr. Merchiers, held a press conference in which he detailed the atrocities allegedly committed in the Congo. In a later publication based on this conference, the official position of the government was as follows:

> The tragic turn taken by events in the Congo has obliged the Belgian Government to act with all speed in order to give the white inhabitants the measure of protection dictated by the supreme laws of humanity and the imperative duty of saving men, women and children in immediate and terrible danger. The Government in all conscience was forced into this course of action by the mutiny of those same Congolese troops whose task it was to maintain order.
>
> Noting that certain Congolese leaders are seeking to discredit the veracity of these appalling events in the eyes of the world, the Government considers itself bound to inform public opinion everywhere of the brutal acts which have taken place—in some cases from the very inception of the disturbances, i.e. as of July 5, 1960, such as, for instance, those at Inkisi.
>
> It should be noted, in regard to the extent of the disturbances, that there seem to have been relatively few cases of homicide, at least on the basis of the information received hitherto, for many people reported missing have in all probability not been killed. However, acts against human dignity, humiliations, and outrages against the profoundest values of mankind and the civilised concept of personal integrity have been the rule, as if the word had gone round that both men and women should be humiliated to the greatest possible extent, but that any indictment of massacre on the part of world opinion should be avoided.
>
> Desirous of shedding as much light as possible on the tragic events in the Congo, the Government submitted to the King for his signature a decree instituting a Commission of Enquiry. Set up by decree dated July 16, this Commission is charged with collecting details of attacks on persons committed in the Congo since the independence which Belgium, voluntarily and of her own free will, generously granted to that country.
>
> To ensure both objectivity and independence of action, the Commission is exclusively composed of magistrates high up in the Judiciary. The chairman is a Counsellor of the Supreme Court of Appeal; the members, numbering three, are all Counsellors of the Belgian Courts of Appeal.

The statement went on to point out that the Commission was not answerable to the government, that a female staff had been appointed to deal with delicate attestations, that appeals had been broadcast to the Belgian people asking those who had been in the Congo to come forth with documentated cases of atrocities, that any statements "tinged with the slightest doubt have been eliminated from this report," and concluded:

> The details contained in the following pages are published with deep regret. Events have been recounted with a maximum of tact, but faced with certain statements which go so far as to throw doubt on the brutal savagery inflicted on the white inhabitants of the Congo, and whatever the shock and revulsion aroused, the Government considers it necessary to place world opinion in possession of those facts concerning which no possible vestige of doubt now exists.

The report then went on to detail cases of rape, abuse, and humiliation suffered by European residents of the Congo, and stated that 291 Belgian women had testified to "the ignoble treatment they had suffered, that about 300 men had been brutalized and beaten and that about twenty men had been killed." (See *95; 96.*)

July 29: Belgium announced that its commanders in the Congo had received orders to begin complying with the U.N. resolution for the withdrawal of their troops; some fifteen hundred were ordered out of the Congo, while the remaining ten thousand were pulled back to the main bases of Kamina and Kitona. Hammarskjold met with the Congolese cabinet, which remained without its chief as Lumumba toured in North America seeking financial aid for his government. Leaving Washington for Montreal, Lumumba reasserted that the presence of Belgian troops in the Congo threatened "the whole of Africa," and that the Congo was in desperate need of emergency funds to operate the government. On his arrival in Montreal he denied Belgian charges that there had been rapes in the Congo disturbances and attributed such reports to fabrications by foreign newspapermen. He said his government had started an inquiry and that they had failed to find "one case of rape."

July 30: In Ottawa, Lumumba held a surprise meeting with Russian Ambassador to Canada, Amasap Aroutunian, and met also with Canadian Prime Minister John Diefenbaker of whom he asked French-speaking technicians for the Congo. He then cut short his two-day visit to Canada and flew back to New York to catch a plane for the Congo. The United States formally dissociated itself from Lumumba's charges that Belgium committed aggression against the Congo, stating, "We are satisfied that the government of Belgium sent its troops to the Congo in order to protect the lives which were endangered and that it had no aggressive intent." In Léopoldville, Deputy Prime Minister Gizenga at an evening banquet told Hammarskjold that U.N. forces had fallen down on the job and had permitted "secession to consolidate" in Katanga province. "The people of the Congo do not understand that we, against whom an aggression has been committed, we who are in our land, we who have made an appeal to international armed forces, are systematically and methodically disarmed while the aggressors, the Belgians, who are here in a conquered country, still have their arms and their power of death and are simply being asked to regroup in certain parts of our Congo which some dare call 'Belgian bases.' " Hammarskjold replied: "We cannot adopt the line of action which in our minds would not correspond with our responsibility to the community of peoples." Guests were reported taken aback by the lavish display of foods at the dinner, and the same day Maurice Pate, head of the United Nations relief mission to the Congo, said that the airlift had staved off famine but that the need would be even more acute in the future: "Even if food is in the shops and markets, where are the Congo's 150,000 unemployed and their families going to get the money to buy it?"

The Congolese cabinet appealed to Hammarskjold to send U.N. troops to the Katanga, and Tshombe replied that "it would mean war." Hammarskjold decided not to visit Katanga, and a delegation from Katanga arrived in Brussels seeking recognition of its independence.

At the United Nations the U.N. and the Congo signed an agreement on the use of the U.N. forces. The agreement read, in part:

> 1. The Government of the Republic of the Congo states that, in the exercise of its sovereign rights with respect to any question concerning the presence and functioning of the United Nations force in the Congo, it will be guided, in good faith, by the fact that it has requested military assistance from the United Nations and by its acceptance of the resolutions of the Security Council of 14 and 22 July 1960; it likewise states that it will insure the freedom of movement of the force in the interior of the country and will accord the requisite privileges and immunities to all personnel associated with the activities of the force. (*13:9*)

July 31: The Katanga mission to Brussels said in a press conference that it would never renege on its declaration of independence from the Congo, and made plans to travel to the United States and the United Nations to correct a "lot of untrue statements about us" made by Lumumba. At the United Nations, pressures on Lumumba from the Soviet delegation were made clearer in a number of moves, and the Congolese delegation conferred with other African states on how to proceed with the Soviet demand for another Security Council meeting. Heavy fighting broke out in Luluabourg and in Tshikapa between Baluba and Bena Lulua tribesmen, and in Elisabethville, the Katanga government created a national bank of Katanga. Casualties in the Kasaï were variously estimated at one hundred in Tshikapa and three hundred in Luluabourg with one hundred thousand fleeing villages and towns. A broadcast by Radio Moscow repeated Soviet threats to the West and accused "the aggressors and their accomplices" of trying to strangle the Congo's economic life and starve its people.

August 1: The United States replied to Russian charges: "The soviet leaders must be aware that this kind of public

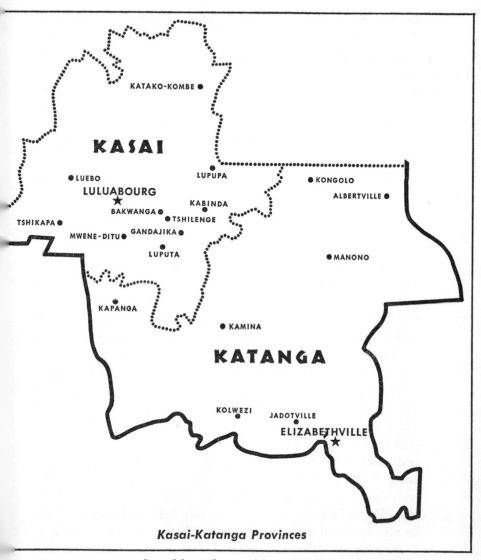

Kasai-Katanga Provinces

statement can only add to the problems of those who are seriously trying to restore peace and order in the Congo. The Soviet Union apparently arrogates to itself the right to judge whether the United Nations is acting with sufficient speed in

the extremely difficult situation in the Congo." In Léopoldville, Hammarskjold finished his talks with Congo leaders
and sent a special emissary, Mr. Heinz Wieschoff, to Brussels for secret talks. At the Léopoldville docks, Ghanaian
troops dispersed a mob which had gathered to demand higher
pay. Fighting continued in Luluabourg and Tshikapa, with
heavy casualties on both the Baluba and Bena Lulua sides.

August 2: France supported Belgium strongly in personal
talks between various dignitaries and Foreign Minister
Wigny. Belgium began pulling 15 per cent of its troops out
of the Congo but made no move to leave the Katanga. Lumumba, still in New York, urged that U.N. troops be sent to
clear out the Katanga, and Hammarskjold delayed his proposed trip to South Africa to await the return of Mr. Weischoff. The Congolese government announced that if Belgian
firms which closed during the violence were not reopened
within eight days they would be considered "abandoned property" and taken over by the state. The Belgian cabinet was
called together to consider the Congo's increasing pressure
on the United Nations to send troops into the Katanga. On the
arrival of Mr. Weischoff, Hammarskjold announced that
U.N. troops would enter the Katanga August 6 "in accordance with the U.N. Security Council resolution calling for
withdrawal of Belgian forces throughout the Congo." He
said that Belgian troops would withdraw from Elisabethville
and other Katanga cities to the Belgian Katanga base of Kamina. In Paris the Katanga delegation said the result would
be a shooting war. In New York Lumumba accused Belgium
of trying to break up the republic and left for London where
he was expected to hold talks with Ghanaian representatives.

August 3: Tshombe declared that his government would
use force to oppose the entry of United Nations troops into
Katanga. "They will have to fight their way in. Katanga
troops will not fire first and we do not intend any aggression.
But if U.N. troops try to land here, that will be an act of ag-

gression and we will oppose it." However, he added that he would welcome the arrival of Ralph Bunche whom Hammarskjold announced he would send to Elisabethville to arrange for U.N. entry.

August 4: Ralph Bunche arrived in Elisabethville where he conferred with Tshombe and other Katangan and Belgian officials. Meanwhile hundreds of white residents were reported to be fleeing the Katanga from Elisabethville, Jadotville, and Kolwezi, in the fear that the entry of U.N. troops would set off new waves of rioting. Tshombe, after conferring with Bunche, announced that the entry of U.N. troops had been suspended for the time being, that Bunche would report back to Hammarskjold, and that the issue would probably be returned to the Security Council. Lumumba held talks in Tunisia with President Bourguiba, and later with Ferhat Abba, leader of the Algerian rebel government in exile at Carthage. In a press interview he repeated many of his charges against Belgium, and threatened "radical" measures should Belgian troops not be withdrawn by August 8. He added that Katanga's secession "cannot be permitted," that Tshombe's mobilization order was "blackmail," and that Tshombe himself was a "traitor."

August 5: An airplane filled with U.N. personnel flying to Elisabethville was given permission to land but the passengers could not get off. After refueling, the plane returned to Léopoldville with Dr. Bunche. Just before Bunche's departure, Tshombe told a news conference: "I have gathered all tribal chiefs of Katanga in Elisabethville in order to explain the internal and external situation of Katanga. I have informed them of the decision to oppose the arrival of U.N. troops. The chiefs agree with me. Dr. Bunche has been informed of my decision and he realizes the situation is dangerous." On hearing Bunche's report, Hammarskjold postponed the entry of U.N. troops into the Katanga, and called for a meeting of the Security Council on August 7. A U.N.

spokesman commenting on the entrance of U.N. forces over the opposition of the Katanga, said: "Such an initiative by the United Nations forces is against the principles established by the Security Council for the operating of the force and against the conditions on which various contributing countries have agreed to send units to the force. In the circumstances, the Secretary-General has instructed the supreme commander to cancel the sending of U.N. military units to Katanga on Saturday, August 6, 1960. Further instructions will be given after the consideration of the matter by the Security Council." In the meantime, during a stopover at Rabat, Lumumba and Crown Prince Moulay Hassan of Morocco signed a joint communiqué promising their countries' support for all peoples struggling for independence, particularly "the heroic Algerian people." The communiqué also condemned South Africa's racial policy and called for cultural, social, and technical co-operation between Morocco and the Congo. In Léopoldville, the Belgian Ambassador was given until August 8 to comply with an expulsion order issued by the Congolese Government.

August 6: From Conakry Lumumba telegraphed his Cabinet to dispense with United Nations forces and assistance, saying that the Congo was assured of direct military aid from other African nations: "The U.N. troops are only parading in the Congo instead of aiding us in the evacuation of hostile Belgian troops." Direct military aid was pledged by Sékou Touré, President of Guinea, and by Kwame Nkrumah who said that Ghana would provide the assistance even if it meant "Ghana and the Congo had to fight alone against Belgian troops. My government, however, believes that if such a struggle did arise, Ghana and other African states would not be without aid and assistance from other countries which value as a principle the conception of African independence."

Hammarskjold arrived in New York, and in an eleven-page report to the Security Council said that he believed the

U.N. force had no authority to shoot its way into the Katanga and that Bunche had reported force would be the only means of entry. He said: "The Security Council may wish to clarify its views on the matter and to lay down such rules for the U.N. operation as would serve to separate effectively questions of a peaceful and democratic development in the constitutional field from any questions relating to the presence of the U.N. force. Were the council to do so, it might well prove to open the door to a speedy implementation of its previous resolutions, also as regards Katanga."

August 7: The meeting of the Security Council was postponed in order to await the arrival of the Congolese delegation which was to include Gizenga, Bomboko, Mwamba, and Thomas Kanza. News reports from Léopoldville indicated that the ABAKO party was pressing for the creation of an independent state in the Lower Congo, and that it had sent a cable to the U.N. saying that Lumumba was incapable of insuring security in the Congo. It urged a federal system of government. Belgium announced that Belgian troops had left all parts of the Congo except the bases of Kitona and Kamina, and that only 8,000 troops remained in the country. In Léopoldville, U.N. troops patrolled the streets as youths demonstrated outside the Belgian embassy and U.N. headquarters. Lumumba arrived in Ghana and immediately began talks with Nkrumah.

August 8: The Security Council went into urgent meeting, and the Russians demanded that the U.N. force be empowered to shoot its way into the Katanga if necessary to force the withdrawal of Belgian troops. Russia introduced a resolution to this effect but it failed. In opening the meeting, Hammarskjold warned that the world might be plunged into war if the Congo problem were not solved: "Achievement of such a solution is a question of peace or war, and when saying peace or war I do not limit my perspective to the Congo." He reported that Lumumba's government was extremely impatient and that when he had argued that he could not act more rapidly, distrust spread: "This dangerous tendency of sowing distrust has not been without support from other quarters outside the Congo. It does not help the U.N. effort if it has to live under a threat of any one contributing government—or more—taking matters in its, or their own hands, breaking away from the U.N. force and pursuing a unilateral policy." Hammarskjold called for the speediest possible complete and unconditional withdrawal of Belgian forces. In Léopoldville, Lumumba returned from Accra, said that he would call an immediate cabinet meeting, and blamed Hammarskjold for the current crisis: "The United Nations is honest. If the secretary had executed the resolutions of the security council, the Congo problem would be solved today. The situation is the fault of the secretary general. . . . Everything the secretary general has done thus far has helped Tshombe and the Belgians." On his way back from Accra, Lumumba had stopped at Lomé to confer with Premier Sylvanus Olympio of Togo, and a joint communiqué condemned the continued presence of Belgian troops in the Congo; but in contrast to Lumumba's later remarks, it congratulated the United Nations "for measures . . . taken thus far to reestablish peace and security."

August 9: At 4:00 A.M., the Security Council adopted a resolution submitted by Ceylon and Tunisia:

> The Security Council, Recalling its resolution of 22 July 1960 (S/4405), *inter alia*, calling upon the Government of Belgium to implement speedily the Security Council resolution of 14 July (S/4387) on the withdrawal of their troops and authorizing the Secretary-General to take all necessary action to this effect; Having noted the second report by the Secretary-General on the implementation of the aforesaid two resolutions and his statement before the Council; Having considered the statements made by the representatives of Belgium and the Republic of the Congo to this Council at this meeting; Noting with satisfaction the progress made by the U.N. in carrying out the Security Council resolutions in respect of the territory of the Republic

of the Congo other than the Province of Katanga; Noting however that the U.N. has been prevented from implementing the aforesaid resolutions in the Province of Katanga although it was ready and in fact attempted, to do so; Recognizing that the withdrawal of Belgian troops from the Province of Katanga will be a positive contribution to and essential for the proper implementation of the Security Council resolutions;

1. Confirms the authority given to the Secretary-General by the Security Council resolutions of 14 July and 22 July 1960 and requests him to continue to carry out the responsibility placed on him thereby; 2. Calls upon the Government of Belgium to withdraw immediately its troops from the Province of Katanga under speedy modalities determined by the Secretary-General and to assist in every possible way the implementation of the Council's resolutions; 3. Declares that the entry of the U.N. force into the Province of Katanga is necessary for the full implementation of this resolution; 4. Reaffirms that the U.N. force in the Congo will not be a party to or in any way intervene in or be used to influence the outcome of any internal conflict, constitutional or otherwise; 5. Calls upon all Member States, in accordance with Articles 25 and 49 of the Charter, to accept and carry out the decisions of the Security Council and to afford mutual assistance in carrying out measures decided upon by the Security Council; 6. Requests the Secretary-General to implement this resolution and to report further to the Security Council as appropriate. (*13:12*)

The Congo representatives, Belgium, and even Russia expressed their willingness to abide by the resolution which passed nine to zero with France and Italy abstaining. But in Léopoldville, Lumumba called the Congo army back to regular duty, proclaimed a state of emergency, and threatened an invasion of Katanga. He called a press conference and lashed out at the ABAKO party, saying "They are fascists who are mad because they did not get any jobs in the administration. . . . The imperialist press is trying to divide me and Kasavubu. But we will continue to lead the nation together toward independence and liberty." He said his own forces would be supported by other African troops and that "If the Belgians . . . shoot, we will be happy to die for our country." The Katanga responded that it could handle anything Lumumba sent its way, and Tshombe added that he was still opposed to U.N. intervention, but in the evening agreed to the entry of U.N. troops, provided none were from communist countries and that they would not interfere in the internal affairs of the province. Belgian civilians began packing for another exodus, and Albert Kalonji was reported to have left for the Kasaï to organize an independent state. In Léopoldville Lumumba said that he was organizing an all-African summit conference to open in Léopoldville August 25. The central government ousted the Belgian Ambassador, and recalled all Congolese students studying in Belgium because they were being "indoctrinated and brainwashed to organize the overthrow of the Congolese government." In New York Hammarskjold delayed his return to the Congo to continue talks with Belgium's Foreign Minister Wigny. In Brussels Premier Eyskens said in a press conference that Belgium was announcing a cut in its NATO commitments. He added that when Belgium set up the Kamina base in the Congo it was told that the base was indispensable for Western defence: "I do not say Belgium will leave NATO, but I now fully understand that generosity does not pay. . . . Belgium does not have the means of recovering financially without reviewing the entire military position."

August 10: Severely conflicting reports announced that rioting had taken place in Léopoldville's African section and that Lumumba had been (1) severely injured; (2) hit in the mouth; (3) uninjured. Rioting was probably caused by ABAKO movements, and it is certain that Lumumba was caught in the midst of it. In Luluabourg, it was reported that four Tunisian soldiers were killed in the continuing Baluba-Bena Lulua struggles. In Léopoldville Lumumba called a press conference to announce that he had cabled Hammarskjold his full support and co-operation in carrying out the new U.N. resolution.

August 11: Hammarskjold left New York for Léopold-ville, saying that he would lead a detachment of Swedish troops into the Katanga on August 12. Tshombe replied by asking for further reassurance that the U.N. would "not pro-voke in any form interference in the internal affairs of Ka-tanga nor favor the intervention of emissaries of the central government." In Léopoldville, Lumumba appealed to the people to "forget their tribal differences" and unite for a peaceable settlement of the Congo crisis; opposition to Lu-mumba was reported hardening. The arrest of Mr. Gabriel Makoso, Congolese editor of the Belgian-owned newspaper, *Le Courrier d'Afrique,* and the seizing of the Belgian news agency, Belga, were reported. In Brussels Premier Eyskens asked Parliament for a vote of confidence in his government which was reported on the verge of collapse. In Accra, Ham-marskjold stopped for talks with President Nkrumah, and in Cairo the formation of an African "peace army" including units from the United Arab Republic, Guinea, and Ghana was announced. Moise Tshombe assured Hammarskjold of his welcome in Elisabethville, but repeated his warnings against support for the central government or interference in internal affairs of the Katanga.

August 12: Hammarskjold arrived in Elisabethville with 220 Swedish troops and was greeted affably by Tshombe but also by a European crowd shouting "Long live Tshombe" and "Down with the United Nations," and by banners of the opposition party which read "Down with federalism, down with independent Katanga, long live the United Congo." Hammarskjold talked with Tshombe for an hour and forty minutes and announced that talks would be continued the following day. In Léopoldville, the French news agency, Agence France Presse, was informed by the government that its activities must "cease at once." Ralph Bunche informed Lumumba that the U.N. intended to carry out its mission in the Congo despite interference by the Congolese army, and Léopoldville was once again disturbed by army members who roved the highway stopping cars and passers-by.

August 13: Swedish United Nations troops began replacing Belgian forces in Elisabethville and taking over guard duties at the airport. Radio Moscow charged Hammarskjold with playing a "disgraceful" role because he held talks with Tshombe while the U.N. troops remained outside Elisabethville proper. In Léopoldville Lumumba bitterly denounced Hammarskjold because the first troops in the Katanga were white and because the Secretary-General had not consulted him during a brief stopover in Léopoldville August 12. Lumumba said that all white troops should be withdrawn from the Congo, accused Hammarskjold of being "a puppet" of Belgium, and said that Belgium "is mounting new plots" against his regime. He accused Belgian agents of disguising themselves as U.N. soldiers, and announced strict new government measures for inspection of newspapers and for banning public meetings which failed to obtain authorizations from the interior ministry six days in advance.

August 14: Katanga military police broke up a demonstration in front of the guest house occupied by Hammarskjold in Elisabethville; the demonstration was in favor of a united Congo and against Tshombe. Swedish troops were sent to Jadotville where demonstrations had taken place. Hammarskjold left Elisabethville for Léopoldville, where Kasavubu was appealing for peace and reconciliation among the Congolese in a radio broadcast, and Lumumba presented Hammarskjold with a letter which expressed dissatisfaction with U.N. operations.

> I submit to you the following request: 1) To entrust the task of guarding all the airfields of the Republic to troops of the National Army and the Congolese police in place of U.N. troops. 2) To send immediately to Katanga Moroccan, Guinean, Ghanaian, Ethiopian, Mali, Tunisian, Sudanese, Liberian, and Congolese troops. 3) To put aircraft at the disposal of the Govern-

ment of the Republic for the transportation of Congolese troops and civilians engaged in restoring order throughout the country. 4) To proceed immediately to seize all arms and ammunition distributed by the Belgians in Katanga to the partisans of the rebel government whether Congolese or foreign, and to put at the disposal of the government of the Republic the arms and ammunition so seized, as they are the property of the Government. 5) To withdraw all non-African troops from Katanga immediately. (*13*:12)

August 15: Hammarskjold rejected Lumumba's letter on the basis of his interpretation of the Security Council resolutions, but this led to a second letter, and then a third in which Lumumba asserted that the "Government of the people of the Congo has lost its confidence in the Secretary-General of the United Nations." He added that Hammarskjold had acquiesced to Belgian demands for the Katanga and repeated previous charges of Hammarskjold-Belgian collusion. Hammarskjold cabled the U.N. to ask for another meeting of the Security Council and departed for Paris and New York. In the meantime, the U.N. announced that river traffic on the Congo River was proceeding normally and that the ports of Matadi and Boma were in full operation.

August 16: In Léopoldville, Congolese police, acting under Lumumba's orders, arrested Europeans and particularly United Nations personnel who, they said, "were Belgians camouflaged under U.N. uniform," as well as some of the few remaining members of the Belgian embassy. Later in the day, Lumumba decreed martial law in the Congo for a period of six months, saying that while military rule was in effect "special military and possibly people's tribunals will hand down summary justice to troublemakers—be they black or white." He also ordered three hundred Congolese troops equipped with armored cars, light artillery and machine guns into Léopoldville from the Thysville garrison. Finally, Lumumba threatened to seize Belgian assets in the Congo as reprisal for Congo funds which he said Belgium had "stolen shortly before independence. . . . If within two weeks we have not recovered our gold, our assets and our patrimony presently frozen, we will be obliged to envisage the confiscation of the Belgian assets in the Congo." Attacking Hammarskjold again, Lumumba said, "Hammarskjold and von Horn are Swedes and everybody knows the close links between Sweden and the Belgian royal family." In Luluabourg there were reports of a heavy exodus of Europeans as inter-tribal fighting continued. In Washington, the Senate foreign relations committee voted unanimously to put an extra 100 million dollars into the President's emergency fund to help restore stability to the Congo. In New York Kuznetsov objected strongly to Hammarskjold's interpretation of the Security Council resolutions as expressed in his exchange of letters with Lumumba.

August 17: In Léopoldville Lumumba called a press conference during which he said, "If no decision is taken on our request to have neutral observers despatched to the Congo, the government will regretfully be forced to consider other and faster solutions. The Congolese government will enter the Katanga, and its army is perfectly able to enter and settle the problem in a week. . . . Unless the U.N. promptly carries out the resolutions of the security council, we will renounce U.N. aid altogether." Lumumba also launched another blast against Hammarskjold: "We condemn him because he has interpreted the resolutions in a personal fashion as if the Congolese government was nonexistent. The contact he had with Tshombe and the assurances he gave are treason. Hammarskjold has no right to deal with Tshombe without first conferring with me. We must separate the United Nations, in which we have complete trust, and a secretary-general whose activities we have denounced in the name of justice and truth." In Brussels the Belgian government defended its policy before parliament with the claim that the alternative to granting independence would have been a colonial war and that good Belgo-Congolese relations would exist if Lumumba had not encouraged disorder. In a press conference in Washington, President Eisenhower called conditions in the Congo "deplorable" but said that the world must continue to support the United Nations actions there.

August 18: In Léopoldville, a group of fourteen Canadian U.N. troops was attacked by a Congolese army detachment and one man was knocked unconscious; the soldiers later explained that they were looking for disguised Belgians. Airport U.N. forces were increased to 1,200 men and U.N. officers gave orders to shoot if another such attack was forthcoming. Shortly after the airport incident, two U.N. soldiers, a Jamaican and a Brazilian, attempted to deliver a message from Bunche to Lumumba; they were arrested, robbed, and put under orders to be executed before being rescued by other U.N. troops. In New York Hammarskjold called one special meeting of representatives of the United States, Russia, France, and Britain to discuss the Congo situation, and another with the remaining powers on the Security Council. In Brussels Premier Eyskens' government defeated a motion demanding its resignation. In Léopoldville, observers felt that opposition to Lumumba's government was beginning to crystallize.

August 19: In Léopoldville, Lumumba held another news conference and said that his cabinet had approved a declaration demanding "the immediate withdrawal from the Congo of all white troops since they are the ones responsible for the incidents." He continued: "We are easily capable of re-establishing order ourselves with our own troops and with the direct help of certain countries who already have pledged to help us." Reacting to a communiqué from Hammarskjold which noted that he would be obliged to ask the Security Council to reconsider its activities in the Congo in the light of recent events, he said, "This blackmail by the secretary-general does not impress us. . . . We are ready to renounce the services of the United Nations." In New York, Hammar-skjold called an emergency meeting of the Security Council for August 21.

August 20: Ralph Bunche resigned as Hammarskjold's personal representative in the Congo, and was replaced by Rajeshwar Dayal of India. In New York, Russia renewed its attacks on Hammarskjold by demanding that Canadian units be withdrawn and declaring that his civilian aid plan was putting the Congo under the thumb of the United States and the so-called colonial powers. Leaders of African delegations to the U.N. were reportedly trying to cool off the Congolese delegates headed by Antoine Gizenga; a number of African governments were said to have been displeased at Lumumba's continuing attacks on Hammarskjold.

At still another press conference in Léopoldville, Lumumba expressed regrets for the attacks on Canadian personnel, which resulted, he said, from an "excess of zeal." He also outlined the Congolese case which would be presented to the Security Council in five points: (1) A demand for U.N. assistance to transport Congolese troops "to any region of the territory where their presence may be necessary." (2) An appeal to the U.N. to allow Congolese forces to control all airfields and ports. (3) A call for the immediate withdrawal of all Belgian troops from the Congo, including Katanga Province. (4) An appeal that the U.N. forces have contacts only with the "sole legal government of the Congo." (5) The withdrawal of all white U.N. troops from the Congo. Meanwhile, the ABAKO party warned that it intended to censure Lumumba's policy and his attacks against the United Nations, and Vital Mwanda added, "If Lumumba is not voted out of office, we shall strike by other means and it will be right on the target." He said the ABAKO intended to rid the country of Lumumba "by legal or illegal means."

August 21: The Security Council went into its fourth series of meetings in New York. In Elisabethville a crowd of

Lumumba sympathizers was arrested by Katanga police. First reports of Albert Kalonji's État Minière (Mining State) in the Kasaï appeared. In Léopoldville Lumumba ordered the stopping of ferry service to Brazzaville and launched a search for spies which resulted in searching some of the U.N. personnel. In the Security Council Russia again attacked Hammarskjold and United States aggression in the Katanga. Hammarskjold was warmly defended by Tunisian and Ceylonese delegates. Hammarskjold exchanged strong remarks with Antoine Gizenga, who presented the five demands of the Congolese government in considerably different form from that proposed by Lumumba on August 20:(1) All U.N. actions should be carried out in co-operation with the central Congolese government. (2) The central government should be constantly kept in touch with U.N. movements. (3) Airports and seaports should be policed by forces of the Congolese army. (4) U.N. forces should entirely disarm all Belgians under rebellious authorities. (5) Withdrawal from Kamina and Kitona should be total and the bases abandoned. Russia introduced a "no-confidence" resolution, but later withdrew it because of lack of support, and no resolutions were passed.

August 22: In Léopoldville, Lumumba spent three hours in conversation with the new Russian ambassador, Mikhail D. Yakovlev, and later announced that he was satisfied with the U.N. policy. "The government sees no reason to press its demands. The government is satisfied that Belgian troops will be withdrawn. The government considers the atmosphere good." In another statement issued by a spokesman at a press conference: "The Premier has noted that the Security Council has not rescinded its previous decisions. The Congolese government once again has confidence in the U.N. because it has promised to get all Belgian troops out of the Congo in a week. The appeal to other friendly countries is not necessary for the moment because the situation is satisfactory." In Elisabethville there was a meeting of federalist forces which included members of Conakat, ABAKO, PUNA, and MNC-Kalonji. In a statement issued by the conference, it was said, "We are determined to overthrow Lumumba . . . I can assure you that Lumumba will fall within fifteen days." In Albertville in the Katanga, heavy fighting was reported between U.N. troops from Mali and Baluba tribesmen. Messages said the Mali troops were in a desperate position and that there were "many dead and wounded." General Alexander criticized the U.N. position that its forces should not be allowed to fire; he said that it placed the troops "in an impossible position." In U.N. headquarters, Bunche responded by saying that the U.N. was in the Congo to co-operate with the Congo government: "The United Nations has neither sought to replace the Congo government nor to make it captive. The United Nations force is in the Congo as a friend and partner, not as an army of occupation. . . . Obviously, if the U.N. force began to use its arms to wound and kill Congolese, its doom would be quickly sealed, for it cannot long survive amidst a hostile public. Indeed, this would defeat its very purpose."

August 24: Mali troops were reported to have calmed the disturbances in Albertville, but Lumumba began sending 600 Congolese troops into the Kasaï to quell disturbances there. The forces were apparently destined to settle Baluba-Bena Lulua fighting and to wipe out Kalonji's Mining State. Lumumba also charged Belgian interference in the Lower Congo and along the Kivu frontiers.

August 25: More than one thousand Congolese army troops were reported massing in the Kasaï in preparation for an all-out attack on Kalonji's Mining State; Kalonji was estimated to have about 450 troops. The Katanga was reported to have mined roads and railway bridges between the Kasaï and Katanga, and to be prepared to blow them up at the first sign of an attempt to invade the Katanga. In Léopoldville the Conference of Independent African Nations convened to anti-Lumumba rioting; demonstrators carried placards demanding the resignation of Lumumba's "fascist government," and stating "Long live a federated Congo." Demonstrators reportedly shouted "Death to Lumumba," and someone in the crowd stated to a news reporter: "Down with communism, down with the government of Lumumba. We demand the liberty of our country. We demand the freedom of the press and we demand the liberty to get to and from Brazzaville at will. We object to being shut up in Léopoldville by that madman Lumumba." Delegates to the conference from Cameroons, Ethiopia, Ghana, Guinea, Liberia, Morocco, Sudan, Togo, Tunisia, the United Arab Republic, and the Algerian rebel national liberation front were reported shocked at the rioting and the measures used to control it.

August 26: In Léopoldville, Lumumba demanded that U.N. troops leave the Congo simultaneously with the last Belgian troops slated to depart by August 29. "We will assure order with our own troops and police. We don't want to replace the Belgian military occupation with a U.N. occupation." In the Kasaï Lumumba's forces were reported to be unopposed as they advanced within thirty miles of the border of Katanga Province. Katanga was reported to have federated in a joint defense and economic union with Kalonji's Mining State. Lumumba said that his security forces had seized a Belgian plane in Luluabourg as it attempted to ferry arms from Brazzaville to Bakwanga, capital of the Mining State, and that a Belgian spy plot had been uncovered in Brazzaville. The United Nations continued to send troops to the Congo, and at the same time the United Christian Missionary Society (Disciples of Christ) announced that its evacuated missionaries were returning to the Congo.

August 27: Lumumba left for Stanleyville in an effort to show the world and the African Congress in Léopoldville that his popularity had not waned. In Stanleyville, eight American airmen were attacked at the airport by Congolese army units; a stiff U.N. protest was immediately released to the

Congolese government. It was announced in Elisabethville that Congolese troops had occupied Bakwanga, capital of the Mining State.

August 28: The American government sent a strong protest to the Congolese government over the Stanleyville incident, but Ambassador Timberlake was unable to find Foreign Minister Bomboko to deliver the note. The American airmen arrived in Léopoldville, where Gen. Von Horn put on a strong show of force, saying, "It is because I was so mad; I promised to fire the first shot myself if there was any interference." In Elisabethville it was reported that Congolese army units were within twenty miles of the Katanga and that Tshombe was flying to his northern border to rally his troops. Tshombe criticized Kalonji for fleeing Bakwanga, and Kalonji in turn charged that three Czechoslovakian army officers were leading Lumumba's troops in the Kasaï. A Swedish physician who had been taken captive in the Lower Congo was released; he noted that the area was in chaos and that "no passports or any other papers are valid in that area." In Brussels, Premier Eyskens was said to have shuffled his cabinet and to have ousted African Affairs Minister August de Schrijver.

August 29: The threat of fighting on the Katanga border grew as Congolese army troops were reported at Luputa. Border rail bridges were said to have been blown up and roads mined. Belgium was reported withdrawing its last 950 troops from the Katanga.

August 30: The United Nations reported that all Belgian combat troops had left the Congo before midnight, with only a number of specialists left at the bases of Kitona and Kamina. Tshombe threatened to take over Kamina; the U.N. announced that the base should be neutralized. In Léopoldville, Lumumba returned from Stanleyville and announced a "profound reform of the ancient structure" of society with the creation of peasant co-operatives to "mobilize all the forces of the country for a vast economic and social program." It

250

was reported that Kasavubu had expressed his regrets to Timberlake and Bunche for the beating of the eight American airmen in Stanleyville, but that Lumumba had taken no such action. One hundred Russian trucks and ten Ilyushin-14 aircraft were reported being sent to the support of Lumumba's forces. News from the Kasaï was confused, with Kasaï Premier Pascual Ngalula reporting that Baluba tribesmen armed with bows and arrows and spears had recaptured Bakwanga, and Katanga authorities denying the report.

August 31: Albert Kalonji said that Bakwanga had indeed been recaptured though he admitted his information was scanty, and the Katanga government threatened to destroy the base of Kamina unless the United Nations guaranteed it could not be used by Lumumba's forces. In Léopoldville the Conference of Independent African States closed after passing a resolution calling for frank and loyal co-operation between the United Nations and the Congo. In his closing speech to the conference, Lumumba praised the work of the U.N. and pledged that his government would do everything possible to assure the security of U.N. forces. He added that both the Congolese army and government were "obsessed" with the idea of marching into the Katanga "to liberate our countrymen."

September 1: Ralph Bunche blamed Belgium for the Congo troubles, saying that it had failed to prepare and educate the Congolese before independence. He added that he was "unaware" of Soviet trucks or planes being used by Lumumba's forces, and stressed the need for "a forbearance and a patience and an understanding far beyond what would normally be expected of any human being" on the part of U.N. personnel in the face of "plenty of provocation."

September 2: The government charged that the opposition PUNA party had tried to assassinate Kasavubu and Lumumba, and jailed Jean Bolikango who was arrested near Lisala. Bolikango was brought by plane to Léopoldville and held in Camp Léopold II, military headquarters for the Congolese army. Three British newsmen were arrested in Bakwanga by government forces.

September 3: A volunteer army, "supervised by white technicians" but officially headed by Albert Kalonji, moved across the Katanga border for the Kasaï. About 250 men comprised the force which was reported heading for Luputa, and it was further announced that the Congolese army was on the defensive and surrounded in Bakwanga. Casualties in the area were reported to have reached about seven hundred wounded and three hundred dead. Some eighty-eight Congolese troops were reported in Luputa, and rebel forces were holding a vital bridge across the Bushimai River which cut off Congolese army supplies to Luputa and Bakwanga. In Léopoldville, Lumumba came under heavy attack in the Senate where he was accused of moving the Congo toward a leftish dictatorship.

September 4: Heavy fighting was again reported in the area of Bakwanga where Congolese troops were reported still pinned down by rebel forces. The Congolese forces were also said to control the villages of Luputa, Mwene-Ditu, and Gandajika as well as areas outside these towns. Fighting was said to be concentrated in the village of Tchelenge, seventeen miles southeast of Bakwanga, and skirmishing was taking place at Kabinda, Luebo, and Gandajika. An American correspondent was reported killed in Bakwanga when caught in a line of fire. The presence of Russian planes in the Congo caused considerable discussion; some reports indicated that they were to be used by Lumumba as troop carriers, and others said that they were to be used only as the basis of a Congo airline. Gen. Ben Hamou Kettani, deputy commander of the United Nations forces, said that Lumumba had accepted a Moroccan plan for reorganizing the Congo army. The plan provided for the training of three battalions of paratroops.

September 5: Léopoldville radio announced that a large mission of Czechoslovakian technicians which would "solve all our technical problems" would arrive shortly. It was also said that fifteen Ilyushin transport planes manned by Russian crews as well as over one hundred Russian built trucks had already been sent to Lumumba, the former using the NATO base at Athens, Greece, for refueling on their way to the Congo. The planes were used to ferry more than two hundred reinforcements from Stanleyville to Bakwanga, via Luluabourg, for Lumumba's army. Fighting was still heavy in the area, and four hundred were said to have been killed on September 3. From Tel Aviv it was announced that farmers from ten former French and Belgian colonies in Africa had begun a study of new patterns of co-operative life developed in Israel; the course, lasting ten weeks, included five Congolese among the students. In Paris, De Gaulle said that the "so-called United Nations" had bungled its Congo peace mission, and also scored Russia heavily for seizing upon the difficulties of newly independent states like the Congo to try to turn the situation "into a chronic chaos."

In Léopoldville, President Kasavubu in a radio address shortly before 8:00 P.M., ousted Premier Lumumba and called on the United Nations to take over all responsibility for law and order. He said that Lumumba had failed and had "plunged the nation into fratricidal warfare," and charged him with curtailing freedom of expression. Shortly after 9:00 P.M., in a broadcast over the same station, Lumumba ousted Kasavubu: "Kasavubu is no longer chief of state. I am still in control of the country, remain faithful to me. . . . Nobody, not even chief of state Kasavubu, has the right to revoke the government of the people, elected by the people, which today has the confidence of the people. . . . Forward youth and workers of the Congo. You must defend the republic." Shortly after the broadcasts, United Nations forces in Léopoldville were put on a state of alert and began patrolling

the streets in greater force. Kasavubu announced the formation of a new government headed by Joseph Ileo. In New
York, a further Security Council meeting was announced as
probable.

September 6: Lumumba called for an emergency session
of Parliament to seek a vote of confidence, and said that he
had the full backing of his cabinet. Anti-Lumumba rioting
took place in Léopoldville as Kasavubu supporters paraded
through the streets shouting "Long live Kasavubu" and
"Down with Lumumba." In the subsequent police action two
persons were reported killed and others wounded; sporadic
street fighting continued throughout the night. Meanwhile the
United Nations shut down the Léopoldville radio station and
closed all Congo airports "to civilian air traffic," that is, to
any planes not serving the United Nations. The immediate
effect was to prevent Lumumba from using Russian aircraft
to ferry troops either into the Kasaï to assist in the fighting, or
to Léopoldville to bulwark his own position. Some African
nations were reported highly disturbed over what they considered to be U.N. interference in the Lumumba-Kasavubu struggle, but U.N. officials answered that their mandate to restore
law and order was overriding. In New York it was expected
that the Russians would try to call another Security Council
meeting, and in Léopoldville it was reported that Kasavubu
had consulted Fulbert Youlou, President of the Congo Republic (formerly part of French Equatorial Africa), before making his move against Lumumba. Late in the evening, Bangala
members of the Congo army walked unopposed into Léopoldville prison and freed Jean Bolikango who was later reported
to be in hiding in the African section of the city.

September 7: After a six-hour debate attended by Lumumba, the Chamber of Deputies voted sixty to nineteen to
invalidate the ousters of both Kasavubu and Lumumba.
Heavy troop and police patrols roamed the streets of Léopoldville, and Kasavubu claimed that a number of troops

loyal to him had entered the city from the Lower Congo region. In a two-hour speech Lumumba denounced the U.N. command for closing the air fields and shutting down the Léopoldville radio, and demanded in a letter that the action be rescinded. His supporters passed out leaflets appealing for national unity, and Lumumba announced the formation of a commission to resolve his difficulties with Kasavubu. ABAKO, PUNA, and MNC-Kalonji announced an alliance, demanded Lumumba's arrest "in the event of insubordination," called for freedom of the press, and warned against communist infiltration by Russia. In Elisabethville a plane carrying nine tons of arms for the Katanga arrived from Belgium.

In Washington the American airmen beaten earlier in Stanleyville arrived home and were awarded medals for devotion to duty. In a news conference, President Eisenhower accused Russia of jeopardizing the restoration of law and order in the Congo, and said that the United States "deplores" and takes "a most serious view" of Russia's unilateral intervention which is "thereby aggravating an already serious situation which finds Africans killing other Africans. . . . The constitutional structure of the Congo republic is a question which should be worked out peacefully by the Congolese themselves. This objective is threatened by the soviet action which seems to be motivated entirely by the Soviet Union's political designs in Africa."

In New York Hammarskjold asked the Security Council to reaffirm its declaration that all member countries must refrain from interference in the Congo situation, and asked the U.N. for clarification of the duties of the U.N. force. United Nations officials reported that the first three months of the U.N. Congo operation would probably cost 40 million dollars, and that by the end of 1960, the cost would rise to 75 millions. It was reported that Hammarskjold would ask the General Assembly to finance the operation by assessing all

255

members according to the scale used in raising U.N. funds; under this scale, the United States would pay 32.51 per cent, the Soviet Union 13.62 per cent. In London the British post office announced that it would no longer insure letters and packages to the Congo.

September 8: In Léopoldville, the Congo Senate refused to be addressed by Lumumba, barred him from the podium, heard Foreign Minister Justin Bomboko denounce Lumumba for bringing anarchy to the Congo, allowed Lumumba to speak, and then voted forty-one to two to keep Lumumba in power; seven senators abstained and thirty-four were absent. Lumumba demanded "the immediate withdrawal of United Nations troops from our country," but said that the Congo reserved the right to receive U.N. technical assistance. He also cabled the U.N. asking that the Security Council hold its next meeting in Léopoldville, and again demanded the opening of airfields and the release of the Léopoldville radio station. In New York, Yugoslavia asked the Security Council to act against any aid to Congolese secessionists and charged that the U.N. had "facilitated" the revolt. Hammarskjold in turn appealed to the Security Council for authority to disarm Congolese troops and to bar Soviet military interference in the Congo. "The internal conflicts which have become increasingly grave in the last few weeks and even days have taken on a particularly serious aspect due to the fact that parties have relied on and obtained certain assistance from outside. This is contrary to the spirit of the Security Council resolutions and is tending to reintroduce elements of the very kind which the Security Council wished to eliminate when it requested the immediate withdrawal of Belgian troops." He also warned that the Congo was on the brink of economic collapse and appealed to the members for 100 million dollars to halt unemployment and run the schools and other government services.

September 9: In Léopoldville, Guinean troops threatened

to withdraw from the U.N. force. Tibu Tunkara, head of the mission, said that the U.N. had "clearly taken sides to influence the results of an internal dispute" and added that the Guinean forces would withdraw provisionally until the U.N. had "ceased its flagrant interference in internal Congo affairs and had gone back to following the security council decisions on the Congo." Sékou Touré, President of Guinea, conferred with Khrushchev in Moscow and the two announced their agreement on Congo and world problems. Russia issued a demand for an immediate United Nations Security Council session and said that Hammarskjold and the U.N. command in the Congo were "systematically violating" Security Council decisions. In Léopoldville, Lumumba said that he had taken over the function of chief of state as well as the premiership, and announced the dismissal of Foreign Minister Bomboko, Finance Minister Pascal Nkayi, and Minister Resident in Belgium, Albert Delvaux; Bomboko and Delvaux had countersigned Kasavubu's decrees dismissing Lumumba as premier. Kasavubu meanwhile declared that parliament had no right to revoke the decree from the head of state which called for firing Lumumba and repeated that Lumumba was no longer premier. He insisted that Joseph Ileo was rightful premier. In New York, Hammarskjold warned that he would oust Guinean troops from the Congo if they carried out their threat to pull out of the U.N. forces. He said that the Congo had only two choices: (1) Take aid from "another state or group of states," (2) "Depend on the . . . U.N. and so remain free." He warned that "the international community . . . cannot be supposed to be willing to foot the bill for political ineptitude and irresponsibility." The Soviets meanwhile charged that Hammarskjold "failed to display a minimum of impartiality" and that he "was most openly working in favor of the colonialists, thus compromising the United Nations in the eyes of the people." The Russians backed Lumumba's demands for return of the Léopoldville radio station and the Congo airports, as well as his demand for a Security Council meeting in Léopoldville. Hammarskjold said that the U.N. operation in the Congo "must continue . . . because of the great risks which exist for the spreading of the Congo crisis over Africa, and even more widely." Meanwhile, it was reported that the United States had informed African diplomats that if the U.N. was forced to give up its Congo operations, the United States stood ready to clash militarily with the Soviets to prevent Moscow's winning the Congo.

In Léopoldville, the ABAKO party called for a general strike at 2:00 P.M. on September 10, and in London it was reported that in recent weeks Belgium had transported to Katanga 100 tons of arms and ammunition and 25 Belgian air force planes, and had assigned 159 Belgian officers and noncommissioned officers to duty there.

September 10: The Congolese army ordered a cease-fire throughout the Congo, including the Katanga, and laid down its arms around Léopoldville. The origin of the order was not known, but the chief of staff, Col. Joseph Mobutu, a supporter of Kasavubu, appeared to be responsible for the action. In New York the Security Council received a cable from Kasavubu and abruptly adjourned. Argentine delegate Mario Amadea said the members "were confused" and Tunisian delegate, Mongi Slim, requested the adjournment. Kasavubu's cable announced the formation of a new Congolese government which included Joseph Ileo as Premier, Albert Kalonji as Interior Minister, and Jean Bolikango as Minister of Information. He said that "the Congolese people do not want, at any price, technical or military assistance from any foreign power unless it is within the framework of the U.N. I ask the U.N. to decide immediately that foreign elements, which have infiltrated here and which our country does not want, be withdrawn." He continued that Hammarskjold's council report "correctly notes the illegality and even the nonexistence

258

of the so-called Lumumba government. The Congolese people congratulates and thanks you for this. . . . Meanwhile, the only lawful and legal government is that consisting of Mr. Ileo, prime minister." The cable asked: "that you do not deal with Mr. Lumumba, the former Prime Minister, and the other ministers whose mandates have been revoked and who by wishing to continue to govern are usurpers. That the U.N. insure the protection of the political leaders and the members of parliament of the Congo so that they might exercise their mandate freely. That the U.N. forces temporarily continue to guard airports, ports, the national radio, and essential public services." In Léopoldville, Averell Harriman said that the Russian Ambassador had told him Russian planes were sent to the Congo with crews on a one-year loan plan, and that Lumumba told him he wanted a loan from the United States and "needed the money quickly."

September 11: In Léopoldville both Kasavubu and Lumumba ordered rival delegations to leave for the United Nations; Kasavubu's delegation was headed by Justin Bomboko, and Lumumba's by Thomas Kanza. Lumumba attempted to broadcast over Léopoldville radio, but was turned back by United Nations forces composed of Ghanaians. In a separate incident, Congolese troops approached the Léopoldville airport road, but did not make any overt move to seize it. Foreign Minister Bomboko was quoted as saying that he would produce pamphlets issued by the Russian embassy as proof of "foreign interference" in Congo affairs, and accused Lumumba of allowing the distribution of communist propaganda in return for Russian air and ground transport. Kasavubu was quoted by the Durban (South Africa) Sunday *Tribune* as saying, "Please warn the west that Russia is busy taking over the Congo." In France, the United States announced that it had flown three million miles in the first two months of the Congo airlift. Planes had hauled 13,325 of the 17,000 U.N. troops and over six million pounds of supplies; 1,367

Belgian troops and 2,478 refugees had also been evacuated by the U.S. planes, and the job was estimated to have cost a million and a half dollars for fuel and lubricants alone.

September 12: In Léopoldville, both Kasavubu and Lumumba claimed victory in the struggle for power. The United Nations was adjourned pending the arrival of the two delegations. While the Parliament continued to support Lumumba, Kasavubu ordered his arrest, and both sides were turned away from the radio station by U.N. troops. In New York the Soviet delegation charged that the United States had "wrecked" the Security Council meeting scheduled for Monday in order to gain time for "criminal plans" to overthrow Lumumba. Hammarskjold's solid African backing appeared to be falling apart as the United Arab Republic announced the withdrawal of its 500 paratroopers from the U.N. force. In Léopoldville, Lumumba was reported jailed and then released after approximately three hours. Kasavubu sent a message to the United Nations asking it to reorganize and train the Congolese army under his supreme command as Chief of State. He also asked for speedy formation of police units, U.N. assistance in reactivating the Congo's judicial system, and U.N. transportation and protection for Tshombe and Kalonji whom, he said, he had invited to Léopoldville for a national conference. A majority in the Congolese Senate and Chamber of Deputies sent a cable to the U.N. discrediting the Bomboko delegation which, it said, "is not recognized by the parliament, has no legal status and cannot be received by the Security Council or speak on behalf of the Congo." In London, Averell Harriman accused Lumumba of running "a reign of terror," and said that "Lumumba is surrounded with left-wing advisers from Belgium and France as well as from the Soviet Union and communist Czechoslovakia. . . . Lumumba is serving his own ambitions and not paying any attention to the economy and other problems of his country."

September 13: The United Nations relaxed its restriction on the Congo airports and Léopoldville's radio station, and Congolese troops favorable to Kasavubu immediately surrounded the latter. In broadcasting his first appeal, Jean Bolikango said that the government would make an all-out effort to find employment and announced that Kasavubu had signed new arrest warrants for Lumumba and six of his ministers. He added that while Ileo's new government would not seek vengeance, Lumumba and others "will have to account for their acts." Shortly before the ban was lifted, Kwame Nkrumah told the United Press International in Accra that Ghanaian troops would be withdrawn from the U.N. forces if Lumumba were not permitted to broadcast. The airports were opened to "all peaceful air traffic" but U.N. personnel continued to man airport installations. A full cease-fire was reported in all the affected areas of the Kasaï and Katanga.

Yugoslavia again demanded a Security Council meeting as rival delegations from the Congo arrived in New York. In Léopoldville Lumumba was given extraordinary powers by Parliament, and sent a cable to Kanza informing him that he had received "full powers" and that Kanza was to leave the U.N. session if Bomboko's group was allowed to address the Security Council. A special meeting of the Security Council was announced for September 14, and the Russian delegation became increasingly hostile to Hammarskjold in another note which said in part: "We are faced with an out and out conspiracy of the colonialists against the independence and integrity of the Congo."

September 14: Hammarskjold was reported trying to patch up the differences between the U.N. and several of its African members. In Léopoldville Lumumba was refused admittance to the radio station by local police. Late in the evening Joseph Mobutu announced that the military was seizing power in the Congo in a "simple and peaceful revolution" which would "neutralize" both Lumumba and Kasavubu until the end of the year. He also ordered Soviet and other communist diplomats to leave the country within forty-eight hours. In the Katanga, 22 Belgians and 140 Congolese were rescued from the town of Manono which was said to be under heavy attack from Baluba tribal units. In New York the Security Council met amidst strong efforts by Russia to discredit Hammarskjold and strong support for Hammarskjold from the United States and most of the African nations.

September 15: In Léopoldville Lumumba's press officer reported that Mobutu had been arrested, but during the day two attempts were made on Lumumba's life. The first attempt was averted by U.N. Ghanaian troops and the second by Congolese police controlled by Mobutu, who announced that he had placed Lumumba under house arrest. In the Katanga, Congolese army troops were reported to have launched an invasion which reached Lubanda, thirty-two miles inside the border. At Manono, fifteen Baluba were killed, but the city was under the control of Irish U.N. forces.

In New York at the Security Council meetings three different resolutions were introduced during rounds of increasing accusations and counter-accusations among Russia, the United States, and Hammarskjold. The first resolution was introduced by Tunisia and co-sponsored by Ceylon; it called for the continued assistance of the Secretary-General to the Congo, as well as financial aid and a "good offices" committee aimed at bringing peace among rival Congo political leaders. The United States resolution urged: (1) The Security Council should encourage Hammarskjold to build up a massive financial and technical assistance program; (2) Action must be taken to safeguard fundamental human rights in The Congo; (3) The Council should urge the parties within The Congo to resolve their differences by peaceful means; (4) The Council should declare that no personnel, supplies, or equipment for military use should be sent into the Congo except by the United Nations. The Russian resolution called for the Council to place itself on record as endorsing Russian charges against Hammarskjold, the channeling of economic aid directly to the Congo government instead of through the U.N., and the firing of the U.N.'s military command headed by General Von Horn.

September 16: In Léopoldville Mobutu took three steps to solidify his control. He warned Russian and Czechoslovakian diplomats that they must leave the Congo by noon, September 17, or be arrested and forcibly deported. Czechoslovakian diplomats were reported to have begun burning documents at the embassy, and late in the evening the Russians announced that the Soviet embassy had received a formal request from President Kasavubu to leave the country. Mobutu also threw a guard around the parliament building and prevented access to all deputies and senators. Finally, he sent troops to Lumumba's residence and administrative offices, and arrested an estimated thirty of his aides. Lumumba was reported to be staying in his home, and Mobutu said he would not arrest the former Premier as long as he caused no trouble; some sources reported that Lumumba had vanished and had taken flight from the Congo.

In the Katanga, the Congolese army force reported to be invading Katanga seemed "to have disappeared," but continuing troubles were reported from an uprising of Baluba tribesmen which had brought disorder and, in some places, open warfare to a number of interior towns.

In New York, the Security Council meetings continued, with the United States diplomatic forces seemingly attempting to force a Russian veto of the Ceylonese-Tunisian resolution in the hope that to the African nations it would show the Russians as obstructers of United Nations actions in the Congo. Late in the day, the Russian delegate indicated that he would veto the resolution, and the United States served notice on Russia that it would not compromise on full U.N. support. A full General Assembly meeting on the Congo crisis developed as a real possibility, and was urged by the United

States in the event that the Russian veto was delivered. Delegates from Ghana, Guinea, United Arab Republic, and Indonesia expressed support of the Lumumba government and several attacked Belgian actions. Averell Harriman arrived in New York and said "The Russians are doing everything they can to take over the Congo."

September 17: In the United Nations, Russia cast its ninetieth veto in the Security Council on the Ceylonese-Tunisian resolution, and an emergency special session of the General Assembly was called for eight o'clock in the evening. The series of events was regarded as a United States diplomatic victory because it undermined the Soviet build-up for the arrival of Khrushchev, forced Russia to cast a veto against the Afro-Asian nations, and rallied the African nations back to support of Hammarskjold and the U.N. At the beginning of the emergency session of the General Assembly, the United States, in a surprise move, proposed that fifteen new members, fourteen of them African nations, be admitted to immediate membership in order to participate in the Congo debate. The Soviet delegate countered that this would deprive the new members of their "ceremonials" and, after brief adjournment, the assembly voted 43–0 with 26 abstentions to adjourn discussion on the membership question.

In Léopoldville, all Russian and other communist diplomats with the exception of the Yugoslavian representative, left the Congo by the noon deadline; special planes were sent to Stanleyville to pick up Russian personnel there. Meanwhile, Lumumba was reported to have disappeared and rumors swept the city that he had been assassinated at a roadblock thirty miles from the city. Other reports indicated that he had gone into hiding in the Guinean embassy. In the Katanga, a new invasion by Congolese troops was reported with estimates of between eight hundred and eleven hundred troops taking part in actions near Kongolo.

The World Health Organization reported that danger was

spreading from a number of localized outbreaks of smallpox.

September 18: In Léopoldville, Lumumba emerged from hiding and announced that he was still the Congo's legal premier and would soon bring back to the Congo the ousted Russian and Czechoslovakian diplomats. He said that Mobutu's actions were illegal and had been supported by "certain powers." He further claimed that he had signed a "declaration of reconciliation" with Kasavubu in which he had agreed to accept foreign aid only through the United Nations, and also to discuss the Katanga and Kasaï questions; Kasavubu denied that he had signed any such agreement.

In the Katanga it was reported that the United Nations had secured an agreement whereby the invading forces would withdraw into Kivu province thus creating a thirty-mile buffer zone on either side of the border. In Moscow, Tass reported that Russia's embassy staff had been temporarily recalled. ". . . To please the egoistic interests of foreign monopolies, the colonizers have by means of fraud and corruption succeeded in establishing a puppet regime in power in the Congo that is obedient to aliens. . . . Colonizers, exploiting their stooges and other political rogues, resort to dirty provocations in order to harm the good relations established between the Soviet Union and the Congolese Republic. Under these conditions, the normal functioning of the soviet embassy in the Congolese Republic has become impossible, as the immunity of the embassy and the security of its staff have become endangered.'' A Czechoslovakian government statement said that its personnel had been recalled because its safety was threatened.

At United Nations headquarters sixteen Afro-Asian nations introduced a resolution into the General Assembly late in the evening expressing confidence in Hammarskjold's Congo policies. The key clause of the resolution called on all parties "to refrain from direct and indirect provisions of arms or other materials of war and military personnel and other assistance for military purposes in the Congo," during the U.N. presence in that country. The countries sponsoring the resolution were Ceylon, Ghana, Guinea, Indonesia, Iraq, Jordan, Lebanon, Liberia, Libya, Morocco, Nepal, Saudi Arabia, Sudan, Tunisia, United Arab Republic, and Yemen. Bulgarian and Polish delegates continued sharp attacks on Hammarskjold, but the Latin-American countries with the exception of Cuba indicated their support for the Secretary-General.

September 19: In Léopoldville, it was reported that five nations, Ghana, Guinea, Morocco, United Arab Republic, and Tunisia, had been engaged in an effort to bring about a reconciliation between Lumumba and Kasavubu, and that certain terms had been accepted.

In the United Nations Russia offered a counter-resolution which, according to press reports, included the following points:

> Condemn "the armed aggression of Belgium against the Republic of The Congo which is being carried out with the support of the Allies under NATO."
>
> Demand that Belgium "and its military allies immediately withdraw their forces and military personnel from the whole territory of The Congo whatever the pretext or shield these elements might use."
>
> Note "with satisfaction" the series of Security Council resolutions "designed to halt the aggression of Belgium and insure the territorial integrity and political independence" of The Congo.
>
> Note that "non-implementation by the secretary-general and the United Nations command of a number of extremely important provisions in the above-mentioned resolutions, particularly provisions regarding non-interference in the domestic affairs of The Congo and regarding the insuring of the territorial integrity and political independence of the country has led to disorganization of the country's economy, exacerbation of the political situation and the overthrow of the lawful government and parliament."
>
> Call on "all governments to refrain from any actions which

might be harmful to the territorial integrity and political independence" of The Congo. (47:4:3–4)

September 20: In the United Nations, both Russia and the United States withdrew their resolutions, and the Afro-Asian resolution was passed by a 70–0 vote which was generally regarded as a sharp victory for Hammarskjold, the United States, and the Afro-Asian bloc, and a severe defeat for Russia.

In Léopoldville, Mobutu tightened his grip on the Congo with the installation of a commission of students and technicians pledged to protect the Congo "from Communist colonialism and from Marxist-Leninist imperialism." The College of High Commissioners was headed by Justin Bomboko and was given a mandate by Mobutu to rule until the end of the year, or until political leaders could reach agreement. Mobutu also moved his forces into the administration building and issued an order for the arrest of Lumumba should he try to fly to the U.N. General Assembly meeting.

In New York, the General Assembly opened with the admission by acclamation of Cameroon, Togo, Malagasy, Somalia, The Congo, Dahomey, Niger, Upper Volta, Ivory Coast, Chad, Republic of Congo, Gabon, Central African Republic, and Cyprus.

CHAPTER VII

Problems of Independence

The situation in the Congo is both tragic and complex, and in viewing it our emotions are pulled in two directions and our intellects are challenged. It is a tragedy from the standpoint both of the Belgians and the Congolese: for the Belgians because of the humiliation of failure and because of the personal indignities suffered by its nationals during the riots, and for the Congolese because of the rude shattering of their dreams for independence and because of the chaos, strife, and anarchy which marked the emergence of their new African state. At the same time, the complexity of the situation raises problems to which we cannot find simple solutions: Why did Belgium give independence when it did? What is the basis for Lumumba's erratic behavior? What part has communism played in it all? What does the future hold for the Congo?

We have noted before that history demands perspective, and perhaps it is only in this perspective that we shall find the answers we seek, but at the moment we must do the best we can with what we have. The problems we pose may help us understand not only the Congo situation, but perhaps where we stand in relation to all Africa south of the Sahara. By looking at the past we may learn something about the future.

Since World War II the world has been swept with an ever-increasing demand not only for independence but for the rights of smaller and so-called underdeveloped nations who wish to take their places on the world scene. Although Belgium attempted to shield the Congo from this world revolution, its efforts were not successful; isolation was not enough, and neither was the substitution of economic for political development. The change in Africa over the past few years

268

shows everywhere on the continent, and in almost every aspect of life. As Melville J. Herskovits has pointed out:

> It is apparent in the drift to newly built urban centers, in the incorporation of Africans into mining, large-scale agricultural schemes, and industry. It is reflected in the continuous increase in world trade as shown in imports and exports, in the growth of schools and school populations, and the number of African university graduates and postgraduate students in institutions of higher learning in Africa itself and in the rest of the world. It is evident in the many nationalist movements that have appeared; in the way in which Africans have learned to employ parliamentary procedures to achieve constitutional reform, where they have been allowed to do so; in the greater pressure of Africans for administrative responsibilities. (*100*:3)

Much discussion has been wasted over whether the Africans are ready for self-government; the answer of many Africans, at least those visiting in America, has been "Were you ready for self-government in 1776?" The question is not so much whether Africans are ready for self-government as it is whether the colonial powers have given to them an understanding of the new obligations, responsibilities, and problems they will meet in the new world in which they are playing an increasing part. For people are *ready* for self-government by one criterion only, and that is when they say they are ready; their *preparation* is another matter. It is clear that by this simple criterion, all of Africa is ready for self-government. The question is not whether they shall have it, but when and how and under what conditions. And Africa is no longer willing to take independence on other peoples' terms or to accept its own role as other people envisage it. The Prime Minister of Ghana has put the case clearly before us:

> Some of us, I think, need reminding that Africa is a continent on its own. It is not an extension of Europe or of any other continent. We want, therefore, to develop our own community and an African personality. Others may feel that they have evolved the very best way of life, but we are not bound, like slavish imitators, to accept it as our mould. If we find the meth-

ods used by others are suitable to our social environments, we shall adopt them; if we find them unsuitable, we shall reject them. (*100:*4)

Looked at from these points of view, independence for the Congo was inevitable. The only question was how and when, and the only question which is apropos in examining Belgium's response to the demand for independence is not whether the Congo was ready but whether it was prepared. We have already discussed this question in previous chapters; the answer is clearly that the Congo was not prepared for independence, and this point of view is by no means limited to the present writer. The Sunday London *Times,* for example, said "For many years the Belgian Congo was held up to us as a colonial model, a benevolent paternalism, happy in having no politics. Suddenly we see how illusory all this was. Self-government comes with a rush—far too great a rush—and finds a people innocent of political experience, without practiced administrators or service officers and indeed short of patriotism. . . ." The London Sunday *Dispatch* noted: "By training Africans for responsibility and authority, we have made sure there are men fit to take over when the white man goes . . . but the Belgians had no such foresight. They knuckled under to militant nationalism the moment it got organized—with humiliating results" (*10:*3:2–3). Indeed, we need go no further than the official statements of Premier Eyskens of Belgium who, according to press reports, "admitted Belgium was guilty of failing to bring about an educated class of Congolese before granting them independence. . . . He compared the Congo's post-independence troubles with the smooth transition of French African territories to independence. France, he said, had trained 7,000 university graduates in its African territories. This compared with only a handful of college graduates in the former Belgian Congo" (*21:*13:1–2).

But these statements imply a more serious question: Granting that independence was inevitable, should the Belgians have given independence when they did, or should they have implemented their plan for a five-year evolution beginning in 1959? We enter here, of course, into the never-never land of second-guessing, and while my own opinion is that Belgium could have persevered, their position is that they could not. In any case, it is clear that the pressures upon Belgium were serious, and it is in these various pressures that we must seek an answer as to why Belgium gave independence on June 30, 1960.

One source of unremitting pressure has been the United Nations which, in acting as a world forum and controlling the trust territories in Africa, has given a constant exposure to basically anti-colonial points of view. Vernon McKay has noted that:

> Because a majority of its members are anticolonial in senti-ment, the General Assembly has been able to expand U.N. ac-tivities affecting Africa far beyond what the colonial powers thought they had agreed to when they signed the United Nations Charter. By creating new committees and commissions dealing with African problems, and by giving new tasks to older organs, it has touched upon nearly all the continent's main areas and issues. . . . The existence of the Assembly as a world forum . . . was a continual encouragement to Tunisian, Moroccan, and Algerian nationalists. To a lesser extent, the non-European peo-ples . . . have found encouragement in the moral support of the outside world as expressed in U.N. discussions and resolu-tions. And a wide range of other political, economic, social, and educational problems comes before the Assembly annually. (*92:65*)

In another context, McKay points out that "The U.N. thus has the effect of inciting political agitation," and "The U.N.'s close scrutiny of the behavior of colonial powers . . . has a tendency to restrain their inclinations to restrict nationalist activities" (*92:65*). The fact that the Congo was not a trust territory but an outright colony mitigates these remarks slightly, but in general the United Nations provided for the world discussion and exposure of Congo problems almost as much as it did those of trust territories, and McKay's point that "a majority of its members are anticolonial in sentiment" is extremely apropos. The pressures upon Belgium from the United Nations have in the past caused some rather sharp reactions in which Belgium accused the U.N. of meddling in affairs which did not concern the organization and pointed out that by the United Nations charter Belgium was obliged to provide the U.N. with Congo data of an informational nature only. (See *48; 7.*) The very fact that Belgium's reaction was so strong is an indication of the pressures she felt from the United Nations.

A second pressure on Belgium and her Congo policies came from the United States. McKay, again, has summed up this aspect of the situation in general terms:

> The United States is inescapably committed to a moderate and responsible policy toward Africa . . . Our government brings pressure to bear through diplomatic persuasion; through our votes on African issues in the United Nations, even when we abstain; through the Voice of America and other propaganda media; through our educational exchange program; and through economic and technical assistance to Africa. . . . And thanks to Africa's new air routes, many thousands of Americans . . . have made their way through much of Africa within the past few years.
> The mingled irritation and uneasiness of Europeans at American pressure is well reflected in the attitude of Andre Siegfried who once suggested . . . that the United States, by fomenting colonial revolts, was as dangerous a revolutionary force as the Soviet Union. (*92:80*)

Belgium has not failed to react, sometimes bitterly, to the pressures of the United States on Africa; thus Raymond Scheyven, writing in 1956, commented:

> The American are fiercely anti-colonialist; their attitude is as much explained by the memories they guard of their own war of independence as by the troubles they have in gaining the sympathies of under-developed countries. Is it too much to hope that in the light of recent developments the men of State

in Washington, taking account of reality, will finally understand that in giving a premature autonomy to peoples who are
too young for it, they do more harm than good in putting them
at the mercy of communism? (*102*:109–110)

Even more outspoken was LaBrique who criticized American
policies, actions and official public pronouncements at considerable length. (See *84:43–7, 49–51.*)

American pressures on Belgium, then, were certainly a
force to be reckoned with and many individuals in the Congo
during recent months have spoken bitterly against America's
supposed role, direct or indirect, in forcing Belgium to give
independence to the Congo.

We shall speak of Soviet pressures on the Congo later, but
at this point, we may turn briefly to McKay once again for a
general assessment of the Soviet role:

> In its occasional articles on Soviet intrigues in Africa during
> the past five years, the American press has given the misleading
> impression that Communism has already made substantial prog-
> ress, and that the Soviet Union has skillfully made the most of
> its African opportunities while a neglectful United States has
> lagged far behind. The facts do not support this view. On the
> contrary, they indicate that neither the Soviet Union nor local
> Communists have made much progress in Africa and that So-
> viet policy, after a generation of feeble efforts marked by an
> inept and doctrinaire ideology, is only now shifting into higher
> gear.
>
> As the Cairo conference foreshadows, Soviet pressure on Af-
> rica will certainly mount in the next decade, if only because
> there will be fewer colonial governments to curtail it. How much
> progress it will make is less easy to foretell. Conditions in Africa
> will no doubt produce more individuals who are looking for
> panaceas but . . . international Communism will have several
> competitors for African allegiance. (*92*:74)

Granting that these more or less general pressures were in-
fluential, there were, however, other and more specific reasons
for the Belgian decision to give independence. According to
news reports, the official Belgian explanation was that "the
alternative to the grant of independence would have been

colonial war . . ." (*15*:3:6). We have no means, of course, of judging whether or not this is a reasonable assumption, for Belgium did grant independence and events moved in their specific channels. We can only call attention again to the fact that even the Congolese seemed shocked at the Round Table Conference when the independence date was announced, and that apparently they had not had the slightest idea their demands would be granted so quickly.

It has been charged that at the time of the January 4–7, 1959, riots in Léopoldville, Belgium fell into a state of panic from which it never recovered. We have already had occasion to point out that in the last year before independence Belgium seemed only to respond to challenges posed by the Congolese rather than to lead the way. She almost always seemed to be behind the situation and overwhelmed by events which she could not seem to control rather than in a position in which she could say to the Congolese: "We are leading the way. Follow us in such and such a manner to your independence." Indeed, the government never seemed to have any firm policy toward independence, except one of caution, delay, and indefiniteness, and the point clearly is that if the Congo was unprepared for independence, so was Belgium. Caught up in a series of events which it seemed to regard as inexorable, the Belgian government found itself with no real policy at all. The result was a series of improvisations where a previously formulated policy could probably have brought an interim period of Belgian-Congolese co-operation which would have provided training for the latter and a graceful exit for the former. Whether Belgium "panicked" or not, it was surely unprepared and turned out to be the led rather than the leaders.

It has been said in some circles that Belgium deliberately made a hasty retreat from the Congo in order to precipitate crisis. Thus the *Chicago Daily News*, in an editorial on July 15, wrote: "There are many who believe that the Belgians, by their precipitate action freeing the Congo, intended only to demonstrate its incompetence at self-government, and 'prove' the necessity for returning it to the status of a colony" (*46*:8:2), and added four days later:

> There is some suspicion in Africa, and to a lesser extent elsewhere, that the Belgians welcomed the breakdown of civil authority in the new republic as an excuse to reassert their own control. It has even been said that the hasty grant of independence was made in the certainty that its chief result would be to prove the Congo's incapacity for self-rule. (*6*:14:1)

I do not find it possible to place much credence in this point of view, both on humanitarian and economic grounds. In respect to the former, it can simply be said that the Belgians are not a bloodthirsty group of people. While we may criticize their actions, there is nothing to make us believe that their fundamental aims were of a savage nature. Even more to the point, however, is the enormity of the risk this would have entailed. It has been estimated that 5 per cent of total Belgian capital was invested in the Congo, and to subject this to the calculated risk involved in pushing the Congo to independence only to be able to take it back again seems unthinkable. Much more logical would be the protection of this investment through peaceable relations with the Congo which, in fact, may itself have been a factor in the granting of independence.

Following this line of logic, it seems possible to believe that Belgium was motivated by the desire not only to avoid any direct military suppression of independence movements, but more important, to retain good relations with the Congolese in order to protect Belgian investment in the Congo. It is impossible to estimate the extent of that investment, but Egon Kaskeline has reported that "during the past 50 years of an until now successful colonization, Belgians have been investing between $3,000,000,000 and $4,000,-000,000 in public and private installations in their former colony. They have been drawing an estimated 10 per cent annual profit from their investments of which, however, most was plowed back into the Congo economy" (*82:*1:2–3). Since independence, Belgian losses have been substantial. *U.S. News and World Report* gives the following figures:

> The surplus earned for the Belgian "balance of payments" from dealing with the Congo averaged more than 200 million dollars a year. This included 80 million dollars in the earnings of shipping and insurance companies, and 60 million in dividends and interest. These are substantial sums for a small nation of fewer than 10 million people.
> The 86,000 Belgians who lived in the Congo earned salaries estimated at 229 million dollars a year. At least 35,000 already have returned to Belgium, and the loss of their buying power is beginning to be felt.
> Belgian investors in Congo shares have been hit hard. The country's biggest commercial bank estimated that, at one time, a fifth of its stock and bond portfolio was in Congo securities. But Congo shares also are widely held by small, individual investors. At the peak, these shares represented 42 per cent of the total value of all shares quoted on the Brussels and Antwerp exchanges. That figure is now down to 14 per cent. The value of Congo shares held by Belgian investors has dropped from 2.1 billion dollars at the market peak on Aug. 16, 1955, to 423 million on July 29 of this year. . . .
> The Belgian Treasury stands to lose 60 million dollars of revenue produced by annual taxes on transactions with the Congo. It may have to pay out 60 million in service charges on Congo loans that Belgium has guaranteed. Government subsidies for shipping and airlines may have to be increased for firms whose profits depended on the Congo run. (*23:*40)

In the first two weeks of July Congo shares on the Brussels Stock Exchange dropped 30 to 50 per cent; the Congo franc in free-trading went down to three-fourths of its official value, and many Belgian and foreign banks refused to accept it at all. Belgium not only has had to write off a part of its investment, but is also faced with finding work and shelter for the Belgians who have fled the Congo. Its loss includes not only capital in the Congo but the livelihood of most of the more than 100,000 Belgians who worked in the colony as public officials, technicians, and businessmen. In view of these heavy investment figures, it seems hardly likely that Belgium turned the Congo loose in order to show its lack of ability to govern itself with the chance that Belgium could then return. The risk is simply too high. It seems much more likely that Belgium rushed the Congo to independence partly in order to retain friendly relations with the Congolese and thus protect its investments.

There is certainly something of this philosophy in the Katanga, where the bulk of Belgian investments lies. To what precise extent Tshombe is supported by the Union Minière we shall probably never know, but it is certain that in Tshombe the Belgians found a man responsive to the Belgian point of view, and that through the secession Belgium has profited in being able to retain her economic investments. This may well explain in more than a casual way Belgium's support of Tshombe, Tshombe's reluctance to allow the entrance of United Nations forces, and Belgium's reluctance to pull her troops out of the Katanga.

The overall budget figures for the Congo reveal other economic problems which Belgium faced.

Year	Credits	Debits	Balance
1948	5,223,085,784	4,698,593,879	524,591,905
1949	5,234,610,000	4,541,920,000	692,690,000
1950	5,332,331,283	4,889,154,939	443,176,344
1951	8,012,685,500	6,355,519,500	1,657,166,000
1952	8,235,500,000	7,004,000,000	1,231,500,000
1953	10,354,000,000	7,737,400,000	2,616,600,000
1955	10,730,578,000	9,496,617,000	1,233,617,000
1956	11,901,268,000	11,314,183,000	587,085,000
1957	11,676,565,000	12,260,569,000	−584,004,000

These figures indicate clearly the nature of the economic curve which was beginning to afflict the Congo. While there was substantial profit in the years between 1948 and 1955, gains in 1956 dropped sharply, and in 1957, for the first time, the budget showed a net loss of 584,004,000 francs, or

11,680,080 dollars. In 1958, the deficit stood at over two billion francs or forty million dollars in a budget of eleven billion francs, and in 1959 it was expected to reach three to four billion, or sixty to eighty million dollars. For 1960, the budget was expected to show receipts of about twelve billion francs, and expenditures of about eighteen billion, resulting in a deficit of approximately six billion francs, or about 120 million dollars. It is clear that for the first time in its history the Congo was becoming an unprofitable undertaking.

There is no reason to suppose, however, that the Congo was destined to remain unprofitable. In the history of a country's economic growth, it is quite likely that plateaus will appear which indicate not that the ultimate development has been attained but rather that a point has been reached at which an infusion of capital is necessary before further growth can be expected. The Congo seems to have been at such a point in its economic history. Its unbalanced budgets were due in part also to world economic conditions which resulted either in more difficulty in obtaining markets for certain Congo products or in lowered prices; thus the price of cobalt, for example, slipped from a peak of $2.60 a pound in 1953 to the current level of about $1.50 a pound. The Katanga, which in 1959 turned out 18,587,000 pounds of cobalt, about 55 per cent of the total world supply, sold most of its production to the United States. But in 1959, total U.S. imports of cobalt amounted to 21,256,000 pounds of which but roughly 9,900,000 pounds were used in industry, while the remainder was stockpiled. Stockpiling cannot continue forever, and if the United States was using less than 50 per cent of its cobalt, it seems reasonable to believe that its imports would probably decrease, with a resultant cut in exports of the mineral from the Katanga.

Thus the Congo found itself at a point at which a number of its products were affected by slumping world prices and consumption, and at which further infusions of capital were necessary if its economy were to continue to expand.

The internal costs of running the Congo were increasing rapidly as well; where in 1948 debits ran to roughly four and a half billion francs, in 1957 they had risen to over twelve billion, and the forecast was clearly for a continued rise. Thus, to cite a relatively small example, while the cost of constructing a mud-and-thatch primary school in the bush and subsidizing missionaries to staff it is relatively small, education had reached a point at which hundreds of secondary schools were becoming a necessity. Economically, a secondary school is a far different proposition from a primary school, and this is to say nothing of the increasing cost of the University at Elisabethville. To take another example, the cost of the Inga Rapids Project which would have dammed the Congo River to produce hydroelectric power was estimated in excess of three billion dollars. While the returns in power for aluminum, ammonia, wood pulp and paper, cement, metal refining, and other industries would eventually have made the project financially rewarding, its initial cost was tremendous.

The argument here, then, is that faced with an unbalanced budget, falling markets, and rising internal costs, Belgium was perhaps not so anxious to hold on to the Congo as it had been in the past. This seems to be borne out by various statements made in Belgium after independence: thus, *Le Soir*, Brussels' leading newspaper, wrote on July 12: "We should remember that holding the Congo is to become an increasingly expensive business in the future and—from the purely financial viewpoint—we should actually be happy to extricate ourselves from a highly non-profitable enterprise" (*82*:1:4). While this attitude, in part at least, can be attributed to bitterness over the turn of events, and while it is clear that the country looked forward to continuing its private investments in the Congo, it is still true that Belgian enthusiasm toward holding its colony had waned.

A number of reasons have been advanced to account for Belgium's abrupt granting of independence to the Congo: pressures from world anticolonial powers, notably the United Nations and the United States; Belgium's own explanation that to fail to grant independence would have meant colonial war; Belgian panic arising from the rapidity of events and particularly the Léopoldville riots; Belgian desire to protect investments; the necessity of pumping financial investment into the Congo at a rising rate; unbalanced Congo budgets; and the charge that Belgium deliberately abandoned the Congo in order to be able to return after the Congolese had demonstrated their inability to govern themselves. With the exception of the last possibility, which I do not regard as valid, all these reasons seem possible, and while we cannot single out any one of them as a dominating motive, in looking at them together we can perhaps understand better the extent of the pressures, legitimate or selfish, which were brought to bear upon the Belgian government.

Given the fact of independence, we must next ask why the Congo fell into a state of anarchy with almost incredible rapidity. Most often overlooked in discussions of this question is the fact that the Congo was already in difficulty before independence. As Belgium's effective control diminished there was no firm Congolese control to replace it. Let us return for a moment to the area of the eastern Kasaï in which I spent the year 1959–60. The local Belgian administrative center was located twenty-five miles from the village of Lupupa; the single agent was responsible for a rather large area in the Sentery Territory. In January of 1960 he was transferred to another post where his talents could be more effectively utilized, and his replacement was a young man who was taking his first Congo post; he was broken into the job by an experienced officer who stayed with him for approximately six weeks. Within two months after he had taken over the position and was the sole authority in the area, he too was transferred, but he was never replaced. Thus after the month of April, the area was without Belgian administration except for that which could be supplied by the agents in Sentery, some fifty miles away. The Congolese in the Secteur did their best to carry on, but their experience was minimal; the result was an almost immediate outbreak of robberies and a realization on the part of the people that effective administration had ended.

In the District headquarters 160 miles away, one Congolese was being trained to take over on June 30; his experience in the training program had lasted only five months. We have already had occasion to discuss what effect independence had upon the village of Lupupa: the people feared an outbreak of war and responded by organizing themselves into bigger, and thus stronger, groups. More important, independence furthered a developing split between the young and old men. In Lupupa independence had the effect not of strengthening the village and its organization, but on the contrary of weakening local government and local human relations.

There is considerable reason to believe that virtual anarchy reigned in the Lower Congo region from the beginning of 1960. It will be recalled that the ABAKO party had long espoused an Independent Republic of Central Kongo, and that an ABAKO representative had written on December 20, 1959: "Don't forget that as of the evening of December 31, 1959, there will no longer be any authority over us, even colonial authority. We will fall into anarchy again, but this time under the direction of our political organization, the ABAKO." It was widely reported in the Congo that from December 31 Belgian administrators in the Lower Congo sat alone in their offices as the people went to the local political offices of the ABAKO to receive their instructions. Belgium no longer had control of the area.

To a considerable extent then, the Congo was in a state of anarchy before independence, and where it was not, local government had broken down. Lupupa was without strong traditional control; Tshofa was without an administrator; Kabinda was preparing but weakly for the Congolese accession to power; the Lower Congo was without effective Belgian control. And this weakening of power did not, of course, go unnoticed by the Congolese. The stage was set long before collapse set in.

A second factor in the situation was the rapid departure of a substantial part of the Belgian population; beginning in May, the exodus assumed extensive proportions. It is true that for the most part the departures were of women and children, but toward the end men also were leaving. The Belgians, many in a state of near panic even before independence, could hardly help but communicate their own insecurities to the Congolese. But as the Belgians left, more and more posts of responsibility were left unfilled, and it was precisely in such posts that the Congolese had had little or no training. Ray Vicker reports that:

> Of the 1,400 civil servants in the top three grades of government service, only three men were Africans, the rest Belgians; in the fourth grade of 5,800 civil servants, only 635 were Africans. About the highest jobs held by Africans were those on a par with postal clerks, meter inspectors and foremen of typing pools.
>
> White men were behind the power plants serving electricity to Léopoldville and other cities, the railroads and riverboat lines linking communities, the wholesaling firms supplying food, the banks handling financial transactions, and the mining firms supplying much of the industry to the country. (*109*:14:1)

As these civil servants and businessmen began to leave the Congo there was no one to fill their posts. Once the post-independence troubles began and the really serious exodus took place, the departure of this key personnel contributed even more dramatically to the collapse of the country.

It has been pointed out by some observers that in traditional Congolese terms the departure of Belgian women and children was interpreted as preparation for war. In some, at least, of the Congolese cultures, any preparation for war involved establishing the safety of women and children. This attitude was unquestionably held in some areas where it doubtlessly contributed to the general state of tension.

Still another factor which contributed to the rapid collapse of the Congo is to be found in the expectations for independence held by the Congolese. It has been charged that various politicians made the most extravagant promises to the electorate, but in the eastern Kasaï, at least, there simply grew up almost out of nowhere a set of generalizations about the meaning of independence to the individual. This represented a pathetic response to the situation in which the people found themselves; without any real understanding of what independence would be, often without the vaguest notion of what the word itself meant, and yet faced with the fact that it would arrive on June 30, 1960, some sort of image had to be created. What emerged was a concept of independence related almost strictly to the individual: independence would mean no taxes, an increase in salary, the ownership of an automobile, and the ownership of a house like those occupied by the Belgians. Furthermore, these miracles would happen overnight.

The effect of this naïve concept was felt almost immediately after independence arrived. The first major outbreak of rioting occurred in Coquilhatville where workers struck specifically for higher wages, but also because their dreams of what independence would mean had not been fulfilled. Subsequent outbreaks followed precisely the same pattern: neither automobiles nor houses appeared and there were no wage increases. Expectations had risen far too high to be fulfilled.

The final factor in the almost immediate disintegration of the Congo after independence was the defection of the Congolese army, the Force Publique: its mutiny was the decisive blow to the country, for both Belgians and Congolese alike had counted upon it as the force which would guarantee order. The Force Publique was created by a decree of October 30, 1885, and its duties, fixed by a decree of May 10, 1919, were ". . . to assure the occupation and the defense of the Colony, to maintain tranquility and public order, to prevent insurrection, to overlook and assure the execution of laws, decrees, ordinances and rules, especially those which are relative to the police and the general security" (*44:4*). The Force Publique was divided by its functions into two parts; each province was assigned a battalion which was used locally almost as police, while artillery, infantry, and commando units formed the core of the army. It was further organized into four major divisions, one at Luluabourg for the Kasaï and Katanga, one at Léopoldville for the Léopoldville and Equator provinces, one at Stanleyville for the Eastern and Kivu provinces, and one, a reserve unit, at Thysville in the Lower Congo. In 1960 the Force Publique numbered 25,-000 men with 1,100 Europeans, primarily Belgians, forming the officer cadre; there were no Congolese officers.

The evidence we have at our disposal indicates that the Force Publique mutinied for the same general reasons noted above, applied, of course, to their own specific situation. Independence Day did not bring the Force higher pay and promotions; it did not see the dismissal of the Belgian officers.

Lumumba himself explained the defection of the Force Publique in the following terms:

> It all started when General Janssens, the Belgian commander of the Force Publique . . . refused to promote Congolese to the grade of officers.
> Even after the entire world recognized our independence, General Janssens refused the Africanization of the army units. This led to the first disturbances and riots.
> Even then, everything could have been settled in calm and

moderation if it were not for the fact that the Belgian officers began making intemperate and provocative statements, insulting the army, our soldiers and young officers.

When I announced our government's decision to dismiss these Belgian officers and to dismiss General Janssens, the Belgian troops began their illegal armed intervention . . . first in the Katanga, then in the port of Matadi which they occupied, Léopoldville and soon throughout the country. The rest you know. (*90*:2:5).

Discounting the questionable remarks in this statement by Lumumba, we still obtain a clear Congolese view of the situation; the Force Publique mutinied because their expectations of promotion and immediate control of the army were not fulfilled.

Even more indicative are some of the statements made by members of the Force Publique *before* independence, statements which indicate not only a general uneasiness but a certain hostility toward Lumumba himself. Thus in *Emancipation* for April 9, 1960, there appeared a letter addressed to the Governor General and the Executive College and signed by "soldiers of the Force Publique":

> There is no human contact between us and our officers, but rather only conditions of dominance and submission which transform us into true slaves. We are considered to belong to an inferior race. There is complete lack of action concerning the Africanization of the army. All the high grades are in the hands of the whites while in actuality there are Congolese in the Force Publique who are capable of assuming the functions of officers and non-commissioned officers. Today the unanimous desire of the Congolese soldiers is to occupy posts of command, to gain a decent salary, to put an end to all traces of discrimination in the Force Publique. We declare publicly and without equivocation that if, before next June 30, you do not provide for an increase in our standard of living and for a massive naming of Negro officers, the independence of June 30 will be crippled . . .

Again, in *Emancipation* for March 19, 1960, a letter signed "African members of the Force Publique" spoke strongly against Lumumba:

From the journal *Courrier d'Afrique* of March 4, 5 and 6, we have learned of the various declarations of M. Patrice Lumumba. . . . In spite of the fact that the Congo will be independent, Minister Lumumba says that we don't have to think that "a second class soldier can become General of the Army." Ah, how shameful to say such things publicly. M. Lumumba judges us incapable of taking our places as officers of the Force Publique . . .
. . . M. Lumumba was never in the Force Publique and will never be in it, and so how can he judge that there is no one in it capable of replacing the officers? . . . Dear Lumumba, beloved brother of the Whites, . . . do not forget that the Government is the Government thanks to the army. The hour of pushing us around like lambs is passed, and since you continue to repel us . . . we guarantee you the ruination of your powers and of your Congo so long as you insult us as ignorant people who are incapable of taking the places of your white brothers. (*44:7–9*)

The collapse of the Congo after independence, then, can be ascribed to the weakening of authority and the departure of the Belgians before independence, the unrealistic expectations of what independence would mean to the Congolese, and the collapse of the Force Publique—the latter, in turn, devolving upon the first three factors. Once the situation had definitely turned into chaos, the continued exodus of the Belgians simply added fuel to the fire; the Belgians were clearly on the run, more and more posts of responsibility were abandoned and could not be filled by the Congolese, businesses were closed and the ranks of the unemployed swelled enormously, and the government leaders were unable to control the situation because they had no forces at their disposal to do so. If the initial collapse can be explained by the points suggested here, it is equally clear that the situation was self-fueling; it gathered momentum, force, and size with the simple function of time, and each new outburst contributed to the general chaos and the increasingly rapid disintegration. The key to the situation, however, seems to have been the Force Publique; had it stood firm, there is a chance at least that most of the chaos would have been avoided. What no one took into consideration was that the members of the Force

Publique were afflicted by the same problems as the rest of the Congo citizenry; their expectations, equally high, were just as equally dashed on Independence Day.

We must turn now to the erratic course Mr. Lumumba pursued after taking over the government of the Congo and search for explanations which will give us some clue as to his behavior. At first glance, he almost seems a madman in his begging for United Nations assistance and then ordering U.N. troops to leave, shouting absurd charges of assassination plots against his person, engaging in wild hunts for Belgian spies hidden among the U.N. personnel, raving against U.N. interference and then blandly announcing his complete confidence in its operations, and literally scores of other contradictions, assertions, and counter-assertions, shouts of rage, and protestations of peaceable intent. We note also his inability to control the situation with which he was faced, and more important, his retreat from facing it. As Smith Hempstone has noted, "Leaving the country civil-war torn, he embarked on a junket to Britain, North Africa, the United States and Canada. While Congolese died, he inspected Cadillacs in Washington and associated with a red-haired Belgian girl" (77:23:1).

We shall probably never know all the reasons for Lumumba's erratic behavior, but there are at least some clues which can aid us in our understanding. First, we must never lose sight of the fact of Lumumba's fragile tenure of office: actually controlling approximately a fourth of the Chamber of Deputies and having support of well under half the electorate, his position as leader of the government was always insecure, and in order to sustain it at all dramatic action was needed. This Lumumba was highly capable of providing, for he is, and has been throughout his career a rabble rouser, capable of moving his listeners to high emotional states in which he participated fully himself. He is a highly excitable person who makes snap judgments and acts upon them quickly and without deliberation as to their possible consequences.

Lumumba, too, is probably a racist, perhaps by inclination, perhaps because nearly every African leader is thrust into this role. Smith Hempstone has remarked on this with extreme cogency:

> His were grievances, some real, some imagined, of every African caught in the limbo between his . . . people, for whom his slight education and tarnished urbanity had deprived him of sympathy, and white society, which would not and could not accept him on terms of equality. . . . Hence, when Lumumba's hard won but thin veneer of culture failed to open the gate to success, power and acclaim, he found the cause of failure not in himself but in the white man's duplicity.
>
> It is this sense of frustration that has made him the elusive and dangerous person he is today. (77:1:1)

From this sense of being a marginal man, caught between two cultures and unable to belong to either, much of Lumumba's sense of insecurity has undoubtedly developed. His constant charges of spies and assassination attempts, as well as his more general theme of the supposed injustices done to him, are evidence of this insecurity. In his thinking these injustices are clearly the fault of the white man for it was the Belgians who jailed him for embezzlement, and it was the Belgians who jailed him for inciting to riot. As Hempstone has suggested, it is not his own inadequacies which are apparent to him, but rather the injustices perpetrated by the white man. In this respect, Lumumba came to regard himself as a martyr, and he played this role to the hilt: he made a considerable production for example, of the marks of manacles on his wrists when he arrived in Brussels for the Round Table Conference straight from prison where he had been held for inciting to riot. His supposed martyrdom probably gave him greater faith in his own public image than he deserved to have, but martyrdom was not a foolish role for Lumumba to play; it provided the drama which the situation required.

288

It is clear, too, that Lumumba visualized himself as a new leader for all of Africa, for he felt the Congo was destined to take its place at the head of the African nations if only because of its size and potential wealth. Personal power was certainly one of his primary goals, not only in reference to his leadership of the Congo, but to all of Africa as well.

Lumumba, too, was genuinely enraged over the failure of Belgium to withdraw its troops once the United Nations operation had begun. While we must look for the sources of this anger in his own personality, this makes his display of rage none the less real. A perusal of his statements through the first weeks of independence show clearly that the Belgian withdrawal became an obsession with Lumumba, and that he felt he could not rest until the troops had left Congolese soil.

Finally, we must look for the reasons for Lumumba's behavior in his own ignorance and lack of experience. He was clearly a man who had little knowledge of what he was doing, of what was expected of him, of how his actions affected the world, and of what constituted a Western government and how it should be run. We see these things clearly in his first major speech made before the world when, speaking before the King of Belgium on Independence Day, he chose to insult Belgium and what it had done in the Congo. ". . . no Congolese worthy of the name will ever forget that independence has been won by struggle, an everyday struggle, an intense and idealistic struggle, a struggle in which we have spared neither our forces, our privations, our suffering, nor our blood. . . . Our lot was eighty years of colonial rule; our wounds are still too fresh and painful to drive them from our memory. . . . We have known ironies, insults, blows . . . We have known that our lands were despoiled in the name of supposedly legal texts which recognized only the law of the stronger . . ."* And so it continued. Lumumba did not re-

* See Appendix IV.

289

alize, I am convinced, that he was for the first time truly speaking before the world, nor did he realize the extent of his gaff until it was explained to him by others and until the King threatened to leave the Congo immediately. That Lumumba finally came to understand is apparent in the graceful little speech which he gave, later on the same day, in the presence of the King: he thanked Belgium for what it had done for the Congo and for granting independence to the Congolese people.

But in short, a grade-schooler had been thrown upon the world and had been expected to act like a mature world statesman. It is no wonder that his course seems erratic, for he had no experience to guide him, and mistakes were inevitable; once made, what could he do but change his tack and attempt to rectify the error? Playing the game strictly by ear and strongly impelled by personal vanity and snap judgments, he tried everything. And attention must be called again here to the obsession with simple solutions to problems which seemed to characterize not only Lumumba's behavior, but that of almost all the Congolese. We have only to recall M who was genuinely convinced that Independence itself would bring the cessation of all inter-tribal conflicts in the Congo, or Lumumba's saying on July 21, "We are sure that if the simple problem of removing Belgian troops can be resolved, the whole problem will be solved." This obsessive idea that there exists a single key which will unlock the solution to every problem surely drove Lumumba into many corners and made his behavior appear especially erratic to the outside world.

Let it be clear that Lumumba, if erratic, is not a stupid man; witness the speed with which he came to understand at least the superficialities of the East-West struggle and to play one side against the other. And some of his behavior is made clearer if we consider the fact that many Africans genuinely wish to remain uncommitted in the East-West struggle for world dominance. The result of his semi-aggressive neutralist stand, coupled with his rudimentary knowledge of world political ideologies was that Lumumba was genuinely prepared to take assistance from any source which proffered it without realizing the consequences. Although we saw him moving into the Russian camp, his move was not necessarily because of a love for communism; probably, it was that in taking proffered Russian unilateral assistance, he saw a way to extricate himself from his difficulties.

No one can understand completely the actions of another, but in searching for clues to Lumumba's behavior we can at least make some progress when we consider his fragile tenure of office, his own volatile personality coupled with a high sense of drama, his habit of making snap judgments and acting on them immediately, his racism, his status as a marginal man, his self-visualization as the emerging leader of all Negro Africa, his own concept of his martyrdom, his genuine discomfiture at the continued presence of Belgian forces, his lack of preparation for the office he held, and his willingness as a neutral to accept aid wherever he could get it.

Quite probably no question created by the Congo situation has been more thoroughly discussed than the United Nations operation which developed some unique features. The first United Nations force was established in the Middle East in the 1956 Suez Canal Crisis to separate the invading British-French-Israeli forces from the Egyptians. This force is still in existence, and there is no indication as to when the United Nations will be able to liquidate it. The U.N. also intervened in Korea to repel the North Korean attack on South Korea, but this was a combat action directed by the United States acting for the United Nations, rather than a peace mission. The U.N. has also sent out a number of peace teams to troubled spots, including Lebanon in 1958.

The Congo mission differs, however, from all previous United Nations efforts in that an international military force intervened to establish law and order within an independent country. If the long run operation is successful, this would seem to set a precedent of considerable proportions and to augur the emergence of a new world role for the United Nations. In effect, the U.N. is acting as army and police force for the Congo, and the question raised is whether the United Nations is actually being gradually built into a superstate which has power over the internal affairs of sovereign nations. While the Security Council resolutions attempted to define the U.N. role clearly, stating that its forces would not "be a party to, or in any way intervene in or be used to influence the outcome of any internal conflict, constitutional or otherwise," it could hardly fail in its role as army and police force to affect the outcome of certain developments. Thus the question remains whether by creating an international army and giving the Secretary-General authority to command it in order to try to run a country which is clearly sovereign, the United Nations role in world affairs has not been considerably expanded. There have been those who have argued that if the U.N. can take such a role, why not do so in cases such as those of Hungary or other captive states?

The answer to these questions seems to lie in the fact that the Congo situation is unique and that the creation of this apparatus can only take place when the two great powers in the United Nations—the United States and Russia—are agreed that the job should be done. Already the two great powers have fallen out in respect to the U.N. role, and the Congo has become another center in the cold war struggle despite the efforts of the U.N. to keep it off the international scene. Thus there is a question as to whether the U.N. operation can continue successfully in the Congo and whether any such intervention as undertaken here can ever be undertaken again.

The United Nations operation in the Congo has weathered one serious crises after another. The first was with Lumumba who continually changed his mind about the U.N. actions and whose criticism forced a reconsideration of position. The second crisis came when the U.N. decided that the Katanga must be entered if the overall operation were to be successful, and the third when the U.N. forced Belgium to withdraw her troops in spite of her obvious reluctance. The fourth crisis, on which we shall elaborate later, has been with Russia and its clearly unilateral action and intentions in the Congo. Thus far the U.N. has triumphed in every crisis; the problem is whether it can continue to do so, for it is clear that without U.N. assistance the Congo cannot at present control itself.

If the philosophical problems concerning the role and function of the United Nations are grave, its practical problems in the Congo itself are perhaps even more complex, for its job encompasses the support not only of law and order but of technical and economic assistance as well. This has meant replacing Belgian technicians as well as restoring facilities and operations which in many cases were partly or wholly destroyed in the first days of independence. It has been reported that in Léopoldville at the end of August, there were 2,500 Belgians left out of 18,000; 300 of 5,000 at Stanleyville; 200 of 6,000 at Luluabourg; 10 of 1,800 at Matadi. Of 333 Belgian technicians who ran telecommunications, an estimated 130 remained; of 800 doctors, almost all departed; of 700 in a transportation firm, only 70 remained; in the Ministry of Finance there were only 3 of 140 Belgians shortly after independence.

The London *Times* on August 31 reported in some detail on aspects of the U.N. operation which are not generally known. In regard to the restoration of port facilities in Matadi, the *Times* reports:

> When General Wheeler arrived in Matadi with a Moroccan assistant in mid-July the town had been thoroughly looted by Congolese, the docks were crammed with broken or abandoned merchandise, including 300 motor cars, and the river channel was already silting up. Within two days General Wheeler had two of the four available dredgers working again with make-

shift Congolese crews, while the docks were cleared and railway trucks moved by hand. A Scandinavian team was flown in to supervise the dredging, an agent for a West African shipping firm was hired to reorganize shipping procedures and warehouse specialists were engaged from overseas to run the docks. Only five river pilots were available, but by flying them back and forth in helicopters after every trip, General Wheeler enabled them to do twice their usual work. As a result, by last week the river channel throughout the eight-hour boat trip from the mouth of the Matadi had been restored to a minimum depth of 29 feet— against its former depth of 30 feet—and already 60 ships have docked at Matadi since the port was reopened. (55:9)

In other spheres of activity, the *Times* report is equally impressive:

> Already the United Nations civilian staff in the Congo, excluding medical personnel, numbers about 350 persons from 43 different countries. Most of these are under the control of Dr. Sture Linner, a Swedish professor designated by Mr. Hammarskjold as chief of the United Nations civilian operations in the Congo. All the specialist agencies of the U.N. are represented, including Unesco and the World Health Organization which is acting at the request of the Congolese Government as the coordinating body for all medical assistance. Over 150 doctors and nurses from 18 different countries have arrived, some through the International Red Cross, and some through bilateral arrangements such as the teams from Ghana, Israel, Tunisia, and Russia. . . .
>
> For the long-term programme of training and administrative advice, Dr. Linner has organized an 11-man "shadow cabinet" of experts in finance (himself), agriculture, communications, education, health, foreign trade, labour, national security, the magistrature, natural resources and industry and public administration. Each of these men works in close consultation with the appropriate ministries, advising on and even proposing policy. This obviously demands the utmost tact to forestall the allegation that the U.N. is running the country. In fact, of course, it is; for in spite of some natural ability, there is no Congolese minister with more than hazy idea of what his job entails, let alone how to do it. (55:9)

The United Nations action in the Congo has been a remarkable operation; without it, it is almost certain that the Congo would have fallen even deeper into difficulty than it did, and there is more than an outside chance that it would have become the scene of a shooting war as Russia made her intentions more and more obvious. We can only note that the Congo operation has been the most responsible and, in some ways, the most successful United Nations operation ever undertaken.

In some quarters there has been severe criticism of United States participation in the U.N. Congo operation and, indeed, in United States concern over African nations and Africa as a whole. This point of view has perhaps been best expressed by editorial remarks in the *Wall Street Journal.*

> Time was when insignificant little nations or areas of the world could have their little upheavals or local border raids and no one else had to pay attention, much less do anything about it. Now, in our brave new world of international togetherness, all that is of course changed.
>
> So it is that in recent days the U.S. has come perilously close to military intervention in—of all places—the Congo. That danger is not necessarily over, but if not the Congo it could be some other place equally remote from American shores and American national interest. . . .
>
> Is it wise for the U.S. to let itself be maneuvered by any or every pipsqueak "nation" into a war situation? Is it wise to permit the Soviet Union, whether bluffing or not, to maneuver the U.S. into war situations in places of no intrinsic importance to this country?

After pointing out that we did not intervene in either Hungary or Tibet, and that the loss of the Congo to Russia might not be of any importance, the editorial continued to discuss the importance of the relative areas of the world:

> To put it another way, is the Congo equal in our scale of values to Western Europe, which we will indeed defend if necessary? Or to Cuba, where we have in our front yard a case of attempted Communist colonialism? It would seem self-evident that Cuba, with all its implications for the Western Hemisphere, is considerably more important than the Congo.
>
> Firmness in dealing with the Communists is one thing, and something this Administration can be proud of. But we must preserve our perspective, we must have priorities, and we must

always reserve our own freedom of action regardless of the Soviets or the U.N.

Otherwise, the way things are going, we may one day find ourselves fighting the wrong war on behalf of the wrong people—and for no sensible purpose of our own. (*54:12*)

This point of view is both serious and dangerous, for it is based upon concepts of the relationship of the United States to the rest of the world which, to put it mildly, are outdated and Neanderthal. We can hardly call the Congo and, by extension, the struggle for the emergence of Africa onto the world scene, "an insignificant little nation or area." Moreover, the Congo must be equal "in our scale of values to Western Europe" and to Cuba, if not in long-developed friendship, respect, historical relationship, and even love, at least in terms of a hardheaded appraisal of the world today. And finally, priorities of the sort this view suggests are probably no longer possible, given the totality of the East-West struggle in which we are engaged. As for our lack of intervention in Hungary and Tibet, let us hope we can say we have learned from our failures in those cases. In any case the Congo and Hungarian or Tibetan situation do not seem comparable, for on the one hand we were faced with a *fait accompli* and our interference would unquestionably have meant war, while on the other, we stepped in through the agency of the United Nations in the hope of avoiding the creation of a situation such as that in Hungary which could lead to war. The point is that without U.N. action which the United States supported, the Congo could easily have become another Hungary or Tibet and demanded much more agonizing decisions on the part of the United States than those it has been forced to make thus far.

The importance of the Congo can hardly be questioned. It is potentially one of the wealthiest nations in Africa in its position as the world's primary producer of industrial diamonds, its previous supply of 60 per cent of the free world's pitchblende, of 55–75 per cent of the free world's cobalt, and so forth. Looked at in the cold hard light of world economics, the Congo is of basic importance. But in even colder appraisal, it seems clear that central Africa, of which the Congo is a part, is of primary military importance, for control of this portion of the continent undoubtedly means control of all Africa south of the Sahara.

Even more, Africa as a whole is emerging rapidly onto the world scene. The Afro-Asian bloc, if it holds together, is destined to play a greater and greater part in world politics and in the U.N. to which, at the moment, the African countries, at least, are firmly wedded. By virtue of its size, its central location in Africa, and its mineral wealth, the Congo will surely come to hold an extremely important position in African affairs. It is quite possible that as the Congo goes, so will go much of Africa.

Finally, our own American ideals of freedom and individual liberty demand that wherever possible in the world the United States lend its authority, prestige, and assistance to whatever nation seeks to realize these same goals and achievements. If we do not always do these things as well as we might, at least our goals must remain clear: we seek for other nations what we feel are universal values in human life, namely, independent strength in liberty and freedom, and our obligation to the world as a free and wealthy country is clear.

As a result of the Congo situation, United States policy toward the emerging African nations has already undergone some changes. Arnold Beichman, writing in the *Christian Science Monitor,* noted this change explicitly:

> Because of its Atlantic-Pact agreements and diplomatic ties, the United States Government has been cooperating with colonial powers such as Britain and France in the evolution of its political and economic policies toward liberated colonies and their freedom.

This has been true in Tunisia, Morocco, and Guinea, former French dependencies where, in a sense, Washington accepted the French line. In British East and Central Africa, the United States has been extraordinarily careful not to offend British or local government sensibilities.

Here in the Congo . . . this policy seems to be reversed. The United States intends—so it appears—to bypass as much as possible the Belgian Government to deal directly with the Congolese Government—whenever it becomes a real government—on economic, fiscal, and technical aid programs, or to funnel such aid through the United Nations or other international agencies. (59:1:5)

It is clear that the United States is slowly maturing in its assessment of the importance of Africa in the world scene and that its policies will be more firmly and pointedly directed in the future.

The initial African reaction to the Congo situation was one of humiliation at the country's collapse, for it was felt that this reflected generally upon the ability of Africans to rule themselves. Both privately and publicly African leaders expressed their chagrin at Lumumba's erratic behavior. This feeling later tended to be submerged as criticism of Belgium's policy in the Congo both before and after independence came to the fore. Most recently, African nations have taken the position, especially in the United Nations where they were drawn together as never before, that the affair should be handled strictly by Africans through the U.N., and it is partly as a result of their opinions that the bulk of the U.N. force was drawn from African nations.

Individually, some countries have been forced to take a closer look at their own relations with colonial countries. Thus the premier of Northern Nigeria stated in Chicago that he was sure Nigeria would not come to independence in a situation parallel to that of the Congo: "We are prepared for self-government—the Congolese were not." Speaking of Belgium's responsibility in the situation, he added "That is the lesson that all Africa should learn from this—and all other peoples, too" (*29:15:2*).

Other countries, and particularly their leaders, saw in the Congo situation a chance for personal gain, and probably the outstanding example in this case was Ghana's Kwame Nkrumah who, in the course of various activities, offered to send troops unilaterally and to send technicians to replace Belgians, kept in close contact with Lumumba, spoke bitterly against Belgium when that country was slow in removing its troops, threatened to pull out of the U.N. force in connection with the Katanga crisis, and urged the United Nations to support the rule of Premier Lumumba. These multiple activities were probably undertaken in order to strengthen Nkrumah's hoped-for position as spokesman for Africa and his dream of the formation of a United States of Africa. That the activities have been primarily political is no insult to Nkrumah; they have represented a point of view and presumably, an honest one.

Finally, the Union of South Africa immediately took the occasion to vindicate its position by pointing out that it was clear from the Congo experience that Africans could not govern themselves. The Union also made a strong bid for permanent settlement of Belgian refugees in South Africa, offering financial assistance and a grant of fourteen thousand dollars for the relief of refugees who fled to South Africa; this was a part of the Union's long-range plan to increase white settlement in the hope of offsetting the dominance of the African numerical majority.

In general, then, the Congo crisis has drawn the African nations together as never before; for the most part, it has also reaffirmed and strengthened their faith in the United Nations, and has showed the growing strength of their voice in U.N. affairs. Finally, crisis has also caused African nations to view from a new perspective the role of Western colonial powers in their past African history, and has given them a good deal of firsthand experience with international communism.

While communist intentions toward Africa have long been a matter of record (*94*), the Congo situation has provided some of the most direct openings in the history of the East-West struggle. Communist ideology toward Africa until 1955 followed a line which, according to McKay, "made it too obvious that African nationalist leaders would be liquidated when the Communists were through using them as stepping stones to power."

> One of the leading Soviet authorities on Africa, I. I. Potekhin, in an article on "The Stalinist Theory of Colonial Revolution and the National Liberation Movement in Tropical and South Africa," published in the journal *Soviet Ethnography* in 1950, wrote that "the bourgeoisie supports the revolutionary movement of the masses . . . only with a view to taking advantage of the fruits of the revolution and seizing political power for the suppression and enslavement of the masses . . ." Potekhin branded Gold Coast Paramount Chief Ofori Atta and the Bamangwato chief, Seretse Khama, as "feudal or semi-feudal lords," and said that the Nigerian nationalist leader, Nnamdi Azikiwe followed "the ideology and policy of petty bourgeoise national reformism," a "colonial edition of the reactionary American philosophy of pragmatism" (evidently a reference to Azikiwe's American education). When Prime Minister Kwame Nkrumah began to turn a cold shoulder to Communist influences in the Gold Coast, his administration was attacked for representing "the interests of the reactionary section of the bourgeoisie and not the workers." (*92:77–8*)

In 1955, however, Russian tactics changed, and Potekhin and other specialists began praising the African leaders they had previously attacked. This change in policy has continued to the present and, at the time of its inception apparently heralded a new drive toward control of Africa by communism. Russian study and research concerning African nations has increased sharply, and in April, 1956, the Oriental Institute in Moscow shifted its emphasis to Southeast Asia and Africa.

300

In September of the same year a separate section of the Oriental Institute was created for Africa, and within the section emphasis was placed upon the study of African languages, particularly Amharic, Hausa, Swahili, and Zulu. In 1957 Potekhin made a short research trip to Ghana, and shortly thereafter there was made public a five-year research plan, including a number of new studies on the theme of "the role and significance of Africa in the colonial system of imperialism." At the 1957 Cairo conference, a twenty-seven-man Soviet delegation was present and, apparently under its general influence, the conference adopted a number of resolutions which were anti-Western in tone. Since 1957, the communist countries have continued their African efforts on an ever-increasing basis, with the most notable success occurring in relation to Guinea.

It is not surprising, then, that communism intruded itself into the Congo crisis but, like so many other questions, that of communist influence in the Congo is not a simple one. Was the Congo situation a communist plot? Is Lumumba a communist? The problem lies in what we mean by these questions. In speaking of communism and Lumumba is our concern to know whether Lumumba himself is actually an ideological, card-carrying communist, or do we wish to know whether he has succumbed to the communist influence? In considering whether the crisis was a communist plot, do we wonder whether the revolt of the Force Publique was engineered by a well-placed communist cadre or whether communism has exploited a situation already developed? In some ways it does not matter in what precise terms our questions are phrased, for what we seek to know is the extent of the communist influence however achieved. The problem is raised, however, because in answering the general question we must take account of a number of specific situations and considerations.

In assessing the communist influence and moves in the

Congo, it is necessary to separate the pre- and post-independence periods. In the former the Congo presented practically the perfect opportunity for exploitation by communism. Tribal organization, general ignorance, fission movements, lack of a strong central government and of experience— all contributed to an extremely volatile situation. This was further enhanced by the Congo's lack of understanding of the world situation in terms of political ideology oriented toward world realities. Indeed, given the general conditions in the Congo, we can only wonder that the communist world has thus far been unable to make significant gains, for the situation was tailored to their requirements.

In the period preceding independence many rumors concerning communist manipulations circulated among the white residents of the Congo. Thus it was widely said that Lumumba had received 10 million francs or 200 thousand dollars from the Belgian Communist Party; it was further suggested that since it was a "known fact" that the Belgian communist party did not have such funds available the money must have come from the Soviet bloc. Another rumor had it that Lumumba's entourage contained seven English-speaking assistants, six of whom were being trained in the pre-independence period in communist nations; it was often suggested that these men were being prepared to replace Lumumba when his own usefulness to communism had ended. It was also said that large-scale Russian offers of scholarships had been made and accepted, and that some three hundred Congolese were already studying in Iron Curtain countries.

If these were only unsubstantiated rumors, some activities were clear. The Czechoslovakian consul in Léopoldville was deeply engaged in politics in that city, and he took every opportunity to influence groups of Congolese. In Elisabethville I spoke to the head of a large commercial concern who related the story of one of his clerks who, from dubious sources, received funds to travel to Belgium; within three

302

days after the clerk's arrival in Brussels, he was embarked on another plane and found himself in Peking where he spent approximately two weeks as a guest of the government. Radio Peking, while I was in the Congo, was broadcasting in French and Kiswahili direct to Africa with an unusually clear beam. An American missionary returned from the Congo reported on a television program in late July that she had personally seen the sale of communist party cards in the Equator Province, although she also reported the cards were not accompanied by communist ideology. Finally, it has frequently been suggested that Lumumba's Independence Day speech derived directly from the communist pattern.

Some other signs point in the same direction, principally in the careers of some Congolese with whom Lumumba was in contact and who later assumed governmental positions. Perhaps the clearest case here is that of Antoine Tshimanga who was co-organizer with Lumumba of the response to the collective audience accorded representatives of various political parties by the Minister on June 24, 1959. Tshimanga was the founder and president of the Union Nationale des Travailleurs Congolais (National Union of Congolese Workers), which, on its formation in April, 1959, included certain aims that might be considered to be patterned both in phraseology and intent after the communist ideology:

> —the safeguarding of the interest of Congolese workers equally in economic, professional, moral and social spheres;
> —the promotion of the working class by the struggle for increase of income for the Congolese workers;
> —the protection of workers in all professions;
> —the assurance to the working class of the more dignified existence of modern man, notably through ennoblement of family life by an adequate family salary;
> —the struggle against all forms of exploitation and oppression of the working class. (*66*:19–20)

While this platform in itself does not necessarily make Tshimanga a communist, it is a matter of record that he was

303

arrested in the Congo for having distributed communist tracts. His defenders, one of whom was formerly a communist Deputy in the Belgian Parliament, pleaded his innocence and his simple desire for knowledge, but Tshimanga was convicted and exiled from Léopoldville to Luisa in the Kasaï Province. It is also clear that Tshimanga had contacts with both the Belgian and French communist parties.

We have previously had occasion to discuss the possible communist leanings both of Anicet Kashamura and Antoine Gizenga; in neither case is there proof of anything further than that both have visited in communist countries and been in contact with communist personnel. *Time* magazine has cited others who have ". . . obvious Red leanings. Of the three, Secretary of State for Defense Jacques Lundula and Lumumba's private secretary, Bernard Salumu, have made junkets to Red China. Information Minister Anicet Kashamura runs the Congo radio and . . . broadcasts endless letters of sympathy from Communist groups in Czechoslovakia, Bulgaria and Russia" (*14:22*). It hardly needs to be added that such vague charges do not make communists of the persons concerned, and yet they sometimes seem to add to the general question.

As for Lumumba himself, we have no direct evidence that he was a communist before independence, or for that matter, after it. His pre-independence actions showed him to be a man of liberal tendencies, and one given to exaggeration, but considering the situation in which he was working, this can probably be attributed to an extreme nationalism which is of course not by any means necessarily to be equated with communism. In short, in the pre-independence period, the evidence for communist infiltration is scanty indeed. And we are further faced with one of the questions posed at the beginning of this part of our discussion, namely, whether we are dealing with full-fledged communists, with communist sympathizers, or simply with persons influenced by their judgment of the nature of current events. Without intending to minimize the dangers of the communist influence, I should like to point out that in the Western world we have come to a point at which we tend to believe that any person who so much as visits a communist country must necessarily be a communist. And I should like to pose, in contrast, the question of whether Mr. Tshombe or Mr. Kalonji, by virtue of their brief visits to the United States are now to be considered full-fledged capitalists? The point here is that while a visit to the country of one of today's great powers may indicate ideological leanings it is by no means an infallible indication: it would seem safe to assume that Mr. Tshombe, for example, is probably not a communist, but whether he learned this from a brief visit to the United States is doubtful. Similarly, it is probably equally safe to assume that Mr. Tshimanga is pro-communist, but it is doubtful that this is the result of a single visit to a communist country or with a communist leader. For certain events and people, we have some fairly substantial evidence, but until that evidence is much clearer than at present we can only subscribe, tentatively at least, to the view that communist influence and penetration before independence was not substantial.

In the post-independence period, evidence for the deep penetration of communist ideology into the thinking of Congolese leaders is not much clearer, but certainly there is much more to substantiate a view that Congolese leaders were swayed toward a pro-communist position as Russia increased her pressures and as the Congolese themselves became more and more aware of the East-West struggle and the possible advantages it might offer them.

The earliest accusations of communist influence came from Mr. Tshombe of the secessionist Katanga Province who on July 11 was quoted as saying that the Congo central government was trying to establish "a ruinous and communist state," and further that the same government had deliberately instituted a reign of terror (*16*:1:1). A day later, Tshombe made his charges more direct, and the *Washington Post* reported that:

> Tshombe later told a news conference flatly that the Lumumba government is Communist. He said that several Congolese members of the Lumumba government have been to Soviet Russia and Red China and received special training there. He did not name any of them.
>
> "The chaos created by the Congolese government is a classic Communist tactic to grab complete dictatorial power," he said. (*88*:8:2)

Similar charges have been made by others. Dr. Bernard Jackson, a missionary dentist returned from the Congo, reported that "Some of the things there seemed too well organized to have been spontaneous," and the July 19 article continued:

> Jackson said he knew of at least one case where a native had been "indoctrinated" by Communists.
>
> The native, son of a local chief, had tried to organize other natives into a guerilla fighting unit, Jackson said.
>
> "He once told the director of the mission, 'If I kill you, it's not because I don't like you, it will be because they tell me to,'" Jackson said. (*33*:4:1)

In a speech on August 3, Dr. Jackson amplified his previous remarks:

> The Congo's independence riots last month were "too well organized to be an accident" and possibly were caused by Communist agitation . . . "In public meetings in the bush country before the uprising we often heard the typical Communist harangue by natives". . .
>
> "I believe the political breakdown was part of a well organized program to discredit the white man . . . It might have been intended to frighten the missionaries out of The Congo, because the Communists cannot do their best work when Christianity is there.
>
> "Some people feel that Congolese Prime Minister Patrice Lumumba's political success is financed by Moscow." (*26*:19:2)

A similar point of view has been expressed by other individuals and also by the Belgian government itself. In a letter

306

which I received from Elisabethville in mid-July, a highly educated and thoughtful Belgian friend wrote to me:

> It seems that another factor played against the Congo: there was a prepared communist plot to wreck Congo. I ordinarily hesitate to charge Russia with the evils which arrive everywhere but this time I think the communists used cleverly the utopic and idiotic attitude of the Belgian government. . . . I think the communists played a role because the timing was too good in the entire Congo, because Lumumba's speeches were definitely inspired by the Communist dialectic, but mostly because radio transmitters were found sending false messages in order to divert planes or to send Belgians out of the Congo. One was found in Elisabethville and I know the Italian who was arrested.

In an article for the *New York Times* published July 15, Harry Gilroy reported:

> The Belgian Government indicated today that it suspected a Communist plot had brought on the turmoil that has torn the former Belgian Congo for the last week. . . . Premier Eyskens said: "As far as the record is complete, it can be stated that the mutiny of the Public Force was not a matter of chance. It seemed to be a provoked and prepared uprising." Foreign Minister Pierre Wigny followed M. Eyskens by denouncing the "Communist influence" in the Congo. (*73:3:8*)

And finally, one missionary in a confidential statement, has suggested that not only was the Congo crisis a prepared communist plot, but that Castro's pro-communist moves in Cuba were deliberately created as a diversionary tactic to Russia's deeper aims in the Congo.

Much more serious seems to be the influx of communist sympathizers into the government since independence and their subsequent influence. Included here are such individuals as Serge Michel, who seems to be a definitely left-wing Frenchman of Russian origin and who became Lumumba's chief press aid, and perhaps even Madame Blouin who became Chief of Protocol in the Congo government and who has apparently associated extensively with Vice-Premier Gizenga.

Nowhere, however, has the possible communist influence been made more apparent than in another personal letter to me from a former Belgian administrator whose deep attachment to the Congo ("I just cannot believe that I cannot be useful any more in a country in which I have worked fourteen years") led him to accept an advisory post to one of the Ministers of Lumumba's government. Writing on August 28, he said:

> . . . the measures taken by the Lumumba government have a definite communist scent. Some examples: Léopoldville radio gives textually the same news as Radio Peking; the word "colonialism" has been replaced by "imperialism," "western decadence" etc.; the press is curtailed and directed to the maintenance of the actual government and against everything which is Belgian or French; all civil, commercial and political societies have to re-register and are authorized only if they are "for the good of the Congolese people."
>
> In the office, it is even worse: I am supposed to be the most important adviser to the Minister . . . You would expect him to follow advice given with the intent to have justice reigning in the country but believe it or not, he does not want order; he listens to the technical advisers imposed on him by Lumumba who are communist recruits from Guinea, Ghana, Egypt and Tunisia. These advisers . . . admit that they have instructions to create what they themselves call "emptiness before construction." My colleagues in other ministries have the same experiences. There is no co-ordination of measures except in view of this principle of "creation du vide." This is the reason why the U.N.'s efforts to establish law and order have no results . . . the U.N. is in Lumumba's way to create the "emptiness" which he needs to maintain his government and the police measures against any opposition.

The principle of destroying, creating a void, and then rebuilding on new lines is a tactic which the communists have employed in a number of cases; this explanation of the situation in the post-independent Congo constitutes the most serious documented charge of communist manipulation that I know.

Certainly one of the most remarkable aspects of the Congo crisis is the rapidity with which it turned from a purely local to an international struggle. First to enter, of course, was the United Nations, and there is substantial evidence to indicate that without the unilateral intervention by Russia, the U.N. mission would have been a relatively swift and forceful triumph. But Russian intervention did occur, of course, and at this point we may recall with profit the various moves and counter moves which characterized Russian efforts.

July 13: Lumumba and Kasavubu threaten to "appeal to the Bandung powers" for military assistance if United Nations forces are not sent to the Congo without delay. Russia accuses the United States and other Western powers of helping Belgium undertake "direct military intervention" against the Congo.

July 14: Lumumba is reported to have received assurances from Chou En-lai that Peking would send help if asked, and also to have sent a message to Khrushchev asking him to follow the situation with care.

July 15: Khrushchev replies to Lumumba's request by saying that Russia would act if "aggression against the Congo" did not stop. The United States labels Khrushchev's remarks "intemperate, misleading and irresponsible."

July 16: Lumumba denies that his calling on Russia means he is a communist.

July 17: The Congolese government threatens to call "Soviet Russian troops" if all Belgian forces are not cleared from the Congo within seventy-two hours. Russia calls for a second series of Security Council meetings.

July 18: The Congolese Senate approves unanimously a resolution rejecting any intervention by the Soviet Union. Russia announces a Congo airlift of food and supplies from Moscow. A meeting of the United Nations African bloc unanimously opposes the Congo threat to call in Russian troops.

July 19: The Congolese threat to call in Russian troops is withdrawn as Belgian troops leave Léopoldville.

July 20: The Congolese Cabinet decides to appeal immediately for Soviet and other Afro-Asian help, specifically including that of Red China.

July 21: In the Security Council, Russia again charges aggression on the part of Western powers. Russia joins the United Nations airlift.

July 22: Lumumba says that passage of the new Security Council resolution obviates the need for any Soviet intervention.

July 24: Lumumba confers in New York with Soviet Deputy Kuznetsov. Russia charges that American businessmen support Belgium in the Katanga, and Chou Enlai is reported meeting with Congolese in Peking.

July 30: Lumumba holds meetings with the Soviet ambassador to Canada in Ottawa.

July 31: Russia demands another meeting of the Security Council. Russian threats against the West are again broadcast by Radio Moscow.

August 1: The United States replies sharply to Russian accusations.

August 6: Direct military aid is pledged by Sékou Touré of Guinea.

August 8: In new Security Council meetings, Russia demands that the United Nations force its way into Katanga; its resolution to this effect is voted down.

August 13: Radio Moscow charges Hammarskjold with playing a "disgraceful" role because he confers with Tshombe while United Nations troops are held outside Elisabethville.

August 16: Kuznetsov again attacks Hammarskjold.

August 17: Lumumba implies that he will call for outside assistance.

August 19: Lumumba again hints at outside help.

August 20: Russia renews its attacks on Hammarskjold and the United Nations Congo operation.

August 21: Russia launches new attacks on Hammarskjold and the United Nations operation in Security Council session, and introduces a no-confidence resolution but withdraws it because of lack of support.

August 22: Lumumba confers with the Russian ambassador in Léopoldville, and later announces that intervention by other countries will not be necessary.

August 28: Kalonji charges that Congolese army units fighting in the Kasaï are led by Czechoslovakian officers.

August 31: One hundred Russian trucks and ten Ilyushin-14 aircraft are reported being sent to the support of Lumumba's forces in the Kasaï fighting.

September 4: Russian planes are reported to be transporting Lumumba's troops from Stanleyville to Bakwanga.

September 5: Léopoldville radio announces the imminent arrival of a Czechoslovakian technical mission. The use of Russian planes to ferry Congolese troops is confirmed.

September 6: The United Nations closes all airports, thus effectively cutting the use of Soviet transports.

September 7: Eisenhower accuses Russia of jeopardizing the restoration of law and order in the Congo. Hammarskjold asks the Security Council for reaffirmation of its declaration against unilateral action by member states.

September 8: Yugoslavia charges the United Nations with "facilitating" Katanga secession, and Hammarskjold asks for authority from the Security Council to bar further Soviet military assistance in the Congo.

September 9: Guinea announces provisional withdrawal of her forces from the United Nations mission. Sékou Touré and Khrushchev announce their complete agreement on the Congo question. Russia charges that the United Nations Congo command and Hammarskjold are "systematically violating" Security Council decisions, and backs Lumumba in his demands for access to Léopoldville radio.

September 12: The United Nations Soviet delegation charges that the United States has wrecked plans for a Security Council meeting in order to gain time for "criminal plans" to overthrow Lumumba.

September 13: Ghana threatens to withdraw from the United Nations force if Lumumba is not permitted to broadcast. Yugoslavia demands a Security Council meeting.

September 14: Mobutu orders Russian and Czechoslovakian diplomats to leave the Congo within 48 hours. Russia continues its attempts to discredit Hammarskjold.

September 15: Russian, United States, and Tunisian-Ceylonese counterresolutions are proposed in the Security Council.

September 17: Russia vetoes the Tunisian-Ceylonese resolution and the United States calls for an emergency special session of the General Assembly. All communist diplomats, with the exception of the Yugoslavian representative, leave the Congo.

September 18: Sixteen Afro-Asian nations introduce a resolution supporting Hammarskjold's Congo actions.

September 19: Russia introduces a resolution condemning Hammarskjold.

September 20: The Afro-Asian resolution passes the General Assembly 70–0, and fourteen new nations, including thirteen from Africa, are formally admitted to the United Nations.

The failure of Russian unilateral action in the Congo is not a simple thing to explain, although a number of viewpoints have been advanced. Lynn Heinzerling, writing in the *Chicago*

Daily News, has attributed the Russian failure to heavy-handedness. He holds that the Soviet ambassador to the Congo, Mikhail D. Yakolev, overplayed his hand badly and made Russia's Congo intentions far too clear by consulting Lumumba, calling in communist newsmen and technicians, bringing in trucks and planes, and other similar actions. The Soviet assistance in airlifting troops to the Kasaï fighting in which the Congolese army looted, burned, and massacred, seems to have mitigated against the Soviets among the Congolese population, according to Heinzerling. And finally, the fact that Russian troops were not easily available to consolidate the temporary gains that their country had made undoubtedly figured in the case (*76:2:*4–8).

Equally important in assessing the Russian setback is the accession to power of Mr. Mobutu. At this point we have no clear understanding of why he insisted the communist nations leave the Congo. This is one of the questions which can only be answered by future historians, but there is no doubt that the emergence of Mobutu as a Congo strongman played heavily against Russian aspirations.

Another factor in the situation was the action of the United States coupled with Russian diplomatic failures in the United Nations. The various moves which forced Russia to veto the latest Ceylonese-Tunisian resolution which in turn took the matter to the General Assembly where the Russians sustained a sharp defeat, represent a combination of Russian errors and, apparently, of United States successes. Perhaps the most significant result of the maneuverings in the Security Council and General Assembly was the reunification of the African nations which decided to stand behind Hammarskjold. How long this firmness will be sustained cannot be predicted, of course, but it seems reasonably clear that the reunification emphasizes the faith of African nations in the world organization. It should also be pointed out that the rebuke to Russian aims, while certainly a triumphant cold war victory for

313

the United States, also represents the emerging force of the neutralist bloc which is rapidly becoming a third world force of diplomatic power equal to that wielded either by the United States or Russia.

Writing in the *Wall Street Journal*, Ray Vicker has summarized some further difficulties of Russian policy toward Africa which underline the recent Congo failure. He notes:

> An assessment of Russian weaknesses made by Western intelligence officials includes: A lack of knowledge about Africa; a lack of business and trading acumen such as that accumulated by Western businessmen through years of free enterprise; language difficulties; and a clumsy approach which stems from the first three weaknesses plus an undisguised jingoism which sometimes grates on African nerves. (*109*:4:3)

Vicker adds to this two further points, first that the Russian drive is now primarily negative, that is, directed toward undermining Western influence, and that this policy may neither pay off nor be self-sustaining as separation of colonial ties fades with the years. Second, Russia faces some difficulties shared by others, namely that its population is white and thus as liable to associations with colonialism as any Western nation.

It is clear that at this point Russia's African ambitions as exemplified by their Congo activities have suffered a setback. But it is equally clear that what we have witnessed to date represents only a single round in what will surely be a continuing battle for the friendship of Africa. Khrushchev's late-September, 1960, actions in the United Nations in which he has continued his attacks on Hammarskjold and made a clear attempt to destroy the growing power of the United Nations by proposing structural changes in that body, indicate again that no cold war battle is ever completely won. The Russian defeat in the Congo has given the United States as well as the neutralist nations a brief breathing space, but it is certain that Africa will continue to be an ideological, if not actual, battleground.

314

What, then, is the future of the Congo? In late September, 1960, the prognosis appeared to be better than at any time since the first flush of independence in early July. In Joseph Mobutu, the Congo appeared finally to have found its leader, a man who acted not only with the force demanded by the situation but with some wisdom as well. In appointing the College of High Commissioners to run the country, Mobutu mobilized almost the entire educated human resources of the country; in placing it under Justin Bomboko, he gave it the direction of one of the best balanced and most thoughtful Congolese. In short, his actions stamped Mobutu as the first Congolese leader with a real sense of responsibility and a real determination to solve his country's problems, but subsequent events have shown that even he could not control the Congo.

The problems faced by the Congo are indeed formidable. In the first place, it is clear that the internal peace of the country can only be maintained at present by the United Nations forces. It must be remembered that the political struggles, which have characterized the Congo since independence and which have resulted in the rise and fall of various leaders, have had effect primarily in Léopoldville and not in other areas of the Congo. The control of governmental machinery in Léopoldville by no means indicates control of the Congo, and the reconciliation of Kasavubu and his Lower Congo, Lumumba and his Eastern Province, Tshombe and his Katanga, and Kalonji and his Kasaï will not be an easy task. Thus far, there has been no truly central government in the Congo save, to a certain extent, the United Nations itself.

The United Nations operation cannot be restricted to military force alone, however, for the Congo is in desperate need both of economic and technical aid. With sources of revenue at practically a standstill, with unemployment at a high level, with the country almost completely disorganized, the economic future is at the moment bleak. Since the Belgians

315

have for the most part departed, the gaps in technical knowledge are almost overwhelming. Without the technical skills which the Belgians took with them, it will be impossible to restore the economy and to take it through the needed period of capital expansion without a great deal of assistance.

It is equally clear that the secessionist areas of the Congo must be returned to the fold if the nation is to be recreated within its former boundaries. The Katanga controls a substantial proportion of the wealth of the Congo, and without it the Congo can only be an economic weakling in Africa. Estimates of the Katanga's share of the Congo's wealth have been variously set at 45–85 per cent; Tshombe himself says 65 per cent, the excellent figures given by CRISP indicate 47 per cent. Whatever the actual figures, it is clear that the Katanga is of primary importance to the Congo. What has not as yet been recognized, however, is the fact that Kalonji's Mining State is also of great importance, for in setting up his capital in Bakwanga he came into control of a substantial proportion of the Congo's diamond production. Recent reports indicate that Kalonji has strengthened his hold upon the Southern Kasaï, and that the Mining State is more of a reality now than it was when first announced in August. While the Katanga problem seems to revolve around questions of governmental structure, Belgian support, and economic problems, the Mining State may demand much more involved solutions because it is founded upon ethnic considerations. It is important to recognize the connection between the Mining State and the Baluba-Bena Lulua struggles which originated primarily in Luluabourg. One of the Belgian solutions to the Luluabourg question was to evacuate an unknown number of Baluba tribesmen from the area; what is not generally recognized is that these Baluba were taken primarily to Bakwanga. Thus in choosing Bakwanga as his capital, Kalonji must have had in mind economic possibilities as well as the concentration of Baluba who represent not only the ethnic group with which he associates himself, but a discontented one as well.

If there is a solution to these problems, it would seem to lie in a change from a centralized to a federal government. The fact that federalism as a concept has never been clearly distinguished from separatism in the minds of the Congolese who espouse it emphasizes the difficulty of finding a federal structure which will appeal to such diverse leaders as Tshombe, Kasavubu, and Kalonji. Yet it seems doubtful that these leaders, assuming they continue to hold their powers, will ever agree to a centralized government, and thus federalism is apparently the only possible compromise which can bring them all together.

Though the first battle against the avowed intentions of Russia has been won, the Congo specifically and Africa in general will surely continue to be a battleground for men's minds, for both sides in the cold war are clearly committed to the fight. To make the struggle successful, we in the United States must understand that Africa has chosen to go its own way and that our job is to help it to develop not as an imitation of our own way of life but in those directions which Africans themselves wish to take. The emergence of neutralism as a force in the world is not necessarily to the detriment of the United States, or of Russia, and in any case, there is little we can or should necessarily do to prevent it. Strong and independent countries are needed in the world, and we cannot expect them all to be just like us. Their own independent strength in liberty and freedom is what we must seek, for we believe that independence and freedom are the goals for which all men search and that these ideals bring with them their own strength.

APPENDIXES

APPENDIXES

APPENDIX I

The Conscience Africaine *Manifesto*

The editorial staff of *Conscience Africaine* has devoted many of its meetings to studying the difficult problems of the future of the Congo.

We are only a small group, but we think we can speak in the name of many because we have voluntarily limited ourselves to delivering and giving form to the aspirations and sentiments of the majority of thinking Congolese.

We have done this in a spirit of sincerity and with a desire to produce a constructive piece of work. What is more, we do not lay claim to any monopoly either of the love of our country or of clairvoyance for her future.

The present manifesto is only a point of departure. We will sharpen and complete it together with those who come later to join us.

OUR NATIONAL VOCATION

In the history of the Congo, the last eighty years have been more important than the millenniums which have preceded them. The next thirty years will be decisive for our future. It would be vain to base our national sentiment on attachment to the past. It is toward the future that we turn our attention.

We believe that the Congo is called upon to become a great nation in the center of the African continent.

Our national vocation: to work in the heart of Africa to establish a new, prosperous, and happy society on the foundations of an ancient clan society which has been vigorously shaken by too rapid an evolution, and which now seeks its new equilibrium.

We will only find this new equilibrium in the synthesis of our African character and temperament with the fundamental riches of Western civilization.

Only the Congolese, with the brotherly assistance of the Western people living in the Congo, can realize this synthesis.

In order to speak of a Congolese nation composed of Africans and Europeans, it is necessary that all be filled with the desire to serve the Congo. We have a right to demand of those Europeans who share in our national life to be, above all, Congolese citizens—that is to say, not to pursue only the good of the Belgian community and their own personal interests in the Congo, but to seek, together with us, the good of the great Congolese community.

321

UNITY IN DIVERSITY

One principle is essential for us: the color of the skin confers no privilege. Without this principle, union is impossible.

But a fundamental equality does not signify identity: we wish to be civilized Congolese, not "dark-skinned Europeans." We understand well that the Europeans wish to maintain their own way of life.

To uphold the privileges for one of the two groups would be a source of conflict. Not to recognize their individual characters, but rather to want uniformity in them, would create equally dangerous tensions. It must be admitted in a spirit of understanding that a difference does not necessarily imply inferiority or superiority.

We reject with vehemence the principle of "equal but separate." It is deeply offensive to us. The European and African milieus must recognize the precise nature of one another. Human relations based on equality must be established—not only at the level of the individual, not only in the associations especially created to maintain these relations, but equally in all family, professional, and social contacts.

A NOBLE TASK TO PURSUE

Out of Belgium's civilizing actions in the Congo will develop a new civilization which will be ours. Already the principal elements of Western civilization are penetrating the Congo more and more intensely. Elementary education is reaching the masses, while an intellectual elite pursues its university study. The unceasing progress of science and technology struggles against illness and misery and establishes the foundations for a growing prosperity. The Christian religion teaches us the profound meaning of life, the eminent dignity of the human being, and the brotherhood of all men.

But we are still only half way—we want a complete civilization. An increasing number of Congolese want to take more responsibility and more initiative in the future of their country. They wish to assimilate in their national life other basic values of Western civilization which are still absent or insufficiently developed: respect for the individual and for his fundamental liberties without racial distinction; a more intense pursuit of social justice; a true democracy based on the equality of all men, and the participation of the people in the government of their country.

This is a long-term program which can be accomplished through the union of Africans and Europeans living in the Congo.

BELGO-CONGOLESE COMMUNITY?

We state as fact that Congolese public opinion reacts with a certain distrust when one speaks of a "Belgo-Congolese Community." These words can cover very different realities.

322

To put it more clearly, the Congolese who reflect on these problems fear that some people distort the idea of the Belgo-Congolese community in order to put a brake on the total emancipation of the Contion, or at least preponderant influence, and thus form a privileged caste.

In the sense that we interpret it, such a community, far from being an obstacle, must be the means by which we realize our total emancipation.

For us the vision evoked by Governor General Petillon is only an ideal of which we dream for the Congolese nation of tomorrow: A human fraternity based on the fundamental equality of men without racial distinction.

PROGRESSIVE BUT TOTAL EMANCIPATION

Belgium must not consider that there is a feeling of hostility in our desire for emancipation. Quite to the contrary, Belgium should be proud that, unlike nearly all colonized people, our desire is expressed without hatred or resentment. This alone is undeniable proof that the work of the Belgians in this country is not a failure.

If Belgium succeeds in leading the Congo to total emancipation intelligently and peacefully, it will be the first example in history of a colonial venture ending in complete success.

But to achieve that the Belgians must realize now that their domination of the Congo will not go on forever. We protest strongly against the opinion sometimes expressed in the press that does not make an essential distinction between the *presence* of the Belgians in the Congo and *their domination* of the Congo.

To those who ask: How long before the Belgians must leave the Congo?, we answer: Why do certain Belgians pose the question either dominate or abandon completely?

To those who pose this question, we would like to propose for the good both of the Congo and of the Belgians in the Congo, that they pack their bags without further delay.

It is time that the European elite react vigorously here in the Congo, and perhaps still more in Belgium, against such a dangerous mentality.

Whose fault is it if already too many Congolese are sure that the Europeans will not be able to abandon their attitude of political domination, economic exploitation, and racial superiority?

POLITICAL EMANCIPATION

We have read that there is a question of a thirty-year plan for the political emancipation of the Congo. Without declaring ourselves on the whole of its component parts, we believe that such a plan has become a necessity if it is the intention to realize emancipation in peace and concord.

This plan should express the sincere will of Belgium to lead the Congo to its complete political emancipation in a period of thirty years.

Only an unequivocal declaration on this point will preserve the confidence of the Congolese toward Belgium.

This plan, which would be a compromise between the impatience of one group and the conservatism of the other, must clearly establish the intermediate stages which it will effect in fixed periods of time. It is the only way to avoid having each reform project give way periodically to discussions, bargaining, and tests of force between two antagonistic blocs, which, finally, would become irreconcilable.

As for political emancipation, we think that there is a way to depart from the existing institutions by having them evolve progressively. The direction is twofold. On the one hand, existing institutions must become more and more representative by replacing progressively the present system of nominations with a system in which the population itself will designate its representatives. On the other hand, the councils which are now purely consultative must receive a true power of decision and control in increasingly extended matters in order to arrive finally at a responsible government at the head of our nation.

Not giving genuine responsibilities to the representatives of the people would only multiply the difficulties and prepare the future poorly. Those who never ought to undertake decisions on their own have always tended to assert exaggerated and unrealizable claims. This would lead inevitably to demagogy.

We are not asking only for a plan of political emancipation, but for a full plan of total emancipation.

At each stage of political emancipation there must be a corresponding stage of economic and social emancipation, as well as progress in education and culture. The parallel realization of these steps is an absolute necessity if political emancipation is to be sincere and effective.

We do not wish that external appearances of political independence be in reality only a way of enslaving and exploiting us.

ECONOMIC AND SOCIAL EMANCIPATION

Who would dare to speak of real emancipation if the direction of all economic life, the ownership of industrial, agricultural, and commerical enterprises, were to remain indefinitely and exclusively in the hands of the Europeans?

We will not accept the maintenance of a policy of low salaries which permits companies to reinvest a large part of their enormous

324

profits. It would be equally inadmissible to confiscate a part of the just salary of the workers for the profit of a state-socialist economy.

Some people extol "nationalization" of the large enterprises. We have no confidence in this capitalism of the State. Besides, are the workers in Europe much better paid and treated in the nationalized enterprises than in the private firms?

Salaries and agricultural revenues must increase in such a way as to allow continually augmented savings. The Congolese themselves will thus also have a way to raise capital by degrees, to have profits from it and to share in its influence.

Congolese artisans, merchants, and farmers must be encouraged and aided. The middle classes are an important element in the economic and social life of the Congo.

For the mass of the population which remains in the villages, consideration must be given to the agricultural economy, and village life must be made more agreeable—beginning by suppressing the loathsome system of forced cultivation.

For the mass of workers, the minimum legal salary which does not permit a decent life must be rapidly raised, especially in the cities where living is expensive. These minimum salaries must be based not on the budget of an unmarried person, but on that of a family. It must be so even for the unmarried adults in order that they may collect the money necessary for marriage without having to deprive themselves to the extent of going hungry.

The possibilities for formation and improvement must be considerably amplified not only by professional education at all levels, but also by a better organization of apprenticeships in the companies.

Beyond the essential minimum, the salaries must bear a realistic relation to the qualifications and efficiency of the worker. For those who meet the qualifications of the Europeans, the chasm which separates the two schedules of remunerations must be bridged.

The Congolese family, which has so much difficulty in liberating itself from the servitudes of the past, is subjected to such conditions of existence in the cities that a bright outlook is impossible. In the domain of housing, particularly, the State has made great efforts, but the problem remains very serious and we have numerous grievances concerning the adopted solutions.

In the past, paternalism has been a necessary thing. The Congolese are beginning to be conscious of the social responsibilities which they can and must take upon themselves. We ask not only that this tendency, which marks a favorable social evolution, not be thwarted, but also that the free organizations which the Congolese have created by their own initiative may be encouraged. We ask, in particular, for the freedom to unionize.

OUR ATTITUDE WITH REGARD TO BELGIUM

We are grateful to Belgium, but an artificial patriotism is not asked of us.

To the question of whether we wish to remain united with Belgium later, we answer: "We do not wish in any way to have the Congo integrated into the united Belgian state. We will never allow a Belgo-Congolese Federation to be imposed on us without our free consent, or as a condition of our political emancipation."

We wish that one day such a community might be the fruit of a free collaboration between two independent Nations which are bound by an enduring friendship.

We do not measure this friendship of Belgium by mounting capital investments, but by the attitude of the Belgians in the Congo with regard to the Congolese, and by the sincerity with which Belgium will help us to realize our total political autonomy.

A year ago the Congo reserved a triumphal welcome for King Baudouin. All the Congolese understood that our King loved his people. Our cheering expressed not only our gratitude, but also our hope that the attitude of the Sovereign would serve as an example to all Belgians in the Congo and in the mother country.

ORDER AND RESPECT FOR AUTHORITY

It is our intention that the Congo's emancipation will be realized in order and tranquility. And we believe that it is possible.

We have decided not to let ourselves be drawn into violence, because violence produces insoluble problems. We have only one aim: the good of the Congolese nation. We will make this aim triumphant in lawfulness and by peaceful means. Those who use violence show that they are not ripe for true democracy.

We wish to continue to respect authority, but we want our opinion to be asked more than in the past; we want it given consideration, and if it is deemed impossible to follow us, we want to be told why.

We ask specially to be directly concerned, in the most formal way, in the elaboration of the contemplated thirty-year plan. Without this participation, such a plan could not have our assent.

APPEAL TO THE EUROPEANS

Europeans must fully understand that our legitimate desire for emancipation is not directed against them. Or national movement is not inspired by hatred but by brotherhood and justice.

We know that the realization of our hopes will depend on our own efforts, and we will not fail to remind the Congolese often of the harsh truth that we are able to demand our rights only if we are fully conscious of our duties and our responsibilities.

326

But the Congolese community of tomorrow, composed of Whites and Negroes, is realizable only in an environment of respect and mutual esteem, as well as sincere friendship.

To achieve this, many Europeans must modify their attitude toward the Congolese. We believe that this is possible. Moreover, we are pleased to acknowledge that there have been some obvious improvements in the last few years; but they are the doing of too small a number to create wholly the environment necessary for a sound community.

We ask the Europeans to abandon their attitude of contempt and racial segregation, to avoid the continual annoyances of which we are the object. We ask them also to abandon their attitude of condescension which wounds our self-respect. We do not like being treated always like children. Understand that we are different from you and, although assimilating the values of your civilization, we still wish to remain ourselves. We ask from you also an effort to understand our legitimate aspirations and to help us in realizing them.

"The hand offered too late risks being refused," proclaimed Governor General Jungers in a solemn warning. We believe that for a sincere joining between Europeans and Congolese, it is not too late, but it is time.

We note with satisfaction that an increasing number of Europeans are inclined to concede progressively to the Congolese all the responsibilities that they show themselves capable of assuming. Many Europeans also, inspired with a sincere spirit of justice, are willing to share the wealth more abundantly with the Congolese as their more qualified and more productive work helps to augment it. Unfortunately these Europeans are too often left powerless because of their compatriots' lack of understanding.

As a willing group of Congolese and Europeans, by our constructive efforts we will convince those who remain indifferent to our community's future. As for those who persist in an attitude of egoism and contemptuous pride, we will constrain them if necessary by the just and worthy use of the invincible force of our united front.

NEED FOR THE NATIONAL UNION

We have only one chance to make our cause triumphant: that is to be and to remain united.

United we will be strong, divided we will be weak; it is the future of the nation which is at stake.

National union is necessary because the whole population of the Congo must, before all else, be conscious of its national character and its unity. How will this be possible if the people are wooed by several competing parties?

This leads us to take a position concerning the introduction of Belgium's political parties into the Congo. Our position is clear: These parties are an evil and they are useless.

Political parties do not fulfill any need in the present political and administrative structure of the Congo, since we have neither a Parliament nor elections. Furthermore, the Belgian political divisions do not have significance for the Congo; they have arisen from historical circumstances peculiar to Belgium.

But above all we do not want parties at present because what characterizes parties is conflict, while what we want is union.

If we let ourselves be divided, we will never realize the ideal of a great Congolese nation. Even if certain parties include political emancipation in their program, the mere existence of these parties is a radical obstacle to this emancipation.

Those Congolese who would be tempted to let themselves get drawn into party politics do not realize the old adage adopted by all dominators: "Divide and conquer"—To divide in order to dominate better.

Let our position be understood: We wish to be neither "a party against parties" nor "an unrivaled party."

We are convinced that it is wholly possible for pagans, Catholics, Protestants, Salvationists, Mohammedans to agree on a program of common good which respects those principles of the natural ethic engraved on the soul of every man worthy of the name. The Congolese can realize this program most surely by being united and by having sincere respect for the convictions of each person.

Later, when the political structures of the Congo make it necessary we can group ourselves according to our affinities, our interests, and our political conceptions. It is highly probable that when that time arrives the specifically Congolese parties will not take the Belgian parties as a model.

HOW TO REALIZE THIS TOTAL UNION?

To begin, we hope that the present manifesto will stir up among the Congolese, and also among the Europeans, a vast movement of opinion which will crystallize around our modest newspaper. We have already decided to enlarge our editorial staff so that it may be more representative of all opinions compatible with the principles here summarized.

Nevertheless, we are convinced that in the more or less near future, it will be necessary to give a more precise form to the advancement of the ideas we wish to promote, and that there will have to be an organization. This organization will be able to form sections, affiliate members, and hold meetings, in order to realize the considerable work of education which is indispensable in the service of the elite and the masses of our people.

The Conscience Africaine *Manifesto*

The organization which we anticipate would come into being in full legality, conforming to the laws and regulations in force.

While waiting, we invite our readers, Africans and Europeans, to write to us in order to begin the colloquy. We would be especially happy to learn their point of view on the opportunity for the *Mouvement Nationale Populaire* which we propose.

May those who share our ideal, even if they do not share all our positions, subscribe immediately to *Conscience Africaine* and become propagandists of our journal.

APPEAL TO THE CONGOLESE

Our appeal is addressed first to the large elite which already exists in the Congo and which we believe truly capable of being the leaven among the masses.

We count on those who have had the privilege of studying and who are in teaching, office work, and administration. We count especially on our Congolese university students who are studying in the universities of the Congo and Belgium.

But we want also the miners, the timber-yard workers, the factory workers, the farmers, the artisans, and the merchants. Among them also there rises a true elite absolutely necessary to the country.

May no one among us seek, in the movement we are endeavoring to create, his own interests or the satisfaction of his own ambitions.

We must accept, generously and disinterestedly, to be at the service of our people. That is not an abstract and vague reality; there is a vast group of men, women, young people, infants who live around us, whom we must love profoundly and whom we must help with all our power to rise and advance.

We must not be satisfied with words. It is not sufficient to write and shout in order to realize our ideal. Extended efforts, sown with difficulties and thwarted by disappointments, will be necessary. Tenacity, perseverence, and patience will be equally necessary.

Through our dignified, intelligent and courageous attitude, through our respect for authority and for the men who represent it, we wish to merit esteem and confidence in order that all will rally to the cause we wish to promote.

We have full confidence in the future of our country. We have confidence also in the men who must live in it in concord and in happiness.

With all the sincerity and all the enthusiasm of our hearts we cry out: Long live the Congo! Long live Belgium! Long live the King!

329

The Counter Manifesto of the ABAOK

Our friends of *Conscience Africaine* have produced a document worthy of this period when people's spirits are restless for a change in the colonial system. We can only congratulate them. However, everyone is aware that no human work is perfect. The principal aim of our study is to set off the weak points and to furnish points of support for this document. For greater facility, we have divided this study in two parts: the part which discusses political questions and that which touches on social questions.

1. POLITICAL QUESTIONS
A. Generalities
Among the weak points of the Manifesto we have noted, above all, that of politics: It is on the political level that the idea of the Manifesto seems to become complicated.

Here are those ideas: "The Congolese want to take more responsibilities and more initiative in the future of their country. They want to assimilate in their national life some of the fundamental values of Western civilization which are still absent or insufficiently developed: respect for the human being and his fundamental liberties, etc." Further on the Manifesto continues: "As for political emancipation, we think that there is a way to depart from the existing institutions by having them evolve progressively. They must become more and more representative by progressively replacing the present system of nominations with an electoral system; the councils which are now purely consultative must receive a true power of decision and control in increasingly extended matters in order to arrive finally at a responsible government at the head of our nation. Not giving genuine responsibilities to the representatives of the people would only multiply the difficulties and prepare the future poorly. Those who never ought to undertake decisions on their own responsibility have always tended to assert exaggerated and unrealizable claims. We are not asking only for a plan of political emancipation, but a full plan of total emancipation. We have only one chance to make our cause triumphant: that is to be and to remain united." How to realize this union? Not even the *Conscience Africaine,* itself, responds to this ticklish question. It is content simply to expose to our thoughts an idea which comes from we-know-not-where: "This leads us to take a position concerning the introduction of Belgium's political parties into the Congo. Our position is clear: These parties are evil and they are useless, because they characterize struggle while what we want is union."

It is on the above statement that we are not in agreement with our friends of the *Conscience Africaine*. They want to govern but they set themselves above the ways by which one directs a country. These soldiers love victory but renounce arms. Now, can a military victory be won by dispensing with weapons? Do the authors of the Manifesto not realize that by trampling politics, or even political parties, under foot, they become enemies of their own projects? Can one participate in government by dispensing with politics? And what do they understand politics to mean? Is it not the art of governing a State? And this union that they hope for: do you believe that we will realize it outside the realm of politics? "Here also lies the question of knowing whether the right way to ameliorate social relations between white and black is not to a considerable extent the recognition of still greater political rights and public liberties," declared Monsieur A. Van Bilsen in his thirty-year plan.

Thus we are convinced that it is by means of politics, and by no other means, that the diverse Congolese tribes could be united. It is purely utopian to try to rally all the Congolese to the same opinion. But, it is the opinion which determines the party and not "the historical circumstances." The struggle of parties, although dangerous, is very necessary in a democracy. It stimulates competition; each party wants to prove to its voters that it knows better than the other what to do to improve the well being of the people. The programs of all the parties aim only at that. At the scholastic level, look at what has happened in one year in the conflict between nondenominational schools and private schools in the Belgian Congo.

Our ears have never ceased being hammered about the so-called evils in the introduction of politics to the Congo. Evidently, you have never employed this conduct? When your child cries or makes other "Matata" do you not seek to calm him by frightening him with the stories of "Dongola-Misu," that Congolese Don Quixote who has accomplished his deeds only against children? Thus we are able to conclude that the ill-omened effects of politics are in reality only the stories of "Dongola-Misu" destined to calm the legitimate aspirations of children.

There must be an end put to the government of arbitrary substitution which has won for the Congo the title of empire of silence. This is why the independent state of the Congo gave only a semblance of independence for twenty-four years. None of us were at the Berlin Conference. And yet everything was decided for us there. And since all was said and done for us, a great value was placed upon freedom of commerce; as for civilizing the natives, a simple platonic declara-

331

tion was offered. Although independent, the Congo had neither a sovereign of its race or even of its choice nor a government to its liking; the citizens were never citizens. "This new Congo State, without correspondence in Europe, is a sure feat, one of the most curious concepts of the new European law," said M. Leroy-Beaulieu. And Father A. Vermeersch added: "It is a type of state absolutely unique in the past, present and probably in the future. The first of its kind, it has a strong chance of also being the last." What an intrigue was the Berlin Conference in 1885 which poorly concealed its exclusive intention of pure and simple exploitation and of free commerce for the signatory countries. Result: The basin of the Congo became in some measure the common inheritance of all nations.

"In colonial matters, our empiricism of that half century is definitely past, and those who consider that this method has succeeded well to the present day must recognize that it could not be re-applied without risk for the future." What do our friends from *Conscience Africaine* think of these words by the author of the thirty-year plan? But in our day, these same politics of substitution continue. No one ignores the Colonial Council. We know that this Council, placed in Brussels far away from us, possesses the legislative power of the Congo; it is there that the drama of our unhappy destiny is played. Nevertheless, none of us is called there to say a word.

No, this political system is too antiquated, it must be made inactive. Our position is clear and we demand: 1. Political rights; 2. All the liberties of the individual, of thought, of opinion, and of the press; liberty of assembly, of association, of conscience, and of religion. By liberty we obviously mean the right to do everything which is in no way harmful to the next person; hence, that which is not forbidden by law. The hour of indecisions, terror, and vain suspicions is ended. The politics of evasion and vague promises can only weaken the confidence which the Congolese have put in the mother country.

These substitutions are falsely justified by the lack of Negro elite graduated from universities. To put it truthfully, these are only expedients. The very wise Monsieur A. Van Bilsen says: "I do not share the opinion of those who affirm that the period of political rights and representative institutions will be achieved only when the qualified natives are in a position to fill all the responsible functions of the administration. I think, to the contrary, that *in a number of cases political maturity precedes administrative capacity.*"

B. Thirty-Year Plan

With respect to this plan, our friends from *Conscience Africaine* declare: "We ask specially to be directly concerned, in the most formal way, in the elaboration of the contemplated thirty-year plan. Without this participation, such a plan could not have our consent."

The Counter Manifesto of the ABAKO

For our part, we do not wish to collaborate in the elaboration of this plan but rather purely and simply to annul it because its application would serve only further to retard the Congo. In reality it is only the same old lullaby. Our patience is already exhausted. Since the hour has come, emancipation should be granted us this very day rather than delayed for another thirty years. History has never known delayed emancipations because when the hour has come people do not wait. If there is hesitation, it is no longer emancipation which terminates the crisis: it is hatred, revolt, separation, says Monsieur P. Ryckmans in his book, *Dominate to Serve.*

C. Congolese Union

Earlier we said that it is purely utopian to want to rally all the Congolese to one same opinion. The author of the thirty-year plan for the political emancipation of Belgian Africa recommends a Congolese Federation. We believe that he is on the right path. Considering the principle from Rousseau that "all which is not in nature has its drawbacks," and since the true union of the Congolese people can only be realized by way of political evolution, this evolution in the sense of democratic progress must begin first on an existing foundation. That means that groups historically, ethnically, and linguistically united or allied organize themselves to form as many political parties. Each "party" would elect its representatives. As in all democratic countries, the number of representatives would be in proportion to the population represented. A percentage would be determined; for example: one representative for 100,000 inhabitants. Only those elected will be able to bring about union and to trace the program of true democratization of the country.

As for the "existing institutions," we recognize with our friends that these have already lingered too long in the politics of evasion. Since 1920 there has been talk about the councils of chieftaincies without their being democratic even in the embryonic sense. Everything depends on the administration which appoints and dismisses the members. At this rate, it will always be possible to speak of us in vain: the Congolese people will remain children forever. The people must become accustomed to voting freely for the councils of chieftaincies. The practical system in Léopoldville for the election of the Ward Council, where no candidate states his candidacy, is a mistake.

D. Belgo-Congolese Community

The problem which seems to preoccupy the Belgian politicans most at this time is that "of the institutional bonds with equal representation, between Belgium and the Congo" in the case where the latter had just gained its emancipation. What is our attitude? We espouse the opinion that the authors of the Manifesto have expressed. In effect, before thinking of the foundation of such a community, the Belgians ought to realize that it must be neither solicited nor imposed but freely chosen and accepted; they ought not to lose sight of the fact that the aims of the founder of their "domain" did not extend to the creation of a colony in the Congo but rather "to the organization of a Negro State."

As for the Congolese population, will it be heterogeneous? We leave the answer to the honorable Vice-Governor General Marzorati: "The Congo is a colony of exploitation and not of peopling. The traditional politics of Belgium are only politics of enlistment. The Congo ought to be reserved to the natives alone and the presence of the whites allowed only temporarily. The permanent installation of Europeans cannot be accepted because it necessarily implies racial discrimination and a color bar which our conscience condemns. Accordingly, we must consider their going there as an enlistment only, and even that will be formed more and more from the native elements. It is not at all proven that the installation of resident colonists in the Belgian Congo necessarily constitutes a service rendered to the country." (Conference of November 17, 1951. See "L'Avenir Colonial Belge," No. 333, November 29, 1951.)

At any rate, is it possible to conceive how this Congo, eighty times larger than Belgium, could become its "tenth province"?

A caricature of the community copied from the famous French Union is not at all plausible for us; it is only a modified form of domination. Is it possible to conceive how this Congo, eighty times larger than Belgium, could become its "tenth province"? Would Belgium be able to tolerate having the inhabitants of her "tenth province" form the majority of the representatives in the Chamber? Perhaps a Commonwealth of the British pattern would be desirable.

2. SOCIAL AND ECONOMIC QUESTIONS

A. Social Life and Salaries

On the purely social level, the division of the population in classes (evolved and mass) is advised against. Although there are the elite, all are of the masses and all are citizens. In no civilized country are certificates given to distinguish the elite from the masses. To borrow the words of one of Belgium's wisest leaders, a former District Commissioner, "if it [the division of classes] flatters the vanity of some, it reduces them at the same time, because, whatever one may say, it creates deserters from the people."

We will not linger long on the question of salaries, a question which our brothers from *Conscience Africaine* have so fully discussed. If true efficiency is sought from the Negro in his work, there is only one remedy: to recognize his labor and to grant him a salary fully in keeping with the service rendered, because a good salary brings true efficiency. A director from a company in Antwerp said to Monsieur

Arthur Pinzi: "As for me, I attend first to the men. When the men are content, the machines turn alone." But, in the Congo, the machines are attended first in order to finish with the men.

As for the pension plan, it is good, but it is necessary to realize that before reaching retirement, the individual must be able to eat. Yet, does one need to underline that the size of the pension depends on the amount of the salary while the person is active? If, then, the salary is low, the pension will be insignificant or almost worthless.

Is it possible to speak of a true assimilation without raising the conditions of subsistence? We give you the words of M. Van Bilsen: "As long as the native peasant earns 2,000 francs ($40.00) a year and the worker or writer 6,400 francs ($128.00) we must not rely on what hygiene, healthful habitation, demographic balance, and civilization indicate to be great progress. An annual revenue of 25,000 francs ($500.00) would appear, at first glance, to constitute a vital minimum for someone whom one prides himself on having civilized." The largest Congolese companies forget their duties and substitute themselves for the state and the unions, and sometimes even for the press. What they call social works are in reality only a reinvestment of profits, a budgetary balance, a refining of the calculations. We know how to build hospitals, schools, foyers where they are not even necessary; we know how to construct city gardens, but we do not dare to add one cent to the salary of the unhappy Negro for fear that the treasury would be ruined. Obviously, one would have to be a fool not to understand that these social works have a purely political end; they constitute "a museum" to distract the tourists and to deceive the visitors of note.

Nationalization of the large business enterprises would be desirable for the parastatals, as well as for the large mineral and agricultural companies, in order to permit the state to fulfill the new needs which have proved increasingly important and complicated.

B. Africanization of the Staffs

There is talk these days in A.E.F. [French Equatorial Africa] of an Africanization of staffs. We think that it is also the moment to reflect on the "Congolization" of staffs in the Administration as well as in private business enterprises. Here again, the lack of university elite must not serve as a pretext for wanting to find a place for the Negroes on lower staffs. Sometimes it is only the color bar, pure jealousy. What places are occupied by the graduates of the school of Administration at Kisantu? Where do those from St. Luke's school of art go? Aren't the medical assistants comparable to the mere sanitary agents from Europe?

We do not ask for such offices as those which have fallen to our well-known city chief in Léopoldville, where the Negro is only an emblem—offices which some shrewd person invented with the unique political aim of falsifying world opinion—but true offices where the Negro assumes real responsibilities with all the usual latitude of the offices. Besides, if we are lacking an elite, it is for them, the Belgians, to confess the fault, as was shown so clearly by Monsieur Van Bilsen when he declared: "It is our fault, not theirs, if among the Negroes there are neither doctors, nor engineers, nor civil servants, nor officers. The Missionaries have, in their own field of action, trained hundreds of priests one of whom has already received Episcopal sanction. In the Belgian Congo and in Ruanda-Urundi, the formation of elite groups and of responsible directing staffs is a generation behind the British colonial territories and the bordering colonies."

C. Academic Politics

In the domain of education, we state that the question of age is contrary to the organization of society at this moment. In the villages there are neither local schools nor means of transportation to permit the six-year-old children to begin their studies. We know what this system has produced and produces now in A.E.F. To dismiss a brilliant child after the sixth year of elementary school because he has reached fourteen or fifteen years of age is inadmissable now; it is "anti-Congolese." Inasmuch as his intelligence permits him, the child should be allowed to pursue his studies. If it is a lack of buildings, there is the Advancement Fund and the funds of the King; why not institute a Study Fund (fonds d'études) granting scholarships to the most deserving?

3. ULTIMATE CONCLUSION

To civilize this country, "is a crusade worthy of this century of progress," wrote King Léopold II. But will the country of Léopold II surpass the atomic century? Indeed, the Belgians will respond proudly that it will not, because they know in the same way as their compatriot, Pierre Kassai knew when he wrote in 1868 that "those who have the honor of contributing to his accomplishment [Humanitarian Mission of Léopold II] should have no other thoughts than those of education, instruction, intellectual development in all its forms for the native populations, with the safeguard of their interests, and their relative independence preparatory to their future liberty."

They know also, just as Monsieur Van Bilsen writes today, that "the time is ended when colonization could be justified by the right of the first occupant or the conqueror or the 'treaties' settled with illiterate and uninformed native princes who were incapable of opposing the colonial penetration. Only one claim justifies colonization and that is consent, the attachment of the native population to those who are their educators, to those who bring them the key to a new and better world, a world of well-being and of liberty."

Resolutions of the Round Table Conference

RESOLUTION NO. 1
Date on Which the Independence of the Congo is to be Proclaimed

Central and provincial institutions in the Congo, as also a central Government, shall be set up by June 30, 1960, so that the independence of the Congo may be proclaimed on that date.

RESOLUTION NO. 2
Organisation of the Congo State

1. As of June 30 next the Congo, within its present frontiers, shall become an independent State whose inhabitants shall, under conditions to be enacted by law, have the same nationality and shall be free to move about and establish themselves within the confines of the said State, and in which goods and merchandise may also circulate freely.
2. As of June 30, 1960, the Congo State shall be made up of six provinces whose geographical boundaries are those of the provinces now in existence.
3. The decision as to the number and geographical boundaries of the provinces which shall thereafter form the Congo State, rests with the Constituent Assembly.
4. The position in regard to certain ethnic groups whose ramifications extend over several provinces shall be examined by the Constituent Assembly and shall be the subject of Congolese laws to be enacted thereafter.
5. Belgium may put at the disposal of the Congo, as part of the technical assistance to be agreed upon by treaty, a scientific commission whose conclusions concerning the problem raised in (4) above shall be designed to facilitate the work of the Congolese legislative assemblies.
6. Alterations to the boundaries of the provinces may be undertaken by the Constitution according to a formula outlined as follows: A law shall fix the new boundaries of the provinces in accordance with the concordant opinions of the provincial assemblies concerned. Should there be a divergence of views between these assemblies, the question shall be settled by Parliament.
   The initiative for proposing such alterations to the provincial

boundaries shall come from that part of the population directly concerned.

RESOLUTION NO. 3
Constitution of the First Central Government of the Congo

1. Without waiting for June 30, the first Congolese Government shall be formed as soon as possible after the elections.
2. This Government may thus present itself to both Houses as soon as they are set up, and obtain a vote of confidence.
3. This Government shall comprise at least one member from each province.
4. It shall be constituted by King Baudouin who, once the election results become known and after consulting the main political parties and leaders, shall designate the person who is to form the government. The latter's task shall consist in submitting to the King for appointment the names of a team of ministers likely to obtain the confidence of Parliament.
5. The Council of Ministers shall be headed by a Prime Minister whose tasks include the following:
   —the conduct of State policy in agreement with the Council of Ministers;
   —the supervision and conduct of Government activity;
   —the submission, to the Head of the State, of proposals relating to the exercise of the statutory powers and the enforcement of laws.
6. The Prime Minister and the Ministers are responsible to both Houses on all matters of policy.
7. In order to ensure a certain measure of stability for the first few governments, it is stipulated that a motion of censure may not be put to the vote until 48 hours after it was proposed, and shall not be considered as carried unless and until it is supported by the vote:
   —either of two-thirds of the total number of members forming one of the two Houses;
   —or of the absolute majority of all members of each of the two Houses;[1]
   —either of two-thirds of the members present in one of the two Houses;
   —or of the absolute majority of all members of each of the two Houses.[2]
8. The censure of one member of the Government shall not necessarily give rise to the resignation of the entire Government.

[1] Cartel, Balubakat, Mongo Union, CEREA, Assoreco, M.N.C. Lumumba.
[2] P.N.P., Tribal parties, Conakat, A.R.P., Congolese Union.

9. Until this point has been settled by means of a Congolese law, Ministers may not be subjected to repressive measures unless and until charges are brought against them by one of the two Houses. In such cases, they shall be brought before a Court of Justice sitting in the Congo. This Court shall comprise three counsellors of the Supreme Court of Appeal in Belgium, who are to be designated by the First Presiding Judge of the Supreme Court of Appeal, and an Advocate General designated by the Attorney General of the same Court.

RESOLUTION NO. 4
Competence of the First Government of the Congo

1. As of June 30, the Congolese Government shall replace the Belgian Government.
2. Both Governments, the Belgian and the Congolese, shall agree on the manner in which mutual representational facilities are to be provided for.

RESOLUTION NO. 5
The Head of the State

Designation of the Head of State:
1. Prior to June 30, the two Houses shall convene in one assembly to decide upon the designation of a Head of State whose enactments shall only be effective when they are countersigned by a Minister of the Congolese Government, who shall be wholly responsible.
2. This regime shall continue until the Constitution becomes operative.
3. Should no agreement be reached with regard to this designation, the functions of the Head of State shall temporarily be assumed:
   —by the President of the Senate,[1]
   —by the President of the House of Representatives,[2]
   —or by the elder of the two Presidents above-mentioned.[3]
   Prerogatives and competency of the Head of State:
4. Under the terms of the basic law, the Head of State shall enjoy certain privileges and shall be acknowledged to hold certain powers, including that of enacting the regulations and decrees necessary for the enforcement of laws, without at any time being empowered to suspend the laws themselves or to grant exemption from their enforcement.

---

[1] Tribal parties, P.N.P., Congolese Union, Conakat, Balubakat.
[2] Cartel, CEREA, M.N.C. Lumumba, Mongo Union.
[3] A.R.P., Assoreco.

RESOLUTION NO. 6
Organisation of the Congolese Parliament

1. The legislature of the Congo State shall be exercised jointly by two national assemblies, temporarily referred to hereinafter as the House of Representatives and the Senate.
2. The House of Representatives, whose members are elected by universal suffrage, comprises one representative for every 100,000 inhabitants irrespective of age, sex or nationality; fractions of the population amounting to 50,000 or more are entitled to an extra representative, the total number of representatives being 137 on the basis of the present population figure.
3. Some delegations[1] would like to see the House comprise twelve co-opted members over and above the representatives elected by universal suffrage, as also tribal chieftains or leaders who would be designated by the provincial assemblies and who would be entitled to two seats per province.
4. The Senate shall be formed essentially of members designated by the provincial assemblies, on the basis of fourteen per province, at least three of whom shall be tribal chieftains or leaders; some delegations[2] are of the opinion that this figure of three seats should be considered as a maximum or as a fixed number.
5. The tribal chieftains and leaders to be designated by the provincial assembly shall be presented on a double list drawn up by the tribal chieftains and leaders in the province. Some delegations[3] recommend, however, that the presentation of a double number of candidates should not be mandatory.
6. By tribal chieftain is meant the heads of chieftaincies. By leaders is meant the heads of groups making up the sectors. Some delegations[4] consider that the heads of sectors should be included under this heading.
7. Members elected by direct vote may be completed by the co-optation, even in the course of sessions, of twelve senators, without the equality of representation between the provinces being affected at any time.
8. Some of the delegations at the Conference[5] also recommend that designations by co-optation be made by the senators of each province.

[1] Tribal chieftains, P.N.P., Conakat, A.R.P.
[2] As a maximum figure: CEREA, Assoreco, M.N.C. Lumumba. As a fixed number: Mongo Union, Cartel.
[3] Tribal chieftains, P.N.P., Conakat (Congolese Union abstained and Balubakat gave no opinion).
[4] Tribal chieftains, P.N.P., Conakat, A.R.P.
[5] Tribal chieftains, P.N.P., Conakat, A.R.P. (Congolese Union abstained).

9. No member of one House may belong to the other.
10. Both Houses together hold full legislative powers, and their competency is identical in scope.
11. The basic law regulates, inter alia, questions relating to:
    —the public nature of all sessions;
    —verification of powers;
    —incompatibilities, except insofar as referred to above;
    —election of the office;
    —voting methods;
    —the right of enquiry;
    —Parliamentary immunity;
    —Pecuniary indemnification and attendance tokens.
12. The first term of office of the Houses entrusted with drawing up the Constitution may not be shorter than three years nor longer than four, except in the case where Parliament is dissolved by official pronouncement in accordance with the Constitution. The latter shall fix the date of the first elections to the legislative Houses, taking into account the duration of mandates as specified above.
13. The language to be used in debates, in the drawing up of official documents and the texts of laws and decrees shall be the French language, and the Presidents of both Houses shall ensure that all interjections in Swahili, Lingala, Kikongo and Tshiluba are translated into French.
14. It is not deemed necessary that Courts of Justice shall be empowered to appraise the constitutional character of national or provincial laws.
15. The Economic and Labour Councils now in existence at central or provincial level shall continue to function until abrogated or modified. Their task is to submit to the national or provincial authorities the opinions and recommendations which are requested of them. The composition and competency of these Councils might usefully be revised prior to June 30, taking account of any conclusions in this regard that might be expressed by the Conference in connection with problems of an economic, financial or social nature.

RESOLUTION NO. 7
The Constituent Assembly
1. The Constitution of the Congo State shall be drawn up by both Houses convened as a Constituent Assembly. They shall be convened in Luluabourg[1] by June 30, 1960 at latest.

---

[1] The Assoreco and the Mongo Union proposed Léopoldville, and the Conakat was in favour of Kamina.

2. Neither of the two Houses shall be held to deliberate officially on the articles of the Constitution unless at least two-thirds of their members are present.
3. No clause may be adopted unless it is supported by the votes of at least two-thirds of the members of both Houses.
4. Some delegations[1] are in favour of allowing the Constituent Assembly, merely by majority vote, to settle the procedure whereby the Constitution is to be adopted. This procedure may take the form of a referendum, or the approval of the draft Constitution by the provincial assemblies, or any other method of consultation and approval.
5. Other delegations[2] would like to see the provisory basic law stipulate that the Constitution shall not be considered as definite until it has been approved by the provincial assemblies.
6. The locality in which the Constituent Assembly is to sit shall be declared a neutral zone under the authority of a special commissioner, so as to protect the Constituent Assembly from all outside pressure.

RESOLUTION NO. 8
The Constitution and Legislation of the Future Congo State

1. In the exercise of its legislative authority, which is unreservedly acknowledged, the Congolese Parliament shall take account of the necessity of guaranteeing the safety of persons and property whether national, Belgian or foreign.
The following principles, notably, shall be included in the provisory basic law, the respect of which shall be ensured by the Belgian Government up to June 30, and which the Conference hopes will be among the basic clauses adopted by the future Congolese Constituent Assembly:
   1) the equality of all in the eyes of the law;
   2) the right of every individual to life and to corporal integrity;
   3) the guarantee of individual liberty, with the exception of sentences pronounced by the judiciary which will be set up by the Constitution and the laws, the latter to guarantee, by inter alia, the right of the individual to legal defence, and to eliminate all risk of arbitrary decisions;
   4) freedom of thought, conscience and religion;
   5) freedom of speech;
   6) freedom of education and all its corollaries;
   7) right of public meeting and freedom of association;

[1] Cartel, Mongo Union, CEREA, Congolese Union, Assoreco, M.N.C. Lumumba.
[2] Tribal chieftains, P.N.P., Balubakat, Conakat, A.R.P.

8) the inviolability of correspondence and of postal, telephone and telegraph communications;
9) freedom of work;
10) the right to own property and, in a wider sense, the respect of investments and acquired estate in accordance with the laws or customs;
11) the inviolability of the home.

2. The legislation in force in the Belgian Congo as at June 30, 1960, shall remain in force until expressly abrogated by Parliament.

RESOLUTION NO. 9
The Partition of Authority Between the Central Government and the Provincial Authorities

1. The basic law provides for a partition of authority between the central government and the provinces in such a way that, by June 30, 1960, and until such time as the Constitution officially establishes them, effective powers are vested in the provinces within the framework of a wide measure of autonomy.

2. To this end, a list of the powers vested in the central government and the provincial authorities respectively is included in the basic law, embodying a first partition established as follows:
   A. in the *central government,* notably everything which concerns:
      1) external relations;
      2) the Army and the national police force;
      3) the nation's finances, whose limits shall be fixed by the provisory basic law;
      4) Customs and excise;
      5) currency, exchange policy, weights and measures;
      6) higher education and the establishment of common standards to ensure the equivalency of diplomas at the following levels; primary, secondary, technical and normal schools, as also the qualifications of teaching staff.
      In regard to pedagogic supervision of education, some delegations[1] consider that this should be entrusted to provincial inspectors approved by the State; other delegations[2] are in favour of seeing such supervision exercised by State inspectors;
      7) public works on a national scale;
      8) ocean shipping, inland waterways, airlines, including ports and airports, telecommunications, broadcasting, me-

[1] Cartel, P.N.P., A.R.P., Tribal chieftains, Mongo Union, Conakat, Balubakat, Congolese Union, Assoreco.
[2] M.N.C. Lumumba, CEREA.

teorology, geodetics, cartography, geology, hydrography, railways, national highways, and the general organisation of the postal services including the issue of postage stamps;

9) the prospection and development of the subsoil; the coordination of various national sources of power, including hydro-electric equipment and resources, it being understood that legislation pertaining to the prospection and development of the subsoil:

a) must provide formal guarantees regarding the expropriation of persons or collective units (ethnic groups) being the owners of the land, such expropriation to comprise equitable and prior indemnification of such persons or collective units;

b) must also guarantee to the provinces in which the development site lies an equitable and direct share of the royalties collected;

c) must acknowledge the right of the provinces to grant concessions within the framework of the general regulations decreed in the higher interests of the nation.

10) The general regulations pertaining to the land tenure system and to the granting of agricultural and forestry concessions on public lands;

11) The regulations pertaining to the organisation of the judiciary, legal procedure and the appointment of magistrates;

12) The settlement of conflicts of authority between the central government and the provincial bodies;

13) State security;

14) medical legislation;

15) general economic policy;

16) scientific policy.

B. in the *provincial bodies*, notably everything which concerns:

1) the provincial police force and any police forces which are adjoined to the Public Prosecution Department of the province;

2) provincial finances, whose limits shall be fixed by the provisory basic law;

3) primary, secondary, normal and technical education;

4) public works on a provincial scale;

5) provincial or local railways and roads;

6) the development of sources of hydraulic power designed to fill the requirements of the province;

7) the granting of mining concessions within the framework of the general regulations provided for by the Constitution;

8) the granting of agricultural or forestry concessions on public lands and their supervision;

9) proposals for the appointment of magistrates at lower levels of the Judiciary, taking account of the conditions fixed by the general legislation in respect of candidates.

C. *Concurrently in the central government and the provincial authorities,* notably everything which concerns:

The establishment of minimum wage levels and regulations pertaining to labor laws and social security.

3. Insofar as unspecified matters are concerned, authority is equally vested in the central and provincial bodies. In case of conflict of authority, the law of the nation must rule.

4. In cases where the central government or the provincial body claim that their respective authority overlaps to a certain extent, they may submit the matter to a Court of Conflict for settlement.

5. Until such time as this point is settled by a Congolese law, the functions of the Court of Conflict are assumed by a chamber of the Belgian Council of State, sitting in the Congo and comprising three members and a recorder designated by the First President of the Council of State.

RESOLUTION NO. 10
The Organisation of Provincial Institutions

1. The provincial institutions are organised by the provisory basic law.

2. The final infrastructure of the provincial administrations must be established by an institutional law passed in each province on the basis of a two-thirds majority vote in the provincial assembly, within the framework of the general conditions fixed by the provisory basic law.

3. A provincial assembly shall be set up in each province prior to June 30, 1960.

4. This provincial assembly shall be composed of sixty, seventy, eighty or ninety members.

5. It shall be complemented by tribal chieftains or leaders directly chosen by elected members, on the basis of 15%[1] of the number of elected members. Some delegations[2] consider that this proportion should be reduced to 10% of the number of elected members.

6. With regard to the first category of members, some delegations[3] consider that these should be elected by universal suffrage. Oth-

---

[1] Tribal chieftains, P.N.P., Conakat, Mongo Union, Congolese Union, A.R.P.
[2] Cartel, Balubakat, CEREA, Assoreco, M.N.C. Lumumba.
[3] Cartel, Balubakat, Mongo Union, CEREA, Congolese Union, Assoreco, M.N.C. Lumumba.

ers[1] consider that the members of the provincial assemblies should be elected by the second degree method, on the vote of territorial or borough councillors.

7. A provincial government shall be set up prior to June 30, 1960. It shall be composed of a president, and of five to ten members elected by the provincial assembly from amongst its own members or from outside itself.

8. A delegate from the central government shall assume the direction of State services functioning in the province.

9. There shall be incompatibility:
   —between the mandate of provincial councillor and that of member of the national assemblies;
   —between the functions of the executive at central level and that at provincial level.

10. The provincial assembly has authority:
    —to modify, if it sees fit, the administrative divisions of the province so as to reunite ethnic groups;
    —to exercise the legislative authority vested in the province.

RESOLUTION NO. 11
THE ELECTORAL SYSTEM
Elections to Designate the Members of the House of Representatives

1. Insofar as the forthcoming elections are concerned, the right to vote is subordinated to the following conditions:
   All voters must be:
   a) male;
   b) 21 years of age or over;
   c) residents of the territory or town for the past six months at least: this condition is not enforced in respect of persons who were forced to leave their place of residence;
   d) Congolese, or born of a Congolese mother. Nationals of Ruanda-Urundi who have been living in the Congo for the past ten years at least are also allowed to vote.
   Some delegations[2] are also in favour of giving the vote to Belgians living in the Congo for six months at least.

2. The right to vote is suspended in respect of prisoners and persons interned or hospitalised by reason of mental derangement. It is not deemed necessary to suspend the vote of persons living under police supervision for political reasons.

3. The electoral lists drawn up in respect of the recent borough and territorial elections shall be brought up to date by the authorities

---

[1] Tribal chieftains, P.N.P., Conakat, A.R.P.
[2] Tribal chieftains, P.N.P., Conakat, A.R.P.

of the native divisions and boroughs under the supervision of representatives of the political parties who may, if necessary, refer to the Supervisory Commission of the District.

4. To present oneself as a candidate for election, it is necessary to be:
   a) Congolese, or born of a Congolese mother.
      Some delegations[1] consider that this right should also be conceded to Belgians, but on condition that the latter adopt Congolese nationality when such nationality is created;
   b) 25 years of age or over, irrespective of sex.
      Candidates may run for election in any electoral division, but in only one division.

5. The following are ineligible:
   a) persons definitely and unconditionally convicted of offences against persons, property, public religious beliefs, family relationships or the guaranteed rights of individuals, and sentenced to a term of penal servitude;
      according to some delegations[2]:
      —of between six months and one year, during the last five years;
      —of a year or more, during the last ten years;
      according to other delegations[3]:
      —of between six months and two years, during the last two years;
      —of two years or more, during the last five years.
   b) persons interned or hospitalised by reason of mental derangement;
   c) declared bankrupts;
   d) convicted prisoners.

6. The existing districts shall constitute the electoral divisions; the towns of Léopoldville on the one hand, Elisabethville and Jadotville on the other, shall also constitute an electoral division.

7. The presentation of a list must be supported by 300 signatures in the electoral divisions of Léopoldville and Elisabethville-Jadotville, and by 200 signatures in other divisions.

8. The voting methods used in the territorial and borough council elections shall again apply.

9. The distribution of seats shall be undertaken according to the principle of proportional representation: the electoral figures obtained in respect of each list shall be divided by 1, 2, 3, 4 . . .

---

[1] Tribal chieftains, P.N.P., Conakat, A.R.P.
[2] P.N.P., Tribal chieftains, Conakat, A.R.P. (CEREA abstained).
[3] Cartel, M.N.C. Lumumba, Mongo Union, Congolese Union, Balubakat, Assoreco.

etc., and the seats shall be attributed to those lists which have thus obtained the highest quotients.

10. Some delegations[1] consider that voting should be made obligatory. Others[2] prefer that voting should be free. Similarly, some delegations[3] would like to see Article 192 of the electoral decree maintained, whereby incitement to abstention is punishable: whereas others[4] would prefer this article to be abolished.

11. One sole date shall be fixed throughout the country for the start of the elections, as also for the deposit of lists.

12. The presidency of the main polling offices shall be entrusted to magistrates, and the presidents of the main offices shall designate the presidents of the polling booths and voting returns offices. The presidents concerned shall be assisted by Congolese assessors. The electoral offices shall be staffed by independent persons, but each list may, however, designate a witness to be present during the various operations.

13. An itinerant supervisory commission shall be set up in each district, composed of a Belgian[5] or a Congolese[6] magistrate and of independent Congolese assessors; this commission shall be vested with real and far-reaching powers and its decisions shall be final.

14. Any complaints concerning the results of the elections shall be laid before a provincial college composed of a Belgian magistrate and independent Congolese assessors.

Elections to Designate the Members of the Senate

15. Candidates for seats in the second House must fulfil the same conditions as those obtaining in respect of candidates for seats in the first House, but the minimum age is fixed at 30 years.

16. The assembly, formed by elected senators, may co-opt members. Some delegations[7] consider that such members shall fulfil the same conditions as those obtained for elected senators. Other delegations[8] are of the opinion that such members should fulfil conditions to be determined by the assembly itself.

Elections to Designate the Members of the Provincial Assemblies

17. The existing territories and towns shall constitute the electoral divisions.

---

[1] Tribal chieftains, P.N.P., Balubakat, Conakat, Congolese Union, A.R.P.
[2] Cartel, Mongo Union, CEREA, Assoreco, M.N.C. Lumumba.
[3] P.N.P., Tribals, Conakat, A.R.P., Assoreco, Congolese Union, CEREA.
[4] M.N.C. Lumumba, Mongo Union, Balubakat, Cartel.
[5] Cartel, Balubakat, Conakat, CEREA, Assoreco, M.N.C. Lumumba.
[6] Tribal chieftains, P.N.P., Mongo Union, Congolese Union, A.R.P.
[7] Cartel, Conakat, CEREA, Congolese Union, Assoreco, M.N.C. Lumumba.
[8] Tribal chieftains, P.N.P., Balubakat, Mongo Union, A.R.P.

18. The distribution of seats shall be undertaken according to the principle of proportional representation in those electoral divisions where there are several seats to be attributed; and to that of the relative majority in those electoral divisions where there is only one seat to be attributed.
19. The presentation of a list must be supported by 100 signatures in the towns of Léopoldville and Elisabethville, and by 50 signatures in the other electoral divisions.
20. With respect to conditions governing the electorate and eligibility, the same requisites are adopted as those obtaining for the election of members of the House of Representatives.

RESOLUTION NO. 12
The Exercise of Executive Authority Until June 30, 1960

1. Effective participation by the Congolese in the exercise of the duties and the authority vested in high administrative offices shall be arranged for at the earliest possible moment and shall continue until June 30 next.
2. Such participation shall take the form of the permanent presence of six Congolese members on the staff of the Governor General, and of three members on the staff of each Provincial Governor.
3. These members, with the Governor General or the Provincial Governor concerned, shall constitute colleges which will be called upon to make the necessary decisions on matters falling within the competency of the Governor General or of the Provincial Governor as the case may be, with the exception of those matters which shall be expressly reserved for the competency of these Governors under the terms of the law.
4. These authorities and colleges are answerable to the Belgian Government.
5. The Provincial Governor and his college shall take all necessary steps to ensure the adjunction of Congolese assistants to the District Commissioners and Territorial Administrators within his area.
6. A commission comprising six members, who will reside in Brussels, shall be set up.
7. The tasks of this commission will be:
    a) to co-operate with the Minister concerned in preparing draft laws, edicts and Royal decrees in the spirit of the agreements reached at the Round Table Conference;
    b) to prepare the drafts of treaties and conventions which are to be signed between the Belgian and Congolese Governments to establish the basis of their future co-operation;
    c) to draw up, with the assistance of members of the record

offices of the Belgian Houses of Parliament, draft regulations on procedure to be submitted for the approval of the Congolese Houses in the course of their June, 1960, session;

d) if possible, with the assistance of Belgian experts, to prepare a draft constitution.

RESOLUTION NO. 13

Future Relations Between Belgium and the Congo

1. A general treaty of friendship, assistance and co-operation shall be signed as soon as possible between the governments of Belgium and the Congo.
2. Within the framework of this treaty, special conventions will be drawn up between the governments of the Congo and Belgium to establish the basis for co-operation between these two states.
3. In respect of matters included in treaties signed by Belgium and which will remain applicable to the Congo, prior consultation shall take place between the two governments as often as may be necessary.
4. A Belgian technical mission in the Congo shall ensure, after June 30, 1960, due coordination of all measures of technical and economic assistance taken by the Belgian Government within the framework of agreements concluded with the Congolese government.
5. Personnel belonging to technical or scientific services undertaken by Belgium at the request of the Congolese government, shall come under the authority of the Belgian government.

RESOLUTION NO. 14

Economic and Financial Problems

1. The Congolese delegations:
   —aware of their immense responsibilities towards their Congolese fellow-citizens;
   —determined to avoid at all costs the possibility of the Congo's accession to independence being accompanied by economic and social regression, troubles and disorders;
   —desiring, on the other hand, that the independence of their country should go hand in hand with rapid economic expansion, accelerated industrialisation and greater improvements to the living standards of the population in conditions of law and order;
   —anxious to maintain the financial and monetary balance so as to preserve the purchasing power of the Congolese franc and the confidence of all in the Congo's economic future;
2. acknowledge the necessity and desirability of obtaining the assistance of technical experts and investments, both Belgian and for-

eign, so that they may contribute, with due respect for the Congolese laws, to the economic development of the Congo and the raising of the people's standard of living.

3. entrust the forthcoming Conference on economic, financial and social problems with the task of preparing the contents of the agreements on technical assistance and economic co-operation which must be concluded between Belgium and the Congo.

RESOLUTION NO. 15
The Status of Belgian Administrative Officials in Africa

1. On June 30, 1960, Belgian civil servants will fall under the authority of the Congolese government.
2. The Congolese government may require these civil servants to take an oath of allegiance, the terms of which will be drawn up by it.
3. The Congolese government shall respect the status of these civil servants, which shall constitute an acquired right.
4. The Congolese government shall, however, be empowered, within the framework of the relevant legislation and the existing statutes, to release certain civil servants for reasons connected with the interests of the service, and on payment of the indemnities provided for in this respect.
5. Any financial problems which might arise in connection with the remuneration of these civil servants, shall be the subject of the assistance agreements which are to be signed between Belgium and the Congo.

RESOLUTION NO. 16
The Exercise of Judiciary Power[1]

1. After June 30, 1960, the Judiciary must of necessity continue to fulfil its functions according to the legislation in force at that date, until such time as the Congolese Legislature has modified the laws governing the organization of the Judiciary and legal procedure with due respect for constitutional principles.
2. Prior to June 30, 1960, the judiciary reforms which have already been the subject of numerous legal documents, shall be put under way with all despatch and to the widest possible extent.
3. Apart from the principles governing these judiciary reforms, arrangements shall be made so that Congolese may attend District law courts in the capacity of assessors.

---

[1] Assoreco reserved its opinion concerning this resolution.

The Speech of Premier Lumumba on Independence Day

Ladies and gentlemen of the Congo who have fought for the independence won today, I salute you in the name of the Congolese government.

To all of you, my friends who have struggled continuously on our side, I ask you to make this day, June 30, 1960, an illustrious date which you will keep indelibly engraved in your hearts—a date of which you will proudly teach your children the significance so that they in their turn may make known to their sons and grandsons the glorious history of our struggle for freedom.

Because this independence of the Congo, as it is proclaimed today in agreement with Belgium—the friendly country with whom we stand on equal terms—no Congolese worthy of the name will ever forget that independence has been won by struggle, an everyday struggle, an intense and idealistic struggle, a struggle in which we have spared neither our forces, our privations, our suffering, nor our blood.

This struggle of tears, fire, and blood makes us profoundly proud because it was a noble and just struggle, an indispensable struggle to put an end to the humiliating bondage imposed on us by force.

Our lot was eighty years of colonial rule; our wounds are still too fresh and painful to be driven from our memory.

We have known tiring labor exacted in exchange for salary which did not allow us to satisfy our hunger, to clothe and lodge ourselves decently or to raise our children like loved beings.

We have known ironies, insults, blows which we had to endure morning, noon, and night because we were "Negroes." Who will forget that to a Negro the familiar verb forms were used, not indeed as with a friend, but because the honorable formal verb forms were reserved for the whites?

We have known that our lands were despoiled in the name of supposedly legal texts which recognized only the law of the stronger.

We have known that the law was never the same depending on whether it concerned a white or a Negro: accommodating for one group, it was cruel and inhuman for the other.

We have known the atrocious sufferings of those banished for

352

political opinions or religious beliefs; exiled in their own countries, their end was truly worse than death itself.

We have known that there were magnificent houses for the whites in the cities and tumble-down straw huts for the Negroes, that a Negro was not admitted in movie houses or restaurants or stores labeled "European," that a Negro traveled in the hulls of river boats at the feet of the white in his first class cabin.

Who will forget, finally, the fusillades where so many of our brothers perished or the prisons where all those were brutally flung who no longer wished to submit to the regime of a law of oppression and exploitation which the colonists had made a tool of their domination?

All that, my brothers, we have profoundly suffered.

But for all of that, we who by the votes of your elected representatives have been approved to direct our beloved country, we who have suffered the colonial oppression in body and heart, we say to you, all of that is henceforth finished.

The Congo Republic has been proclaimed and our beloved country is now in the hands of its own children.

Together, my brothers, we are going to begin a new struggle, a sublime struggle which is going to lead our country to peace, prosperity, and grandeur.

Together we are going to establish social justice and assure that everyone receives just remuneration for his work.

We are going to show the world what the black man can do when he works in freedom, and we are going to make the Congo the center of radiance for the whole of Africa.

We are going to awaken to what the lands of our beloved country provide her children.

We are going to re-examine all the former laws and from them make new laws which will be noble and just.

We are going to put an end to the oppression of free thought so that all citizens may enjoy fully the fundamental liberties provided for in the declaration of the Rights of Man.

We are going to suppress effectually all discrimination, whatever it may be, and give to each person the just place which his human dignity, his work, and his devotion to his country merit him.

We are not going to let a peace of guns and bayonets prevail, but rather a peace of courage and good will.

And for all that, beloved compatriots, rest assured that we will be able to count not only on our enormous forces and our immense riches but also on the assistance of many foreign countries with whom we will accept collaboration so long as it is honest and does not seek to impose any politics whatever.

In this domain, even Belgium who after all understands the meaning of history has not tried to oppose our independence further and is ready to give us her help and her friendship; and a treaty with this understanding has been signed between our two equal and independent countries. This co-operation, I am sure, will be profitable to both countries. While remaining vigilant, we will be able for our part to respect the promises freely given.

Thus, as much at home as abroad, the new Congo which my government is going to create will be a rich, free, and prosperous country. But in order that we may arrive at this goal without delay, I ask all of you, legislators and Congolese citizens to assist me with all your strength.

—I ask all of you to forget the hazardous tribal quarrels which exhaust our strength and make us contemptible to the foreigner.

—I ask the parliamentary minority to help my government with a constructive opposition, and to stay strictly in legal and democratic channels.

—I ask all of you not to retreat in the face of any sacrifice necessary to assure the success of our great undertaking.

—I ask you finally to respect unconditionally the life and well-being of your fellow citizens and of the foreigners settled in our country; if the conduct of these foreigners leaves something to be desired, our courts of justice will be prompt to expel them from the territory of the Republic; if on the other hand their conduct is good, they must be left in peace, because they also work for the prosperity of our country.

The independence of the Congo marks a decisive step toward the liberation of the entire African continent.

There, Lord, Excellencies, Ladies, Gentlemen, my brothers in ancestry, my brothers in struggle, my compatriots, there is what I have wanted to tell you in the name of the government on this magnificent day of our complete and sovereign Independence.

Our government, strong, national, popular, will be the hope of this country.

I invite all Congolese citizens, men, women, and children, to devote themselves resolutely to their work with a view toward creating a national economy and building our economic independence.

Homage to the Champions of National Liberty!

Long live African Independence and Unity!

Long live the Independent and Sovereign Congo!

APPENDIX V

MINISTERS, SECRETARIES, AND COMMISSIONERS OF STATE APPOINTED TO THE FIRST CONGOLESE GOVERNMENT

MINISTERS
Prime Minister and National Defense: Patrice Lumumba (MNC)
Vice Prime Minister: Antoine Gizenga (PSA)
Minister of Foreign Affairs: Justin Bomboko (UNIMO)
Minister of External Commerce: Marcel Bisukiro (CEREA)
Resident Minister in Belgium: Albert Delvaux (PNP—LUKA)
Minister-Delegate to the United Nations: Thomas Kanza
Minister of Justice: Remy Mwamba (Balubakat)
Minister of the Interior: Chrystophe Gbenye (MNC)
Minister of Finance: Pascal Nkayi (ABAKO)
Minister of Economic Affairs: Robert Yava (Conakat)
Minister of Economic Coordination and Planning: Alois Kabanga
    (MNC)
Minister of Public Works: Alphonse Ilunga (UNC)
Minister of Communications: Alphonse Songolo (MNC)
Minister of Agriculture: Joseph Lutula (MNC)
Minister of Labor: J. Masena (PSA)
Minister of the Middle Classes: Joseph Mbuyi (MNC)
Minister of Public Health: Gr. Kamanga (COAKA)
Minister of Mines: Rudahindwa (REKO)
Minister of Land Affairs: Alexandre Mahamba (MNC)
Minister of Social Affairs: Antoine Ngwenza (PUNA)
Minister of National Education and Fine Arts: Pierre Mulele
Minister of Information and Cultural Affairs: Anicet Kashamura
Minister of Youth and Sports: Maurice Mpolo (MNC)

SECRETARIES OF STATE
Secretary to the Presidency: Joseph Mobutu (MNC)
                            Jacques Lumbala (PNP)
Secretary to Foreign Affairs: André Mandi
Secretary to External Commerce: Antoine Kiwewa (MNC)
Secretary to Finance: André Tshibangu
Secretary to Justice: Maximilien Liongo
Secretary to Interior: Raphael Batshikama (ABAKO)

Secretary to Economic Co-ordination and Planning: Alphonse
   Nguvulu (PP)
Secretary to National Defense: Albert Nyembo (Conakat)
Secretary to Information and Cultural Affairs: Antoine Bolamba
   (MNC)
State Ministers: Members of the Council of Ministers:
   Kisolokele (ABAKO)
   G. Grenfell (MNC)
   Paul Bolya (PNP)
   André Genge (PUNA)

COMMISSIONERS OF STATE (PROPOSED)
Commissioner of the Province of Léopoldville: Sylvain Kama
Commissioner of the Equator Province: Tamusu Fumu
Commissioner of the Kasaï Province: Isaac Kalonji
Commissioner of the Katanga Province: Jason Sendwe
Commissioner of the Kivu Province: Hubert Sangara
Commissioner of the Eastern Province: Christophe Muzungu

356

BIBLIOGRAPHY

Reference system: References are cited in the text by number. Thus *1*:12, refers to the first listing in the bibliography, p. 12. In the case of citations to articles in newspapers, *14*:IV, 16:3–4, would refer to the fourteenth listing, Part IV of the newspaper, p. 16, columns 3 and 4; in such a citation, any part may be omitted depending on the circumstances.

1. Anonymous. "Actualités Congolaises. (élections, Congrès de Kisantu, table ronde)," *Courrier Africain* (CRISP), 2 (22 January, 1960), 2–14.
2. ———. "L'affaire Kalonji et les problèmes du Kasaï," *Courrier Africain* (CRISP), n.d., 6–8.
3. ———. "African Manifesto Stirs Congo," *Africa Special Reports*, I (October 26, 1956), 1–5.
4. ———. *The Belgian Congo: Its Past, Its Future.* Bruxelles: Inforcongo, n.d. 63 pp.
5. ———. "The Belgian Congo on the Eve of Independence," *The Belgian Congo To-Day*, IX (April–May, 1960), 5–15.
6. ———. "Belgian Troops in Congo should Withdraw Quickly," *Chicago Daily News*, 19 July, 1960, 14:1.
7. ———. "Belgium Provides Full Facts to U.N.O. on Congo Administration," *The Belgian Congo To-Day*, VII (January, 1958), 3–16.
8. ———. "Belgium Warned to Move Quickly on Lower Congo," *New York Times* (Overseas Edition), 17 December, 1959.
9. ———. *The Belgo-Congolese Round Table Conference.* Bruxelles: Inforcongo, 1960. 63 pp.
10. ———. "British Press Blames Belgium for Congo Riot," *Chicago Daily Tribune*, 11 July, 1960, 3:2–3.
11. ———. "La Conférence de la Table Ronde Belgo-Congolaise," *Courrier Africain* (CRISP), 6 (25 March, 1960), 1–20.
12. ———. "La Conférence de la Table Ronde Économique," *Courrier Africain* (CRISP), 10 (3 June, 1960), 1–20.
13. ———. "Conflict in the Congo," *Africa Today*, VII (September, 1960), 5–13.
14. ———. "Congo: Back from the Precipice," *Time*, LXXVI (1 August, 1960), 21–2.
15. ———. "Congo Freed to Avoid War, Belgians Told," *Chicago Tribune*, 18 August, 1960, 3:6.
16. ———. "Congo State Pulls Out of New Republic," *Chicago Tribune*, 12 July, 1960, 1:1, 16:1–2.
17. ———. "The Congo's Educational System," *The Belgian Congo To-Day*, VI (October, 1957), 21–5.
18. ———. "A Congolese 'Scholastic Pact'," *Belgian Congo 59*, 9 (September, 1959), 10–11.
19. ———. "Decrees on Civic Liberties and 'Inga'," *Belgian Congo 59*, 9 (September, 1959), 4–6.
20. ———. "Election Results," *Belgian Congo 60*, 1 (January, 1960), 5–7.
21. ———. "Eyskens Wins Vote on Policy Toward Congo," *Chicago Tribune*, 19 August, 1960, 13:2

22. Anonymous. "The Fight Against Unemployment," *Belgian Congo 59*, 2 (February, 1959), 3–4.
23. ——. "For Belgium: High Stakes in the Congo," *U.S. News & World Report*, XLIX (22 August, 1960), 40.
24. ——. "La Formation du Premier Gouvernement Congolais," *Courrier Africain* (CRISP), 12 (1 July, 1960), 1–22.
25. ——. "Further Claims on the Part of Congolese Political Parties," *Belgian Congo 59*, 7–8 (July–August, 1959), 14.
26. ——. "Hints Reds Caused Congo Riots," *Chicago Daily News*, 4 August, 1960, 19:2.
27. ——. "The Hopes and Aspirations of the People of the Congo," *Belgian Congo 59*, 2 (February, 1959), 4–7.
28. ——. "The Incidents at Léopoldville," *Belgian Congo 59*, 1 (January, 1959), 1–4.
29. ——. "Independence Won't Spark Nigeria Riots, Leader Says," *Chicago Daily News*, 20 July, 1960, II, 15:1–4.
30. ——. "Le Kimbanguisme," *Courrier Africain* (CRISP), 1 (8 January, 1960), 1–21.
31. ——. " 'King' of the Congo: Joseph Kasavubu," *New York Times* (Overseas Edition), 23 January, 1960.
32. ——. "Message Broadcast to the Congo on October 16, 1959, by Mr. A. E. DeSchrijver, Minister of the Belgian Congo and Ruanda-Urundi," *Belgian Congo 59*, 10 (October, 1959), 1–7
33. ——. "Missionary Thinks Reds Spark Violence in Congo," *Chicago Daily News*, 19 July, 1960, 4:1.
34. ——. "Mr. A. DeSchrijver, New Belgian Minister of the Congo and Ruanda-Urundi," *The Belgian Congo To-Day*, VIII (October, 1959), 3–5.
35. ——. "1950–59: The Congo Ten Year Plan," *The Belgian Congo To-Day*, VIII (January, 1959), 22–7.
36. ——. *Nous nous y sommes sentis chez nous; notes de voyage des 15 notables congolais qui visiterent la Belgique en 1953*. Kalina: Service de l'Information, 1954. 254 pp.
37. ——. "L'organisation et l'Action des Colons au Congo: La Fédacol," *Courrier Africain* (CRISP), n.d., 9–14.
38. ——. "Parliamentary Enquiry on the Troubles," *Belgian Congo 59*, 4 (April, 1959), 1–4.
39. ——. "The Political Situation on the Eve of Elections," *Belgian Congo 59*, 12 (December, 1959), 2–6.
40. ——. "Pour Comprendre le Telex Schöller," *Courrier Africain* (CRISP), n.d., pp. 2–5.
41. ——. "Problèmes du Bas-Congo. II," *Courrier Africain* (CRISP), 8 (22 April, 1960), 1–19.
42. ——. "Les Problèmes du Katanga," *Courrier Africain* (CRISP), 5 (4 March, 1960), 1–19.
43. ——. "Programmes Economiques des Partis Politiques et des Syndicats Congolais," *Courrier Africain* (CRISP), 9 (26 April, 1960), 14–18.
44. ——. "La Répercussion des Evénements Congolais sur la Situation et les Décisions Politiques en Belgique," *Courrier Africain* (CRISP), 14 (15 July, 1960), 1–16.
45. ——. "Resolutions Adopted by the Round Table Conference," *Belgian Congo 60*, 2 (February, 1960), 4–20.
46. ——. "Restoring Order," *Chicago Daily News*, 15 July, 1960, 8:2.
47. ——. "Russ Blast Dag Policy on Congo," *Chicago Daily News*, 19 September, 1960, 1:5, 4:3–4.
48. ——. *The Sacred Mission of Civilization*. New York: Belgian Government Information Center, 1953. 64 pp.

49. Anonymous. "Schools for the Congolese in 1951," *The Belgian Congo To-Day*, II (January, 1953), 11–16.
50. ———. "A Survey of the Congolese Press," *Belgian Congo 58*, 11 (November, 1958), 9–13.
51. ———. "Table III: Foreign Students: Home Country, Sex, Year Studies in U.S. Began, Financial Support, Academic Status," *Open Doors* (June, 1957), 35–7.
52. ———. "Text of the Resolutions Adopted by the Economic, Financial and Social Conference," *Belgian Congo 60*, 4–5 (May, 1960), 13–24.
53. ———. *Thirteen Million Congolese*. Bruxelles: Inforcongo, n.d. 79 pp.
54. ———. "Too Much Togetherness," *Wall Street Journal*, 26 July, 1960, 12:1–2.
55. ———. "U.N.'s Giant Task in the Congo," London *Times*, 31 August, 1960, 9.
56. ———. "Unemployment Drops in Léopoldville," *Belgian Congo 59*, 10 (October, 1959), 9–10.
57. ———. *Universities of Belgian Congo and of Ruanda-Urundi*. Brussels: Inforcongo, n.d. 47 pp.
58. Artigue, Pierre, *Qui Sont les Leaders Congolais?* Bruxelles: Editions Europe-Afrique, 1960. 139 pp.
59. Beichman, Arnold. "U.S. Focus Turns to Congo: Changed Tactic Emerges," *The Christian Science Monitor*, 18 July, 1960, 1:5–6.
60. Carpenter, George. "Belgian Congo and the United States—Policies and Relationships," *in* Calvin W. Stillman (Ed). *Africa in the Modern World*. Chicago: Norman Wait Harris Memorial Foundation, Proceedings of the Twenty-Ninth Institute, 1953, pp. 306–32.
61. Chomé, Jules. *Le Drame de Luluabourg*. Bruxelles: Editions de Remarques Congolaises, Collection 'Etudes Congolaises' No. 1, 1960. 52 pp.
62. ———. *Indépendance Congolaise Pacifique Conquête*. Bruxelles: Editions de Remarques Congolaises, Collection 'Etudes Congolaises' No. 3, 1960. 52 pp.
63. Davidson, Basil. *The African Awakening*. London: Jonathan Cape, 1955. 262 pp.
64. DeBacker, M. C. C. *Notes Pour Servir à l'Etude des 'Groupements Politiques' à Léopoldville*. Bruxelles: Inforcongo, 15 March, 1959, 1ère Partie. 63 pp.
65. ———. *Notes Pour Servir à l'Etude des 'Groupements Politiques' à Léopoldville*. Bruxelles: Inforcongo, 30 June, 1959, 2ème Partie. 85 pp.
66. ———. *Notes Pour Servir à l'Etude des 'Groupements Politiques' à Léopoldville*. Bruxelles: Inforcongo, 15 September, 1959, 3ème Partie. 160 pp.
67. ———. *Digest de l'Evolution et de la Situation Actuelle des Partis Politiques au Congo Belge*. Bruxelles: Inforcongo, 24 November, 1959. 28 pp.
68. Demany, Fernand. *S.O.S. Congo (Chronique d'un Soulèvement)*. Bruxelles: Éditions Labor, 1959. 172 pp.
69. Freudenheim, Milt. "U.S. Warns: We'll Shoot Russ in Congo," *Chicago Daily News*, 21 July, 1960, 1:1–2; 4:5–7.
70. ———. "U.N. Hears Grim Details of Atrocities in the Congo; Belgian Envoy Tells His Side; Congolese Accuse Whites," *Chicago Daily News*, 22 July, 1960, 2:1–4.
71. Gérard, Jo. *La Monarchie Belge Abandonnera-t-elle le Congo?* Bruxelles: Éditions Europe-Afrique, 1960. 95 pp.
72. Gérard-Libois, J. (Ed). *Congo 1959: Documents Belges et Africains*. Bruxelles: Les Dossiers du C.R.I.S.P., 1960. 319 pp.
73. Gilroy, Harry. "Belgians Suspect Red Plot in Congo," *New York Times*, 15 July, 1960, 3:8.
74. Goris, Jan-Albert. "John Gunther on the Belgian Congo: A Boner a Page

or Better," *in* Jan-Albert Goris (Ed). *Belgian Congo-American Survey 1956–57.* New York: Belgian Chamber of Commerce, 1957, p. 61.
75. Gunther, John. *Inside Africa.* New York: Harper & Brothers, 1955. 952 pp.
76. Heinzerling, Lynn. "Why Russ Bungled Attempt to Control Congo," *Chicago Daily News,* 20 September, 1960, 2:4–8.
77. Hempstone, Smith. "What's Making Lumumba Tick?" *Chicago Daily News,* 20 August, 1960, 1:1; 23:1–2.
78. Huge, J. "Economic Planning and Development in the Belgian Congo," *in* William O. Brown (Ed). *Contemporary Africa: Trends and Issues.* Philadelphia: The Annals of the American Academy of Political and Social Science, Vol. 298, March, 1955, pp. 62–70.
79. Kadijk, Jozef. "What Price Independence?" *The Belgian Congo To-Day,* IX (January, 1960), 3–5.
80. Kalanda, Mabika. *Baluba et Lulua: Une Ethnie à la Recherche d'un Nouvel Equilibre.* Bruxelles: Editions de Remarques Congolaises, Collection 'Etudes Congolaises' No. 2, 1959. 106 pp.
81. Kanza, Thomas R. *Tôt ou Tard (Ata Ndele...).* Bruxelles: Le Livre Africain, 1959. 85 pp.
82. Kaskeline, Egon. "Brussels Evaluates Losses in Congo," *The Christian Science Monitor,* 15 July, 1960, 1:2–5.
83. Kennedy, Raymond. "The Colonial Crisis and the Future," *in* Ralph Linton (Ed). *The Science of Man in the World Crisis.* New York: Columbia University Press, 1947, pp. 306–46.
84. Labrique, Jean. *Congo Politique.* Léopoldville: Editions de l'Avenir, 1957. 275 pp.
85. Legum, Colin. "The Belgian Congo (I): Revolt of the Elite," *Africa South,* IV (October–December, 1959), 104–13.
86. ———. "The Belgian Congo (II): Towards Independence," *Africa South In Exile,* IV (July–September, 1960), 78–91.
87. Lenain, R. E. "A vos Poches!" *L'Echo du Kivu* (Bukavu), 5 February, 1960, 1, 12.
88. Lindsay, Robert N. "Belgian Troops Seize Airport in Léopoldville," *Washington Post,* 14 July, 1960, 8:1–5.
89. Lumumba, Patrice. *Les Incidents de Stanleyville.* Liège: Jacques Yerna, and others, 11 January, 1960. 31 pp.
90. Malley, Simon. "First Congo Chief Interview: Calls Africa Key to Peace; Lumumba Warns that Continent Must be Allowed to Develop," *Chicago Daily News,* 25 July, 1960, 1:1–2.
91. Marres, Jacques et Pierre De Vos. *L'Equinoxe de Janvier: Les Emeutes de Léopoldville.* Bruxelles: Éditions Euraforient, n.d. 261 pp.
92. McKay, Vernon. "External Political Pressures on Africa Today," *in* Walter Goldschmidt (Ed). *The United States and Africa.* New York: The American Assembly, 1958, pp. 63–88.
93. Mendelsohn, Jack, Jr. " 'Uhuru' Comes to the Congo," *Africa Today,* VII (September, 1960), 6–7.
94. Mendiaux, Edouard. *Moscou, Accra et le Congo.* Bruxelles: Charles Dessart, 1960. 198 pp.
95. Merchiers, L. *Congo July 1960 Evidence.* Brussels: Ministry of Justice, 1960. 30 pp.
96. ———. *A Preliminary Report on the Atrocities Committed by the Congolese Army Against the White Population of the Republic of the Congo Before the Intervention of the Belgian Forces.* New York: Belgian Government Information Center, 1960. 22 pp.
97. Merriam, Alan P. "The Concept of Culture Clusters Applied to the Belgian Congo," *Southwestern Journal of Anthropology,* XV (Winter, 1959), 373–95.

98. Miller, John. "Soviet Charges Intervention in Congo," *Washington Post*, 14 July, 1960, 10:1–8.
99. Perin, Francois. *Les Institutions Politiques du Congo Indépendant au 30 Juin 1960*. Léopoldville: Institut Politique Congolais, and Bruxelles: C.R.I.S.P., 1960. 151 pp.
100. Program of African Studies, Northwestern University. *United States Foreign Policy: Africa*. Washington: 86th Congress, 1st Session, Printed for the use of the Senate Committee on Foreign Relations, 1959. 84 pp.
101. Ritner, Peter. *The Death of Africa*. New York: Macmillan, 1960. 312 pp.
102. Scheyven, Raymond. *Et le Congo?* Bruxelles: La Libre Belgique (?), c. 1956. 111 pp.
103. Slade, Ruth. *The Belgian Congo: Some Recent Changes*. London: Oxford University Press, under the auspices of the Institute of Race Relations, 1960. 55 pp.
104. Stanley, Henry M. *In Darkest Africa*. New York: Charles Scribner's Sons, 1890. 2 vols.
105. Van Bilsen, A. A. J. *Vers l'Indépendance du Congo et du Ruanda-Urundi; Réflexions sur les Devoirs et l'Avenir de la Belgique en Afrique Centrale*. Kraainem: The Author, n.d. 294 pp.
106. Van Bol, J. M. *La Presse Quotidiènne au Congo Belge*. Bruxelles: La Pensée Catholique, Etudes Sociales, 23–24, 1959. 112 pp.
107. Van Reyn, Paul. *Le Congo Politique; les Parties et les Elections*. Bruxelles: Editions Europe-Afrique, Collection "Carrefours Africains" No. 1, 1960. 75 pp.
108. Van Wing, J. (Ed). *Le Congo 1959: Documents*. Bruxelles: DeLinie, n.d. 40 pp.
109. Vicker, Ray. "Congo Lesson: Strife in Newly-Independent State Suggests Self-Rule Cannot Precede Education," *Wall Street Journal*, 12 July, 1960, 14:1
110. ———. "African Adversaries: Russia Also Has Its Weaknesses in Battle with the West over New Nations," *Wall Street Journal*, 19 August, 1960, 4:3.

INDEX

ABAKO (Alliance des Bakongo): 75–
77, 78–79, 93, 99, 107–108, 116, 119–
126, 131, 132, 150, 237, 239, 240,
246, 248, 255, 258, 281; dissolution of after Léopoldville riots: 88;
publications of: 123
ADAPES (Association des Anciens
Elèves des Péres de Scheut): 117,
120, 121, 158
APIC (Association du Personnel In-
digène du Congo Belge et du Ruan-
da-Urundi): 118, 156, 158
ARP (Alliance Rurale Progressiste):
172
ASSANEF (Association des Anciens
Elèves des Frères des Ecoles Chré-
tiennes): 117, 165
Atcar (Association des Tshokwe, Ka-
tanga): 137
Action Socialiste: 128, 171
Albertville, fighting in: 248
Alexander, Henry: 216, 248
Anciens Elèves des Pères Jésuites:
117–118
Aroutunian, Amasap: 231
Atrocities, reports of Congolese by
Belgium: 218, 221–222, 228–230;
denied by Lumumba: 230

Balubakat (Baluba du Katanga): 99,
133, 136–137
Baker, Samuel: 5
Bakwanga: 249, 251, 252, 253, 316
Banana Point: 10
Banningville: 220
Bantu: 18–19, 20–23
Banzyville: 9
Batshikama, Raphael: 172
Belgium, cabinet crisis in, as result of
Congo independence: 241, 244, 245,
250; threatens to withdraw forces
from NATO: 240

Belgo-Congolese community: 68, 73,
76, 134–135
Berlin Conference: 7
Bisukiro, Marcel: 168
Bolamba, Antoine-Roger: 162, 165
Bolikango, Jean: 24, 118, 141, 143,
158–161, 163–165, 251, 254, 258, 261
Bolya, Paul: 103, 165–166, 197–198
Bomboko, Justin-Marie: 170–171, 209,
210, 221, 237, 256, 257, 259, 261,
267
Brussels International Exposition of
1958: 80–81, 148
Bunche, Ralph: 216, 217, 219, 235,
237, 241, 246, 248, 251
Business interests and their role in
Congo government: 36–38; Banque
Empain: 37; Brufina: 36; Cominiè-
re: 37; Huilever: 36–37; Société
Générale: 37

CEREA (Centre de Regroupement
Africain): 109, 168, 170
COAKA (Coalition Kasaïenne): 172
Conakat (Confederation des Associa-
tions du Katanga): 99–100, 132–
136, 137, 248
Cameron, Verney Lovett: 6
Cão, Diego: 4–5, 24
Catholic Church, its role in Congo
government: 36
China, requested to intervene in Con-
go crisis: 215, 220; visit of Congo-
lese to: 302–303
Chou En-lai: 227
Collapse of Congo after independ-
ence: 280–287
Colonial policies: 29–51; Belgian: 32–
51; British: 30–31; Dutch: 29;
French: 31; Portuguese: 31; Span-
ish: 31–32; United States: 29–30
Comité National du Kivu: 13

Index

Comité Spécial du Katanga: 13
Communism, charges of its influence
on the Congo: 216, 218, 220; Congolese influenced by: 302; ideology
toward Africa: 300–301; in political parties: 132; influence on the
Congo: 301–307, 309–312. See also
under: China, Czechoslovakia, Lumumba, Russia, United States.
Compagnie des Chemins de Fer du
Congo Supérieur aux Grands Lacs
Africains: 13
Conference of Independent African
Nations (All African Summit Conference) : 240, 248–249, 251
Congo, Belgian administration of: 12–
16, 35–36, 78; centres extracoutumiers in: 15; Chieftaincies in: 15;
climate and rainfall: 10–11; culture
clusters in: 23–27; Districts of: 14;
education in: 15, 40–48, 59–60, 174,
279; elections in: 78–79, 90, 94, 98–
100, 108–109, 133, 150, 185–186;
flora and fauna: 11; geography of:
8–11; health services in: 15–16, 48;
history of: 3–8, 23–27; importance
of in world: 296–297; justice in:
15; land tenure in: 12–13; languages of: 23; mineral wealth in:
11–12, 278; missions and missionaries in: 16; Native Cities in: 15;
peoples of: 18–28 (See also under
Tribes, in Congo); population of:
16–17; prehistory of: 3, 18, 24;
provinces of: 14; territories in: 14;
transportation: 12; vegetable products of: 12; voting in: 14, 35, 99–
100, 103, 182–186
Congo Free State: 8, 13
Congo River: 4, 5, 10
Conscience Africaine Manifesto: 71–
75, 76, 77; reaction to: 77; text of:
321–329
Coquilhatville: 18, 98, 220; rioting in:
208, 217
Counter Manifesto of the ABAKO:
75–77; reaction to: 77; text of:
330–336
Cristal Mountains: 9
Czechoslovakia, army officers reported
leading Congo troops: 250; consul

in Léopoldville: 302; diplomats ordered to leave Congo: 261–262, 263,
264, 265; reported influencing Congo government: 260; technicians reported in Léopoldville: 253

Dayal, Rajeshwar: 246
De Gaulle, Charles: 81–82, 139, 253
De Schrijver, Auguste: 94, 215
Delvaux, Albert: 166, 257
Departure from the Congo, Belgian:
106–107, 210–212, 214, 217, 227, 235,
240, 244, 282–283
Dequenne Report: 96, 149
Dericoyard, Jean-Pierre: 162, 166–167
Detwiler, Edgar: 224, 225, 226, 228
Diefenbaker, John: 231

Economic decrees, affecting credit:
106–107; affecting transfer of monies to Belgium: 106
Economics, situation of Belgian in
Congo after independence: 275–280
Eisenhower, Dwight D.: 212, 226, 245,
255
Elections, of December, 1959: 98–100,
150, 184–185, 198, 199; of May,
1960: 108–109, 185–186
Elisabethville, Independence Day in:
206; population of: 17; rioting in:
211
Epidemics and health in Congo: 226,
228, 264–265
Eratosthenes of Syena: 3

Fédacol (Fédération Congolaise des
Classes Moyennes) : 169–170
Fedeka (Fédération des Associations
tribales des originaires du Kasaï) :
137
FUB (Front de l'Unité Bangala) :
163–164
Federalism, as discussed in the Thirty-
Year Plan: 70; as means of Congo
unification: 317
Federalist political parties: 132–138
Fonds du Bien-Etre Indigène: 49
Food shortages, in Congo: 217, 219,
220–221, 231
Force Publique, mutiny of: 208–211,
213, 216, 225, 283–287; revolt

363

Index